Developing Focus Group Research

Developing Focus Group Research
Politics, Theory and Practice

edited by
Rosaline S. Barbour and Jenny Kitzinger

SAGE Publications
London • Thousand Oaks • New Delhi

First published 1999. Reprinted 2001

SAGE Publications Ltd
6 Bonhill Street
London EC2A 4PU

SAGE Publications Inc.
2455 Teller Road
Thousand Oaks, California 91320

SAGE Publications India Pvt Ltd
32, M-Block Market
Greater Kailash – I
New Delhi 110 048

British Library Cataloguing in Publication data

A catalogue record for this book is available from the British Library

ISBN 0 7619 5567 4
ISBN 0 7619 5568 2 (pbk)

Library of Congress catalog card number 98–61656

To Mike and Alasdair, with grateful thanks for their encouragement and tolerance [RB]

To my parents, Sheila and Uwe, and my sisters, Celia, Tess, Nell and Polly, with thanks for providing me with a childhood training in group discussion at every family meal! [JK]

Contents

Notes on contributors

Rachel Baker works with the DFID team in the Department of Social Anthropology at Edinburgh University, where she also teaches on methodology and childhood. Prior to this she was based in the Department of Anthropology at Durham University, where she wrote her doctoral thesis on the well-being, lifestyles and careers of homeless street children in Nepal. While at Durham she also taught a course in applied medical anthropology.

Rosaline Barbour has just taken up appointment as Senior Lecturer in Primary Care in the Department of General Practice at Glasgow University. Prior to this she was Senior Lecturer in Health Services Research in the Department of Public Health and Primary Care at the University of Hull. Her research career spans both health and social services research and includes an appointment as a researcher with the London Borough of Lambeth, in addition to research posts in the Public Health Research Unit at Glasgow University and the MRC Medical Sociology Unit (both in Glasgow and Aberdeen). She has maintained an interest in professionals' responses to change, having studied the process of training for social work, midwives' perceptions of their roles and responsibilities, reactions to various new service developments (including methadone prescribing in general practice), and the demands of HIV/AIDS work. She is co-editor (with Guro Huby) of *Meddling with Mythology: AIDS and the Social Construction of Knowledge* (Routledge, 1998) and has published in a range of social science and medical journals.

Michael Bloor is Professor of Medical Sociology in the School of Social Sciences at Cardiff University. His recent publications include *The Sociology of HIV Transmission* (Sage, 1995) and a selection of his past papers *Selected Writings in Medical Sociological Research* (Ashgate, 1997).

Lai-Fong Chiu is a project manager with Wakefield and Pontefract Community Health Trust. Before starting her career in the NHS she worked as English as second language tutor, interpreter, patients' advocate and community project co-ordinator. This experience, particularly with minority women, motivated her subsequent research interest. She was the principal researcher on two participatory action research (PAR) projects. She has shared her practical and research experiences through a range of publications including training packs developed from the two PAR projects. She is currently completing her PhD at the University of Leeds.

Sarah Cunningham-Burley is Senior Lecturer in Medical Sociology at the Department of Public Health Sciences, Medical School, University of Edinburgh. Her research interests span medical and family sociology, with a particular emphasis on lay knowledge and experience. She has used a range of qualitative methods, including focus group interviews. Her current research includes 'The Social and Cultural Impact of the New Genetics' (funded under the ESRC Risk and Human Behaviour Programme); 'Life as a Disabled Child: A Qualitative Study of Young People's Experiences and Perspectives' (funded under the ESRC's Children 5–16 programme), and 'Smoking in Transition: A Prospective Study of Young People of School Leaving Age' (funded by the Scottish Office DoH). She has published widely in both social science and medical journals, and is co-editor (with Neil McKeganey) of *Readings in Medical Sociology* (Routledge, 1990) and *Enter the Sociologist* (Avebury, 1987).

Rita Das is a Scottish-born Indian dyke. She is angry and energetic, passionate and compassionate. She presently works as a doctor in London, and challenges prejudice every day by being herself boldly. Her research has included homophobia in medical education; lesbians and health; and South Asian lesbians. She has presented papers at conferences in York, London and Toronto. Her political activism has included involvement with the Zero Tolerance campaign against violence against women (Edinburgh) and the Lesbian Avengers (London). She is cycle-mad and delights in standing on her head.

Clare Farquhar has spent periods of her life as a teacher, woodworker, health promotion worker and HIV/AIDS trainer. She also worked for ten years as a research officer at the Thomas Coram Research Unit, Institute of Education, University of London. Her main interest is in feminist research on gender, sexuality and health. She is currently a Research Fellow at South Bank University, where she has recently completed a PhD on the construction of lesbian sexualities in sexual health discourse.

Jane Frankland is currently completing a PhD at Cardiff University on lay management of illness. She was previously a Research Associate, working with Professor Michael Bloor on an evaluation of a peer-led smoking intervention in secondary schools in Wales.

Judith Green is Lecturer in Sociology at the London School of Hygiene and Tropical Medicine. She has researched and published on primary care, the sociology of accidents and the organization of health services. She is author of *Risk and Misfortune: a Social Construction of Accidents* (UCL Press, 1997) and co-author (with Nicki Thorogood) of *Analysing Health Policy: a Sociological Approach* (Longman, 1988).

Laura Hart is a Research Officer with Cornerstone Research Services and part-time lecturer in Sociology at South Bank University. Her research interests include the new sociology of childhood and developing research methods which engage with young people.

Rachel Hinton is a lecturer and Social Development Consultant working with the DFID team in the Department of Social Anthropology at Edinburgh University. Her doctoral research at Cambridge University examined the interplay between modern and traditional medicine in the refugee camps of Nepal. She teaches courses on refugees and childhood.

Anne Kerr is currently conducting research on the social history of cystic fibrosis, funded by the Wellcome Trust. She followed her PhD studies, on gender, feminism and science at Edinburgh, with a research fellowship working with Sarah Cunningham-Burley and Amanda Amos on 'The Social and Cultural Impact of the New Genetics' project. She is now based at the Science Studies Unit, University of Edinburgh.

Jenny Kitzinger is Senior Research Fellow in the Sociology Department, Glasgow University. She specializes in researching the design, implementation and impact of health promotion campaigns as well as studying the general role of the mass media in the social construction of public issues. She has worked both as an academic and as an activist against sexual violence and is co-author of *The Mass Media and Power in Modern Britain* (Oxford University Press), *Great Expectations* (Hochland and Hochland) and *The Circuit of Mass Communication: Media Strategies, Representation and Audience Reception in the AIDS Crisis* (Sage).

Deborah Knight graduated with a degree in Social Policy and Social Services and developed an initial career in Health Promotion, in which much of her work centred on women's health, breast and cervical screening, attitude and belief systems in the adoption of health-seeking behaviour and action-research with ethnic minority women. Deborah has also been involved in the development and writing of education and training materials using a variety of media. She now works in a Health Commissioning role within the National Health Service.

Phil Macnaghten is a Research Fellow at the Centre for the Study of Environmental Change at Lancaster University. He is co-author (with John Urry) of *Contested Natures* (Sage, 1998).

Lynn Michell has a degree in English and Drama and further degrees in Educational Psychology. She has worked as a teacher, research fellow, university lecturer, educational psychologist, freelance journalist and writer. She has a long track record of focus group and interview based research with adolescents in the fields of cognition, language and health education. The common thread in her writing is the search for sensitive ways of recording and reflecting other people's experiences. She has published a number of books – fiction and non-fiction – including a language scheme for schools. In 1994 she was funded by the Scottish Office to carry out a longitudinal study of smoking and peer group structure based in the MRC Medical Sociology Unit in Glasgow. She has been unable to work for the past two and a half years.

Greg Myers teaches in the Department of Linguistics and Modern English Language at Lancaster University. He is author of *Writing Biology: Texts in the Social Construction of Scientific Knowledge* (1990), *Words in Ads* (1994) and of *Adworlds* (1998).

Stephen Pavis completed his PhD in the Department of Social Policy at the University of Edinburgh in 1993. Since then he has worked as a Research Fellow on several projects. He is currently employed in the Research Unit for Health and Behavioural Change, University of Edinburgh, where he is looking at the health impact of rapid social and economic change, with a particular focus on social exclusion.

Claire Waterton is a research fellow at the Centre for the Study of Environmental Change, Lancaster University. She has worked on many aspects of environmental policy and politics, using focus groups as one of a range of qualitative research methods. Her current research is an investigation of scientists' own perspectives on contemporary science and its interaction with environmental policy issues.

Sue Wilkinson is Reader in Feminism and Psychology and Director of Women's Studies in the Department of Social Sciences, Loughborough University. She founded and edits the international journal *Feminism & Psychology* and the book series *Gender and Psychology: Feminist and Critical Perspectives* (both published by Sage). Her books include *Feminist Social Psychologies* (Open University Press, 1996) and, with Celia Kitzinger, *Heterosexuality* (1993); *Feminism and Discourse* (1995); and *Representing the Other* (1996) (all Sage publications). Her current research interests are in the areas of breast cancer and threatened sexual identities.

Brian Wynne is Professor of Science Studies at Lancaster University, where he is Research Director of the Centre for the Study of Environmental Change, and Director of the Centre for Science Studies and Science Policy. Most of his work has been in the fields of social understanding of scientific expertise as deployed in public decisions about risk and environmental issues. Thus he has studied and published about environmental controversies such as nuclear risks and attempted novel interpretations of the divergences between expert and lay public understandings of what are described as risk problems. This has involved extensive empirical and theoretical contributions on ways of understanding public perceptions of risk, understanding the social and cultural roles of modern expertise on risk and environmental questions, and public understanding of science. This has centrally depended upon interpretive qualitative approaches to social science research. Some of his books are: *Rationality and Ritual* (1982); *Risk Management and Hazardous Wastes: Implementation and the Dialectics of*

Credibility (1987); and, jointly edited, *Expert Evidence: Interpreting Science in the Law* (1989); *Misunderstanding Science* (1996); and *Risk, Environment and Modernity* (1996). He is currently editing a book on risk and reflexive modernization and another (with Sheila Jasanoff) on sociology of science and global climate change.

Acknowledgements

Firstly we would like to thank all of the contributors to this volume for their commitment to the project and for their patience throughout the lengthy process of preparing such a manuscript and getting it into print. We are grateful to Northern and Yorkshire Regional Health Authority's R&D Directorate for funding a day meeting on focus groups which enabled us to bring together around half of our contributors for a stimulating and extremely productive discussion. Thanks are due to our partners, Mike and Diana, and Rosaline's son Alasdair, who have provided a constant source of encouragement and have tolerated our absences and preoccupation with good humour. We would also like to acknowledge the practical help provided by Mike Barbour in the form of literature searches and in providing our index. Maria (Winnie) Wilson deserves special mention for her excellent continuous secretarial support. Thanks are also due to Liz Bradley, whose calm and competent presence helped our day meeting to run smoothly, and who transcribed one of our discussion sessions. Last, but not least, the enthusiasm and support of Krysia Domaszewicz at Sage has been crucial in helping us to turn our initial ideas into an integrated edited collection.

1 Introduction: the challenge and promise of focus groups

Jenny Kitzinger and Rosaline S. Barbour

Background and outline

This volume is a response to the unprecedented popularity currently being enjoyed by focus groups. Traditionally embraced most enthusiastically by market researchers, this technique has gained a high profile as a method for guiding political campaign advertising and governments' image-management. North American politicians have long used focus group research to inform their self-presentation strategies. This technique is now increasingly being adopted in the UK, prompting political commentators to declare that politicians are 'bewitched by focus groups' which unleash 'monsters' and are a 'short cut to anarchy' (Jenkins, 1997). British Prime Minister, Tony Blair, famously declared, 'there is no one more powerful than a member of a focus group' (cited in Ferguson, 1996: 46) and has had to publicly deny that he is attempting 'government by focus groups' (*World at One*, Radio 4, 29 July 1997). This research method has even attracted the satirical pen of the political cartoonist (see Figure 1.1).

In academia, too, focus groups have attracted increasing attention. Although group work has a relatively established pedigree in social anthropology, media/cultural studies and health research, the method is now being adopted and developed in a wide range of social sciences. Over the last few years there has been a three-fold increase in the number of focus group studies published in academic journals.

However, in our view, a great deal of focus group work adopts a formulaic approach which fails to develop the full potential of this method. In particular, social scientists are in danger of uncritically adopting market researchers' models of such research rather than adapting and expanding them, taking into account our own purposes and theoretical traditions.

This book casts a critical eye over focus group research and suggests ways forward in harnessing this versatile and powerful method. We dispute some of the emerging orthodoxies about how to conduct such research, question the uncritical celebration of this data collection technique and challenge simplistic statements about its 'inherent' qualities. Focus groups have great potential. Like any other research method, however, they are

FIGURE 1.1 *One of several cartoons parodying focus groups which appeared in the press in the late 1990s*

Source: *Guardian* 16 July 1997: 5

open to careless or inappropriate use, the results may be manipulated, and 'subjects' of the research can be exploited.

We have compiled this edited collection in the hope that it will encourage 'good practice' and help to develop the creative use of focus groups. The book draws on the collective experience of 21 researchers who have used focus groups to explore a wide range of issues with a variety of populations in a range of settings. The studies represented here include projects exploring children's experiences of their social worlds, 'community' attitudes towards the nuclear industry, refugees' negotiation of identity, lesbian sexual health, professional decision-making, and public understandings of science, AIDS, sexual violence and genetics.

In preparing this book, the editors and contributors met for a thoroughly enjoyable and very lively all-day discussion about group research methods (thanks to funding from Northern and Yorkshire's Research and Development Directorate). Rather than simply reflecting the editors' views, this introduction is thus the product of the shared expertise of the contributors (although not every contributor necessarily agrees with all the arguments presented here). Dialogue between the authors has also helped to inform individual chapters (indeed several previously single-authored contributions became joint endeavours during the course of producing this collection).

The book is structured to take the reader through the whole process of planning, conducting and analysing focus group studies. Each chapter explores a different methodological issue. The first few chapters address questions of research design: How does the venue influence the data generated? (Judith Green and Laura Hart) When can individual interviews usefully complement focus groups? (Lynn Michell) Are focus groups suitable for exploring sensitive topics? (Clare Farquhar with Rita Das).

We then move on to examine the potential of focus groups to contribute to radical political research agendas including feminist and participatory paradigms (Sue Wilkinson, Chapter 5 and Rachel Baker and Rachel Hinton, Chapter 6). The next three chapters address specific substantive issues. Lai-Fong Chiu and Deborah Knight (Chapter 7) explore ways of using focus groups to access the views of ethnic minority groups and address issues around working with interpreters. Rosaline Barbour (Chapter 8) discusses focus group research into professional decision-making and organizational change. Claire Waterton and Brian Wynne (Chapter 9) examine the use of focus groups to access 'community views'.

The final section of the book focuses on analysis. Jane Franklin and Michael Bloor (Chapter 10) describe thematic analysis and outline ways of using computer-assisted coding techniques. Jenny Kitzinger and Clare Farquhar (Chapter 11) examine the interaction between focus group participants, and expound on the analytical potential of 'sensitive moments' in group discussions. Greg Myers and Phil Macnaghten (Chapter 12) demonstrate the advantages of discourse analysis. The last chapter reflects on the political context of focus group research in locating people as 'consumers' or 'citizens' (Sarah Cunningham-Burley, Anne Kerr and Steve Pavis).

The contributors come from a wide range of disciplinary and professional backgrounds and employ different models of how to work with focus groups. Some use them to document experience; others to explore discourse. Some write up practical reports documenting service provision or needs; others are conducting in-depth theoretical, even literary, analysis. What the contributors share, however, is commitment to the critical interrogation of focus group research and what might be called a 'sceptical enthusiasm' for this method. We hope that this volume will enthuse readers with the same excitement about focus groups, encouraging researchers to employ this technique reflexively, and facilitating the continued development of focus group research within the social sciences.

An introduction to key questions about focus groups

The following section provides a brief overview of ways of approaching focus group research. Here, we address common questions and highlight the differences between focus groups and other data collection techniques. This section points to key elements in the book and demonstrates the interconnections between decisions taken at different points in the design, conduct and analysis of focus group research. We would advise readers new to the field to use this volume alongside basic guides to focus group research. As we go to press Sage is publishing a revised edition of *The Handbook for Focus Group Research* (Greenbaum, 1998) and a comprehensive introductory *Focus Group Kit* (Morgan and Krueger, 1997). The usefulness of such guidance notwithstanding, we would, however, urge focus group researchers not to be constrained by the advice offered, but to reflect on its appropriateness for the research project in hand and would encourage researchers to think creatively about developing focus group approaches.

What are focus groups?

Focus groups are group discussions exploring a specific set of issues. The group is 'focused' in that it involves some kind of collective activity – such as viewing a video, examining a single health promotion message, or simply debating a set of questions. Crucially, focus groups are distinguished from the broader category of group interviews by the explicit use of group interaction to generate data. Instead of asking questions of each person in turn, focus group researchers encourage participants to talk to one another: asking questions, exchanging anecdotes, and commenting on each others' experiences and points of view. At the very least, research participants create an audience for one another.

With the increasing popularity of group methods comes a bewildering array of terms, made all the more confusing by lack of consistency in their usage. In addition to focus groups and group interviews, one hears of 'brainstorming sessions' (which involve little in the way of preparation) and 'nominal groups' (which are specially convened rather than naturally-occurring groups and often include ranking exercises to establish participants' priorities or concerns). There are also 'Delphi groups' (involving selected panels of experts responding to results from complementary research) and 'consensus panels' (designed to develop agreed professional principles or protocols).

Perhaps the resulting confusion has contributed to the apologetic tone which accompanies many researchers' acknowledgement of group methods. Research presentations are often accompanied by partial disclaimers such as, 'Well, I'm not sure if we used *proper* focus groups'. Certainly, focus group research is not the same as work involving 'Delphi groups' or 'consensus panels' where these are employed simply to facilitate an *outcome* of an agreed response rather than to observe the *process* of prioritization and decision-making. However, any group discussion may be called a 'focus group' as long as the researcher is actively encouraging of, and attentive to, the group interaction. Focus groups can involve different group compositions (including strangers or friends, 'lay people' or professionals) and diverse group tasks (including brainstorming, ranking exercises or attempting to reach a consensus). Indeed, the creative use of focus groups could include developing – where appropriate – hybrids of the various group types on offer and using focus groups in multi-method studies as well as refining stand-alone group methods to address a wider range of issues.

When is it appropriate to use focus groups?

Focus groups are ideal for exploring people's experiences, opinions, wishes and concerns. The method is particularly useful for allowing participants to generate their own questions, frames and concepts and to pursue their own priorities on their own terms, in their own vocabulary. Focus groups also enable researchers to examine people's different perspectives as they operate within a social network. Crucially, group work explores how accounts are articulated, censured, opposed and changed through social interaction and how this relates to peer communication and group norms. Indeed, depending on the researcher's theoretical approach, focus group data can go further and challenge the notion that opinions are attributes of subjects at all rather than utterances produced in specific situations (see Chapter 12).

In general, questionnaires are more appropriate for obtaining quantitative information and explaining how many people 'hold' a certain (predefined) 'opinion'. However, focus groups are better for exploring how points of view are constructed and expressed. In-depth ethnographic work may be more appropriate for documenting broad cultural issues, but focus groups are particularly suited to the study of attitudes and experiences around specific topics. Interviews are more effective for tapping into individual biographies, but focus groups are invaluable for examining how knowledge, ideas, story-telling, self-presentation and linguistic exchanges operate within a given cultural context. Even these generalizations, however, should not be treated as if they were cast in stone and combining different data collection techniques into a single project can be highly productive.

Combining focus groups with other *qualitative* methods

Even if focus groups are not the most appropriate primary research tool, including some focus groups in a study can be fruitful (or vice versa). In this volume Rachel Baker and Rachel Hinton (Chapter 6) examine the value of conducting focus groups after lengthy ethnographic research and

Lynn Michell (Chapter 3) describes the importance, in her research, of combining focus groups with individual interviews. The key aspect to remember is that all data are context-bound and the same individuals are likely to answer questions differently, depending on whether we access them individually, through a researcher-convened group, or through a 'naturally-occurring' group. In weighing up the relative merits of focus groups and interviews for a particular study (or deciding how to compose each group), the researcher should consider how the group context and broader cultural and institutional features operate to encourage or suppress the expression of certain points of view.

Several contributors to this volume note differences between statements generated in individual and group work. Rosaline Barbour (Chapter 8), for example, found that the most vituperative comments about social workers were made by general practitioners and health visitors in the group setting, whereas, in one-to-one interviews, the same individuals were more likely to take a sympathetic view of the difficulties faced by other professionals. Differences between focus group and interview data were also revealed by Lynn Michell's (Chapter 3) work with school-children. Whereas focus groups were invaluable for teasing out details of the peer group 'pecking order', it was only in interviews that she was able to access individual experiences of bullying and victimization. However, the way in which group work differs from individual interview data cannot always be predicted in advance. Jenny Kitzinger found that group work could facilitate discussion of 'deviant' experiences and the naming of abuse (Chapter 11) and Rachel Baker reflects that in her work with street children in Nepal she was suspicious of normative responses in interviews (the responses the children were used to giving to journalists and aid workers) and decided to use focus groups to explore these further (Chapter 6).

Combining focus groups with *quantitative* methods

Focus groups can also be combined with 'quantitative' methods such as questionnaire surveys. At the outset of such research, group work can be employed to help construct questionnaires: developing an understanding of key issues and refining the phrasing of specific questions. Focus groups can also provide fertile ground for eliciting anecdotal material and are therefore ideal 'seedbeds' for germinating vignettes for use in question-naires. Such vignettes, which may allow the researcher to vary significant details or develop unfolding scenarios, can be incorporated into large-scale questionnaire studies, so that their precise impact on responses can be systematically studied (Barbour, in press). Focus groups can also be used in the latter stage of quantitative projects. They can help to tease out the reasons for surprising or anomalous findings and to explain the occurrence of 'outliers' identified – but not explained – by quantitative approaches, such as scattergrams or 'box and whisker plots' (Barbour, in press).

Group work can not only complement data collected via other methods, but may actually challenge how such data are interpreted. Jenny Kitzinger's study of public understandings of AIDS demonstrates how focus groups can suggest different ways of interpreting survey findings through revealing the 'readings', 'facts' and value systems that inform respondents' answers to survey questions (see Kitzinger, 1994b). Similarly Clare Waterton and Brian Wynne (Chapter 9) challenge the nuclear industry's use of particular opinion poll findings by exploring the same questions in focus groups. They argue that the polls constructed a misleading view of local feelings by assuming that 'attitudes' and 'risks' are objects whose basic meanings are stable and universally accepted. Their focus group data, by contrast, demonstrate that, when people talk about the risks from nuclear power, they do so in a highly complex way which highlights the 'relational construction of beliefs'.

Sample size and sampling strategies

Focus group studies range from just three or four groups, to over fifty. Although some research projects rely on less than ten groups in total, all of the contributors to this volume ran considerably more sessions than this. The appropriate number of focus groups will depend on the research question, the range of people you wish to include and, of course, time and resource limitations.

Statistical 'representativeness' is not the aim of most focus group research. Usually focus group researchers employ 'qualitative sampling' (Kuzel, 1992) in order to encompass diversity and compose a structured rather than random sample, guided by the particular research questions which they are addressing.

Within most projects it is important to include demographic diversity and to make particular efforts to consider the voices which might be excluded. It is also useful to develop a topic-specific sampling strategy. Thus a study about attitudes to nuclear power could include groups of those working for the nuclear industry and those not; a study of AIDS might include groups of those who have tested HIV positive and groups of those who have tested negative. Different sampling strategies have been adopted by the various contributors to this volume and the decision-making process is explained in several chapters. Clare Farquhar and Rita Das, for example (Chapter 4), document their efforts to include different types of lesbian groups in their research, while Lai-Fong Chiu and Deborah Knight (Chapter 7) compare two sampling strategies for reaching ethnic minority women.

Maintaining a flexible approach to the sampling frame is desirable. This can be built in at the planning stage. Having determined your ideal sample in an original grant application it is useful to cost in funds for a couple of extra 'wild card' groups to explore hypotheses as they emerge. So, for example, researchers may decide to work with a group not included in their original sample, such as incomers to an area (within a project which focused on local people) or short-stay patients (in a project focused on long-stay 'patients'). Such strategies can lend greater depth or scope to a study and test emerging hypotheses.

Group size and composition

Advice about group size and composition in existing guides to focus group research is often didactic. This can seriously hamper imaginative – or even appropriate – application of focus group methods. One orthodoxy emerging from the market research literature stipulates that the ideal number of participants is between 8 and 12. However, this number is too large for many sociological studies. Several of the contributors to this volume prefer to work with groups of five or six participants, or even as few as three.

Focus group researchers are also faced with the perennial problem – given much attention in all of the 'how to' books – of deciding whether to aim for homogeneity or heterogeneity among group participants. Bringing together people on the basis of some shared experience is often most productive; however, differences between participants are often illuminating (Kitzinger, 1994a). As with many other aspects of focus group design, though, the guidelines overemphasize the extent to which the researchers can control for all characteristics of participants which are likely to be relevant. Some details are likely to emerge only once discussion has been initiated and the precise composition of groups will often be a product of circumstance rather than planning. This is not necessarily a disadvantage. Khan and Manderson (1992) report that difficulties in stimulating discussion of reproductive issues among a group of young women in India were resolved when an older woman (a mother-in-law who arrived as chaperone to one of the women) started talking. Similarly, Jenny Kitzinger found unexpected advantages in including (by mistake) one short-term resident in a group of long-term residents of a hospital unit for the elderly. The participation of this individual mobilized criticisms and suggestions from the group which might not otherwise have been expressed (as groups composed entirely of longer-term residents adopted a more resigned and institutionalized attitude).

The third issue to consider is whether or not to work with people who already know each other. Market research texts tend to insist on focus groups being held with strangers in order to avoid both the 'polluting' and 'inhibiting' effect of existing relations between group members. However, many social science researchers prefer to work with pre-existing groups – people who are already acquainted through living, working or socializing together. These are, after all, the networks in which people might normally discuss (or evade) the sorts of issues likely to be raised in the research session and the 'naturally-occurring' group is one of the most important contexts in which ideas are formed and decisions made.

Pre-existing groups are not, however, a prerequisite for successful focus group research. Indeed, many projects bring together people who might not otherwise meet. Studies into the experience of living in a particular tower block, having a particular illness, or winning the lottery, might involve people who are virtual strangers. Even in a study where it has been possible to recruit pre-existing groups, the researcher might want to intervene to bring together other participants who do not know each other and whose voices and common experiences might otherwise be muted or entirely excluded from the research. In some cases, too, researchers deliberately opt to observe the talk generated by strangers or set up one-off groups to ensure that participants will talk without fear of making revelations to members of their own social circle.

If pre-existing groups are chosen then consideration should be given to the types of networks used. For example, an investigation into school sex education programmes could access the same 16-year-old boy through a variety of networks. He could participate in a focus group with his parents and sister; with a selection of his schoolfriends; or he could become involved in the research via a support group for gay teenagers. Each type of group may give a different perspective on this same young man's views and experiences or access different discourses.

Pre-existing groups are likely to have established their own norms as to what can and cannot be said and hierarchies within groups and in broader society may inhibit the contributions of members in particular structural positions. This does not, however, necessarily preclude utilizing pre-existing groups or, indeed, using group work at all. Indeed, the 'sensitive moments' within the group can be a source of insight (see Chapter 11 and also Chapter 8). However, it is often useful to ensure that participants have ways of communicating their points of view outside the group. For example, participants may be provided with a questionnaire or the opportunity to talk one-to-one to the facilitator after the group or in a subsequent tele- phone debriefing session. Researchers can also adapt their sampling frame to create the context which will facilitate access to particular voices in order to 'fill the gaps' (such as a gay youth group in the earlier example).

Recruitment, access and the role of gate-keepers

There are some issues around recruitment and access which are specific to focus group research and bring both advantages and disadvantages, often involving the adoption of new strategies. For example, although some people may be intimidated by the prospect of a group discussion (or feel that it devalues them as research participants), group methods offer reassurance to others. Focus groups are ideal for individuals whose views you wish to elicit, but who protest they do not have much to say on the topic in question. Focus groups are also good for involving people who might be nervous of being the sole focus of a researcher's attention.

There are also important *practical* differences between interviews and focus groups. Interviewers can go to a respondent's own home at a time of his or her choice. However, focus group work often relies on research participants travelling to a common venue and co-ordinating with others. This can make people less likely to co-operate. Researchers may therefore need to recruit several more potential participants than are actually needed and reimburse participants' travel expenses or offer payment. It is well worth fitting your research session into established meeting slots where this is an option (for example, existing staff meeting times, youth club nights or support sessions).

Focus group work also often involves increased dependency on gate-keepers. This has two main problems. The first problem is an access and recruitment issue: the gatekeeper may screen potential participants. For example, if the researcher leaves it up to a teacher to ask for volunteers in a school, then she or he may find that the entire group is made up of prefects or members of the school debating society. Similarly, line managers in an organization may try to exclude potential critics (see Chapter 8). Gate-keepers may also view group discussions as far more threatening than interviews: for example, employers of casual labour may worry that group discussion between workers will disrupt existing employer–employee relations or doctors may worry that bringing patients together in a group will result in them telling each other 'horror stories' or engaging in the 'inappropriate' exchange of information. Sue Wilkinson, for example, found that some clinicians were concerned to prevent women who were about to undergo surgery for breast cancer meeting with those who had already had such treatment.

The second issue for focus group recruitment is an ethical one: far from denying access, an enthusiastic group contact may facilitate access without passing on all relevant information. One of us (JK) had a problem when she met with a group set up for her by a market research company. The group, members of a football club, was convened in order to discuss sexual abuse. However, on arrival she discovered that the men had been told by the group contact that they would be discussing football hooliganism. (He had resorted to this strategy because he had found it difficult to recruit participants in any other way.) The other one of us (RB) turned up at a health centre under the impression that the practice manager had secured agreement for a focus group discussion to be conducted in a slot generally used for team meetings. However, she then discovered that staff expected to carry out their usual business at the meeting and viewed the research task as an imposition. In Chapter 4, Clare Farquhar and Rita Das question whether permission granted on behalf of a 'group' can really involve 'informed consent' on the part of all its members. Their chapter suggests ways of addressing this problem.

Research settings

Alongside research design and recruitment, consideration also needs to be given to where the group sessions are actually going to take place. Researchers should choose a venue easily accessible to the people they wish to include in the research. In our experience, people are more likely to turn up for a group which takes place in a familiar venue (such as their community centre) rather than having to travel to an unfamiliar place (such as the university). However, this has to be counterbalanced with consideration of the value of working with groups outside the institutions which bring them together (for example residential care, school, workplace, prison).

Ideally, the room needs to be quiet and comfortable, free from interruptions and protected from observation by those not participating in the research. Social anthropologists are used to conducting informal group sessions in the village square, the market-place, or on the bank of the river where the clothes are washed, recognizing the advantages of such 'natural' set ups. However, it is difficult to conduct a discussion with school pupils constantly interrupted by their teacher, or with in-patients under the scrutiny of staff. The interventions of those who have not agreed to participate, and may be suspicious of the research, can also be a problem if the venue is too 'public' (see Chapter 6).

However, researchers need to be flexible in their use of venues and often have little choice. The contributors to this volume have used a wide range of sites including classrooms, play-group premises, refugee camp committee rooms, prison recreation rooms, health centres, community centres, and people's own homes. Concerns about selecting a suitable venue have led several writers of focus group guidelines to recommend 'a neutral setting, where participants will not feel influenced by the surroundings' (College of Health, 1994: 86). We would argue that there is no such place. Rather than aiming for 'neutrality', researchers should consider, instead, the different messages that are being given to participants when we select different venues. This is discussed in depth by Judith Green and Laura Hart (Chapter 2), where they explain how the 'formal' and 'informal' settings chosen for their focus group sessions influenced the content of discussions. They note that 'different contexts produce different types of stories . . . and different repertoires of social competencies'. Questions about venue are thus, they argue, 'not merely technical questions about validity and reliability, but involve rather more theoretical decisions about research aims.'

Using stimulus materials and exercises

The group facilitator should approach the group discussion with a basic outline of key questions. Over and above this, specific group exercises are sometimes useful. This can be as simple as providing participants with a flip chart and pens to list key concerns, or showing them advertisements, leaflets, cartoons or newspaper clippings as stimulus material. Alternatively, the researcher may wish to use quite developed exercises such as vignettes.

Several of the contributors to this volume developed their own ways of stimulating discussion. Rosaline Barbour (Chapter 8) used vignettes to explore team members' understandings of each others' roles and how they allocated professional responsibilities. Lai-Fong Chiu and Deborah Knight (Chapter 7) took a speculum into their group discussion about cervical smears and encouraged women to pass it around. In her work on AIDS and on child sexual abuse, Jenny Kitzinger used still photographs from news bulletins and asked groups to try to reproduce typical news reports. This task was specifically developed to trace media influence on public understandings. However, working with pictures can be useful for other types of projects too, particularly because they engage people in discussion without the researcher providing any vocabulary or terminology. (For in-depth discussion of this technique see Kitzinger, 1993.)

Another common exercise consists of presenting participants with a series of statements on large cards, which they are then asked, as a collective exercise, to rank or assign to different categories. For example, Jenny Kitzinger used such cards to explore the views of Greenham Common peace campaigners (asking them to sort statements about gender and violence into different 'agree'–'disagree' categories), to explore public understandings of AIDS (placing statements about 'types' of people into different 'risk categories') and to examine midwives' perceptions of their professional responsibilities (placing a series of statements about midwives' roles along a continuum of importance). (For further discussion of this technique, see Kitzinger, 1990.)

Collective tasks, such as these, encourage participants to concentrate on one another (rather than the group facilitator) and may force them to explain and defend their differing perspectives. They focus discussion around key points of interest to the researcher and facilitate comparison across groups. However, stimulus materials are not always necessary and can make people feel uncomfortable ('it's like being back at school'). As with other features of focus groups, they should be selected judiciously and their usefulness monitored throughout a project.

Facilitators' skills

One reason for researchers' hesitation in using focus groups is the notion that the group facilitator must be inordinately skilled. Certainly skill in conducting focus groups increases exponentially with experience. However, pilot group discussions can be attempted by novice researchers, provided the topic is straightforward, 'safe' and of obvious interest to the research participants. Indeed, this may be an even easier starting point than one-to-one interviews because the group will have its own momentum, and the researcher's role is to allow the interaction between participants to develop unencumbered by heavy-handed interventions. One simple way of beginning to develop group facilitation skills is to start off by conducting group discussions with your own friends, students, relatives or colleagues just to try out the method.

For difficult (that is complex or fraught) subjects, greater experience is necessary (see Chapter 11). However, most experienced qualitative researchers already possess many of the skills needed for successful focus group moderating. As with interviews, researchers should avoid being judgemental, presenting themselves as experts or making assumptions which close off exploration. A group facilitator also needs skill in balancing keeping quiet with knowing when to intervene. In addition, facilitators need to be able to think on their feet to clarify ambiguous statements, enable incomplete sentences to be finished, encourage everyone to participate and ensure that interesting and unexpected avenues are pursued. One of the key skills is ensuring that interaction between research participants is encouraged.

Prior knowledge (or the ability to pick up on, or interpret) the language, terminology, gestures and cultural meanings of the particular groups with whom one is working is also crucial. This is true both for group facilitation and subsequent data interpretation. For some research projects this will involve working with interpreters (see Chapter 7) and considerable preparatory research. For example, in their work with street children in Kathmandu and with refugees from Bhutan, Rachel Baker and Rachel Hinton (Chapter 6) point to the importance of conducting observational fieldwork before setting up group discussions. Without such background preparation the researcher may not only misinterpret the discussion data after the event but also, at the time, lose credibility with the research participants who may simply decide to 'take the researcher for a ride'.

The potential for researchers to 'lose control' of group discussions is a common concern expressed in the literature. However, the validity of such concerns depends on whether you want to keep control in the first place (see Chapter 5). It also depends on what one means by 'losing control'. The 'freer' and more dynamic situation of a focus group may actually access 'better data' than a more subdued and formal encounter. In addition, it is incorrect to assume that total anarchy will ensue unless the researcher handles the group situation with consummate poise. This worry ignores the skills of the other participants. We all operate in a wide variety of group situations in the context of our everyday lives, and can call on our stock of experiences in dealing with potentially difficult situations. In most focus group settings, participants – as well as the researcher – have a vested interest in avoiding unpleasant confrontation or open hostility. Focus group researchers need to be prepared for the fact that group work may involve 'sensitive moments' and may elicit painful exchanges and revelations (see Chapters 4 and 11). Certainly, the facilitator should think, in advance, about how to lead group discussion on to safer ground if necessary. However, in practice, many difficult situations are actually 'managed' by the group participants themselves.

The group facilitator's persona and self-presentation

Traditional research approaches encouraged researchers to present themselves as faceless, objective nonentities. This paradigm has now been challenged (see, for example, Oakley, 1981). Alternative models for conducting, understanding and theorizing researchers' relationships with their 'subjects' are increasingly being explored (Whitehead and Conaway, 1986; Edwards, 1990; Phoenix, 1990; McKeganey and Bloor, 1991; Green et al., 1993). Many of these debates revolve around one-to-one interviewing but are equally applicable to focus group research. The only difference is that, on the one hand, group work may 'dilute' the effect of the researcher's own persona because group participants are usually addressing each other as much as (if not more) than the researcher. On the other hand, the researcher's persona may be highlighted as the group members position themselves in relation to their collective identity and in 'opposition' to the researcher's. This can sometimes happen, for example, when a woman facilitates a men-only group or an 'outsider' runs a group with people living close to a nuclear power station (see Chapter 9).

There is no 'correct' persona for focus group facilitation, although some facilitators will be more appropriate for some topics and for some research populations. It is crucial, however, to consider how the researcher's persona influences the data collected. If you've brought together a group on the basis of shared characteristics or experiences, how are you located in relation to this? Are you seen as 'one of us' or an outsider? Are you perceived to be related to 'authority' or the institution under study? How do your own identity, dress, accent and behaviour influence how you are seen (such as displaying heterosexuality by wearing a wedding ring)?

White, heterosexual, able-bodied researchers rarely theorize, or are even aware, of how their own identities or self-presentations impact on research participants, except where they are researching 'the other'. Indeed, being white or heterosexual is seldom a thought-out 'identity' in the same way as being black or gay. 'Minority' researchers are often more sensitive to this dimension, whatever the context. Particularly revealing dynamics may be evident where the researcher's identity is sometimes 'ambiguous', 'hidden' or made invisible and/or when research participants' assumptions become explicit. Lai-Fong Chiu, for example, finds that she is often not seen as 'black' and therefore white research participants feel free to air their prejudices in front of her without feeling that she is implicated by their statements. Indeed, some of the white groups with which she worked were resistant to her self-definition when she did expressly identify herself as a black woman.

While we would not argue that there necessarily needs to be close correspondence between researcher and researched, theorizing about research participants' perceptions of the researcher is a valuable part of the research process. This is discussed in Chapters 4 and 7 in relation to lesbian and 'black' and 'white' identities. These examples throw into sharp focus issues of identity and self-presentation which are pertinent to all research encounters.

Recording and transcribing focus group discussions

The most basic level of recording focus group discussions depends on note-taking and the use of a flip chart to construct, with group participants, a summary of the meeting. Tape-recording provides far richer research access to the discussion and we would advise this, even if it is only used as an *aide-mémoire*. Some researchers recommend video-recording. While this can provide additional information, it can also be cumbersome, may be particularly inhibiting and can give a misleading illusion of comprehensiveness. If you are relying on audio-tape, however, it is useful to note down your own impressions and the most obvious elements of body language. For example, in one group discussion about 'slags', the only female member of the group started to tug at her short skirt until it was stretched right over her knees (Kitzinger, 1993).

Audio-taping needs a high-quality recorder and, ideally, a multidirectional microphone (the flat mikes are excellent). Tapes of group discussions are invariably more difficult to transcribe than are one-to-one interviews. They will take an experienced audio-typist in excess of the four hours per hour of taped material generally calculated for transcription of interviews. This will be even longer if one is aiming for the sophistication of transcript required for conversation analysis with all the pauses and interruptions marked in (see Myers and Macnaghten, Chapter 12, for an example of this). Sometimes, however, the tape may be used simply to refresh one's memories and clarify notes. The amount of transcription required can be cut down by employing a judicious mixture of written and tape-recorded sections (see, for example, Barbour, 1995).

One of the challenges for transcribers is identifying individual speakers. A voice check, where the facilitator simply asks people to go round and give their first names on the tape at the beginning of the session, can be very useful. It can also be helpful if the person who transcribes the tape was also present at the group or if an observer takes notes of the sequence of talk. Some of the contributors to this volume have opted to work with simple male/female identifiers for speakers and only attempt to identify individual speakers for key sections of text (noting in counter numbers during transcription will help locate the relevant sections of tape later on).

Focus group transcription can also be difficult because participants tend to make sudden, apparently 'illogical' leaps, and interrupt or shout over each other. This happens especially when discussion becomes animated – and, consequently, often when it is of most interest to the researcher. Ideally, researchers should transcribe at least one of the group discussions themselves, and, of course, many do not have the luxury of doing anything else. Transcription by the facilitator will help her to adapt her facilitation style if necessary. (A facilitator who has transcribed her own tape is more likely in subsequent groups to intervene to ask participants to finish off their comments, or to ensure that individual voices are not drowned out.) It will also improve the facilitator's ability to liaise with whoever is transcribing further tapes if this task is subsequently delegated. In any case, it is useful to listen to the tape once more while reading the transcript in order to correct it, and to add in additional notes or impressions. It can also be useful to listen to the tape while coding the transcript – especially where tone of voice and the nature of the interaction is important.

Analysing and presenting focus group data

Focus groups can generate large amounts of very rich and dynamic data. This very richness and complexity can, however, make it unwieldy and, again, adequate time must be allowed for analysis. Analysing focus group data involves essentially the same process as does the analysis of any other qualitative data. However, the researcher needs to reference the group context. This means starting from an analysis of groups rather than individuals and striking a balance between looking at the picture provided by the group as a whole and recognizing the operation of individual 'voices' within it. The researcher should try to distinguish between opinions expressed in spite of, or in opposition to, the group and the consensus expressed or constructed by the group.

Analysis will involve, at the very least, drawing together and comparing discussion of similar themes and examining how these relate to the variation between individuals and between groups. A more developed analysis can use systematic coding and packages such as NUD•IST or Ethnograph. This is documented in detail by Jane Frankland and Michael Bloor in Chapter 10. Alternatively, transcripts can be subjected to conversation analysis. This is discussed in depth by Greg Myers and Phil Macnaghten in Chapter 12. Attention should also be paid to the group dynamics, including examining jokes, anecdotes, agreement, disagreement (see Kitzinger, 1994a). Close attention to 'sensitive moments' can be very revealing and this is discussed in Chapter 11.

Several of the contributors to this volume raise issues relating to how best to present focus group data in talks, reports and published papers. Myers and Mcnaghten argue for presenting larger chunks of transcripts to illustrate the context in which remarks were made. It may also be important to include a sense of dynamic change during the course of the group (as people shift their position, accommodate to, or challenge one another). Sue Wilkinson (Chapter 5) is critical of the tendency for some focus group researchers to bow to the supposed requirements of journals for data in the form of tables and numbers. Asbury (1995: 418) comments: 'Focus groups are not oral surveys: that is, participants' comments should not be tallied, counted, or otherwise taken out of the context in which the comments originated.' Nevertheless, systematic counting prevents impressionistic assumptions and can be useful in some cases, depending on our sample. For example, the 'Cleveland scandal' was spontaneously raised in over half the focus group discussions about sexual abuse in Jenny Kitzinger's research. This study involved 49 groups from a wide range of backgrounds. Only seven groups could not recall the Cleveland case, and these consisted predominantly of participants under 18 or who were not resident in Britain during the time when this case received extensive media coverage. Noting the persistent reference to this case and the role it played in how participants understood more contemporary child abuse cases was relevant to developing a theory about media influence and the role of historical reference points and 'conceptual templates' (Kitzinger, in press, a).

Ethical issues

Ethical issues are relevant to all stages of focus group research design, implementation and presentation. The question of informed consent has already been raised. A second issue is the question of confidentiality. Unlike interviewees, focus group participants cannot be given an absolute guarantee that confidences shared in the group will be respected; the temptation to 'gossip' may be strong if participants are part of the same social network. In addition, vicarious disclosure takes place. For example, in one research session one participant informed the group that one of the young women present had worked as a prostitute. A third issue is that group members may voice opinions that are upsetting to other participants (for example, in one group, the suggestion that incest survivors should be sterilized because they were deemed to be 'unfit parents').

A related problem is that participants may actually provide each other with misinformation during the course of the group; information which may be implicitly legitimized by the presence of the researcher. It is clearly inappropriate simply to walk away from a group after having silently listened to people convincing each other that HIV can be transmitted by casual contact or that anal intercourse is safer than vaginal intercourse. In such cases the researcher has a responsibility to provide accurate information.

Such ethical issues can be addressed through attempting to set ground rules prior to the group, and through debriefing and supplying literature after the group. During the course of the session itself it may very occasionally be necessary to intervene but, as noted earlier, groups often have their own way of responding to difficult dynamics and individuals within groups may be used to 'putting up with' particular offensive remarks or may, within the group, develop their own robust defence (for a more extensive discussion see Chapters 5 and 11).

The politics of focus group research

Although focus groups introduce some new ethical challenges for qualitative researchers, they also bring new political possibilities. Focus groups are welcomed by some because of their potential for transforming the researcher–researched relationship. In contrast to one-to-one interviews, group work can shift the balance of power in favour of the participants (see Chapter 5). Focus groups may involve participants in helping to define research questions and can even involve them in collaborative writing projects.

However, it would be naïve to suppose that power differentials are thereby entirely dissolved. Sarah Cunningham-Burley, Anne Kerr and Stephen Pavis point out that we need not only to interrogate relationships between research participants and researchers, but also those between researchers and funders (Chapter 13). In addition, Rachel Baker and Rachel Hinton (Chapter 6) argue that participatory research is not a discrete activity, 'rather it is a cycle followed by researchers and participants that begins and ends in shared activities and understanding'. Their chapter shows group discussion as just one of a series of ethnographic and participatory endeavours, and they caution against assuming that focus groups automatically lead to participatory action research practice.

Similarly, Rosaline Barbour (1995) makes the distinction between working *on* people and working *with* people to effect change, and several of the contributors discuss the practical strategies which they employed to this end. Claire Waterton and Brian Wynne held public meetings at which findings were fed back to the communities studied, Lai-Fong Chiu and Deborah Knight recruited and trained bilingual moderators who not only became involved in their research but acted as health educators. They also worked with research participants in analysing transcripts of focus group discussions – a process which proved particularly important in working with white health workers to analyse their own racism. If the potential of focus group work to change relations between research participants and researchers is to be realized, this can only be done through additional practical acts, it cannot be assumed to be an 'inherent' quality of this data collection technique.

The dynamics within focus groups are also heralded as a useful addition to developing a 'new politics of knowledge' by accessing uncodified knowledge and stimulating the sociological imagination in both researchers and participants (Johnson, 1996). Certainly, focus group work can disrupt researchers' (and commissioning bodies') assumptions and encourage research participants to explore issues, identify common problems and suggest potential solutions through sharing and comparing experiences. Focus group participants have the opportunity to piece together the fragmented experiences of group members and may come to view events in their own lives in a new light in the course of such discussions (see particularly Chapters 5 and 11). Group work can help individuals to develop a perspective which transcends their individual context and thus may transform 'personal troubles' into 'public issues'. The group process can also foster collective identity and provide a point of contact to initiate grass-roots change.

It is these qualities which made group discussion, in the form of 'consciousness-raising groups', such a powerful political tool in the black power and women's liberation movements. It is this potential that has also attracted community activists, action researchers and feminists (see Sue Wilkinson's discussion in Chapter 5). In addition, the ability of focus groups to involve those without access to formal channels of communication and who might resist individual interviews has also led to group work being adopted by some as a means of 'citizens' consultation'. For example 'A Citizens' Inquiry: The Opsahl Report on Northern Ireland' (1993) collected the views of around 3000 people about the troubles, using focus groups alongside public hearings (cited in Johnson, 1996).

The other side of the coin, however, is that focus groups can also be co-opted as a powerful public relations tool. Since focus groups have all the right credentials, it is relatively easy for them to be presented as consultation exercises or for findings to be manipulated to justify decisions which have already been made (Barbour, 1995). Alternatively, the insights from focus groups can be employed to massage the presentation of an unpopular government policy, rather than change the policy itself. Several of the contributors to this volume question whether focus groups are inevitably 'empowering' or 'politically correct' and suggest that this may be an overly extravagant claim for focus group research. At the same time, however, many are engaged in trying to realize the radical potential of this research method. Some are trying to create new critical ways of engaging with discourse and society or are explicitly committed to research which reflects 'citizenship as opposed to consumerism' and harnesses the power of focus groups to 'contribute to greater public engagement with policy decisions' (Sarah Cunningham-Burley et al., Chapter 13).

Concluding remarks

In this introduction we have tried to provide a basic guide to some of the key questions around developing focus group research. We have resisted providing definitive answers in favour of suggesting ways of considering alternatives. If our answers have often seemed merely another way of saying 'well, it all depends', that is because it does! Every decision in the course of designing, conducting and analysing focus group research is interdependent. A 'one-size fits all' formula would be no substitute for serious critical engagement with the political, theoretical and practical issues around group work. We hope that the following chapters will provide readers with a solid basis from which to make their own decisions and to confront both the promise and the challenge of focus group research.

2 The impact of context on data

Judith Green and Laura Hart

Discussion group interviews have attracted some interest recently as a method for accessing the ways in which people arrive at social knowledge through interaction with their peers (see, for instance, Kitzinger, 1994a). Unlike traditional focus groups (Basch, 1987), discussion groups bring together peers, ideally participants who have relationships which pre-exist the research setting. The findings from the study on which this chapter is based suggest that such groups can provide data that are useful for health promotion professionals as well as for social theory development. The use of group interviews has a long history in qualitative research (see, for instance, Hargreaves, 1967; Willis, 1977; Hammersley and Woods, 1984, for studies in which talking to groups has generated as least some of the data). Many classic studies in sociology have relied on group discussions of various kinds to generate their data, but the impact of context on data collection is rarely addressed explicitly (Buckingham, 1993). As Morgan points out, 'social science and evaluation of research are still at a stage at which most of our knowledge about focus groups comes from personal experience rather than systematic investigation' (Morgan, 1988: 3). With the increasing use of group interviews as the method of choice in much community health research (Coreil, 1995) as well as qualitative sociology, such investigation is perhaps long overdue.

As we were interested in how children's knowledge about accident risks is produced in local contexts, discussion groups seemed to offer a useful method. Previous work (Green, 1995) suggested that 'accident stories' are an important vehicle for producing knowledge about both accidents and appropriate responsibilities for accident prevention. It also suggested that discussion groups are a more effective method than traditional one-to-one interviews for accessing these stories. The Children and Risk (Green and Hart, 1996) study aimed to explore children's views of accidents risks and the possibilities for accident prevention. The main findings of the study are reported elsewhere (Green, 1997; Green and Hart, 1998) and are not discussed in this chapter, which is concerned solely with methodology. In order to contribute to an investigation of how context influences the data produced, this chapter draws out some of the implications of various sampling strategies and institutional contexts used in this study. After describing the methodology, we will focus on three particular issues. The first is the notion of 'naturalism' in focus group research. This raises questions of how to balance the production of 'naturalistic' data with more pragmatic concerns (such as producing transcribable audio-tapes), and wider questions about the theoretical status of naturalistic data. The second is the ethical considerations of discussion group research, particularly with young people. The third is an exploration of the impact of context on the data produced.

Method

In this study, children aged between 7 and 11 were invited to participate in discussion groups. The sample of 16 groups, although not statistically representative of any larger population, was designed to reflect a range of factors which might impact on attitudes to risk, including social class, gender, rural or urban residence and ethnicity. The focus groups were held in the schools, play scheme and youth clubs from which the participants were recruited (see Table 2.1). All were from the southeast of England. All schools were state schools. School 1 was a small village school with an intake from a nearby council housing estate and from houses in and around the village. Schools 2 and 3 were inner-city primary schools, with a predominantly working-class intake, and School 4 was a Catholic school in a rural area. The Saturday club was located in a town. The children using it came from the town and outlying villages and farms. The play scheme was located near several large city housing estates where the children live. The Cub Scout group was an urban one, taking boys from a socially diverse area including council estates and privately-owned housing. Six groups were single sex, with the others mixed. Some groups were 'friendship groups': groups of children who reported playing together. Others consisted of children who knew each other less well. The size of the groups ranged from 3 to 13.

In order to recruit children to the discussion groups, contacts in the play scheme, youth clubs and schools were provided with an information sheet about the project. They were then asked to obtain parental permission (via a consent form) to ask children to participate. In some schools teachers then 'chose' children to participate, in others we were given permission to ask for volunteers in the classroom. Participants from the youth clubs and play scheme were volunteers. We also asked children's permission to tape the discussion, and many asked to hear the tapes after the session had finished. Group facilitators (who were all female) used a series of prompts to generate discussion (see Figure 2.1).

Audiotapes of the discussions were transcribed as fully as possible. Analysis of the transcripts was mainly qualitative. The transcripts were first examined closely to identify the range of ways in which children referred to accidents, and how they accounted for accidental misfortunes. They were then coded for recurrent themes, such as blame, responsibility and cause.

TABLE 2.1 *Focus groups*

Group	Place	Number of children	Rural/ Urban	Gender[1]	Age range
1	Saturday club	8	Rural	M	7–8
2	School 1	8	Rural	M	7–8
3	School 1	7	Rural	M	7–8
4	Play scheme	5	Urban	M	7–11
5	Play scheme	6	Urban	B	7–11
6	School 2	6	Urban	M	7–8
7	School 2	13	Urban	M	7–8
8	School 2	3	Urban	M	10
9	School 2	4	Urban	G	10–11
10	Play scheme	5	Urban	G	7–10
11	School 2	3	Urban	B	7–8
12	School 3	7	Urban	M	10–11
13	School 3	8	Urban	M	7–9
14	School 4	5	Rural	M	9
15	School 4	5	Rural	M	9
16	Cub Scouts	6	Urban	B	7–10

[1] G = Girls, B = Boys, M = Mixed.

Introduction
Can anyone tell me what they think an accident is?
Has anyone had an accident recently?
Seen one?
What happened/how did it happen?
What causes accidents to happen?
How do you know if something happened 'by accident?'

Follow up to stories
Could anything have been done to stop that accident happening?
Was it anyone's fault?
Does everyone agree that that was an accident?

When everyone who wants to has told their story
How can we stop accidents happening?
What kind of advice do adults give you about avoiding accidents?
Is this good advice? Do you always follow it? Why not?
Do some children have more accidents than others? Who? Why?

FIGURE 2.1 *Focus group prompts*

Excerpts related to these key themes were then grouped together with the aid of a word-processing package, with a tag listing their source. We then identified the key dimensions by which these themes were organized (for instance, blaming known others, blaming unknown others, blaming self) and explored the conditions under which they occurred (for instance, in response to direct questions, or when telling certain kinds of story).

Analysis continued throughout the data collection process. Some emergent ideas were validated using basic quantitative methods such as counting the frequency of particular stories told by participants.

Excerpts from the transcripts in this chapter are tagged with the group number (see Table 2.1), and use the following transcription conventions:

–	(at end or beginning of utterance) interrupted speech
. . .	material omitted by authors
[ ]	material inserted by authors
—	material inaudible on tape
?	unidentifiable speaker

'Naturalism' and discussion groups

Using peer discussion groups allowed us access to children's interaction with each other, which would clearly not have been possible using one-to-one interviews. Participants in the group setting (children, in our case) obtain immediate feedback on their own views and constructions of reality, as their stories are challenged, corroborated or marginalized by their peers. Peers provide an appropriate audience for the 'stories' which are told about accidental occurrences, and which are less likely to be told in individual interviews. As Kitzinger (1994a) notes, however, focus groups are artificial situations which would not exist without the intervention of a researcher. Clearly a discussion group conducted for research cannot be an unproblematically naturalistic setting. The discussions we transcribed were 'artificial' to the extent that they were guided by the facilitator, and there is no way of knowing how far the rhetorics used in our discussions reflect those utilized in more natural settings without more detailed ethnographic fieldwork of the sort done, for instance, by Christensen (1993) on children's behaviour in the playground. We cannot know the extent to which stories told in our transcripts were 'tailored' for an adult audience. This does, of course, raise the issue of what is meant by 'naturalistic' data, with its assumption that there could be a 'natural' social field untainted by the research process. There are, perhaps, relatively few social settings in which children in late 20th-century Britain interact solely with other children, in a 'children's domain', without the presence of adults (Mayall, 1993). However, even if the presence of adults does not itself compromise 'naturalism', the focus on one topic surely does. The setting is artificial in that there are a limited number of situations in which children will themselves spontaneously discuss accidents (or, indeed, many health related topics) in such depth. One exception is perhaps detailed arguments about the likely consequences of accidents. One example from our data was a lengthy discussion about what to do if a fire broke out in your flat, which does have the flavour of 'naturalistic interaction'. As the excerpt below indicates, however, the discussion in this case was too heated to identify any but the loudest speakers, and the participants interrupted and spoke over each other in their eagerness to contribute:

Ben:	Would you jump out of the window or get burnt to pieces?
Leyanne:	I'd jump out the window
Ben:	But if you lived on the fourth floor you'd be scared –
Cindy:	If you live in the top floor, the fourth floor, yeah . . . and your house is on fire, and it's by the toilet door, yeah, how you gonna get out? You can't jump out the window because you'd be dead!
Tracey:	If you –
Ben:	No listen, if you could jump from the balcony –
?	– you'd go splat on the floor and die –
?	– no, you wouldn't die –
?	– you will die –
?	– jump carefully! –
?	– you could land on your feet! –
?	– Your legs would break –
?	– how would your legs break? –
Ben:	– if your legs would just break like that, you wouldn't be able to walk for the rest of your life. (Group 7)

Such interaction may be the most 'naturalistic' (in that it might closely resemble children's interaction when away from an adult-led agenda), but as research data it is, perhaps, limited. Not only is the audio tape almost impossible to transcribe, but there is a limit to how useful analysis of the transcription can be. Beyond noting that certain questions produce animated discussion, a cacophony of children's voices produces little in the way of 'meaningful' social interaction for the qualitative analyst.

Conversely, the sections of transcript which look most 'useful' in terms of data analysis may be the ones that are least like natural interaction. They are the sections where the tapes were audible, there was little interruption or children talking at the same time, and where children's utterances were most comprehensible. The danger here is that fragments of discussion can readily be reified, separated out from the surrounding discussion as 'opinions' or 'views', and used merely to illustrate a 'theme' in the final report. Here, for instance, is an 'opinion' which could have been abstracted from the lists of extracts we produced, on accepting dares:

| *Facilitator*: | If somebody did dare you to do something dangerous, would you do it? |
| *Tunde*: | No, I wouldn't (Group 9) |

To do this, though, undervalues and even distorts the data produced by discussion groups. Of more interest is how such opinions are received by others, and what participants achieve in social interaction through such utterances. In this particular example, note the agreement in the echoed comments of the two friends here, in the interchange surrounding the previous quote, as they come to a shared understanding of what 'they' do:

Facilitator:	Do you ever dare people to do things?
Emma:	Yeah, but not dangerous things like that
Tunde:	Not dangerous stuff
Facilitator:	If somebody did dare you to do something dangerous, would you do it?
Tunde:	No, I wouldn't
Emma:	No, never
Tunde:	No
Emma:	If they dared me to do something dangerous, and I was worried about losing my friends, well they're not my friends really (Group 9)

Discussion groups tap into this *process* of social knowledge formation, rather than fixed attitudes, and are more useful for examining how such knowledge gets used in social interaction (here, for instance, in reiterating peer group boundaries) than what the content of that knowledge is. Clearly the peer group discussion transcriptions do not represent naturalistic data of the sort that would be collected using more ethnographic methods, but they do provide insight into the social processes of both belief formation (how certain beliefs are accepted, rejected or modified by peer groups) and the role of utterances about beliefs in peer groups. The practical advantage of the method is that we were able to collect the data in a much shorter period of time than ethnographic fieldwork would normally allow, given that discussion is focused on the area of interest

Rather than attempting to recreate a 'natural' field, we suggest a more productive methodological strategy would be to explore explicitly the impact of context on data, if necessary, by using different settings for the groups, and to examine carefully what impact these settings have on the kind of interaction recorded. Although this was not an original aim of our study, our opportunistic site selection resulted in a range of settings which provide an opportunity to do this.

Formal and informal contexts

The main differences between the groups included in our study seemed to relate to a dimension we have labelled 'formality'. The degree of 'formality' of the institutional context influenced several aspects of the research process, including recruitment (whether strictly voluntary or not), the relationship between facilitator and participants, and how explicit the 'rules' of conversation were (for instance, whether children took turns to speak). These factors, we argue, had considerable impact on the data produced in

TABLE 2.2 *Institutional context of group*

	More formal	Less formal
Example of context	School	Play scheme
Arena	'Public'	'Private'
Recruitment	Less voluntary	Voluntary
Research relationship	'Teacher'–'pupil'	Peer/uncertain
Rules for conversation	Explicit	Implicit
	e.g. turn taking	e.g. interruptions
	Adult led	Peer led
Language	Formal	'Naturalistic'

the study, evidenced by the different styles of story-telling in different transcripts. Table 2.2 summarizes some of the differences between the 'formal' and 'informal' ends of this dimension.

In short, our data indicate that the terms of involvement in the research impacts on the production of data in discussion groups. Discussions were, perhaps inevitably (at least in the context of British state schools), more formal in school settings than in the play schemes (where participants clearly felt on 'their turf'), and the Cub Scout group fell somewhere in between. The most striking aspect of formality was the rules for discussion, which were more explicit in the schools than other settings, and almost chaotic in the play scheme groups. In the school settings participants themselves became anxious if the discussion became too unruly and attempted to return to the order of the classroom. Although this 'policing' of what the participants felt was an appropriate style of discussion for school meant a less stressful job for the facilitator, it made it more difficult to get children to talk to each other in a more interactive way. In one of the rural schools, for instance, Lauren was concerned because her peers are having a very animated debate about accident prevention, in which they talk over each other, and she asks:

Lauren: Why can't we go round in circles? We can't all talk together – there's not so much to shout about then. (Group 14)

In another school, children admonished their peers for playing with Plasticine once the facilitator had started the discussion. In the school environment, children were more likely to wait for permission to speak (by raising hands, however enthusiastically) and take turns to contribute, whereas in the play scheme and Saturday club group participants joked with each other, interrupted and even fought. In the Saturday club, seven- and eight-year-old participants who were bored with the discussion simply got up, moved around and in one case removed themselves completely, announcing 'I'm going now!'. This is clearly their space, not the researcher's or the teacher's, and they behave accordingly, with a freedom that would be inappropriate in the school environment.

Although the less explicit rules for conversation in the least formal groups (with shouting, joking, interrupting, all accepted behaviour) meant that parts of the tapes of these discussions were difficult to transcribe (as children shouted together, or moved around the room while talking), they did provide access to stories which may not have been reported in a more constrained school setting. In several of the schools, it was difficult to find a private room for discussions. Rooms designated 'quiet space' often doubled as resource rooms, libraries or dining rooms, and group discussions could be interrupted by teachers or school meals staff. Such interruption (or even the potential for them) may inhibit disclosure of certain kinds of stories, particularly if they relate to risk-taking behaviours which may be forbidden or disapproved of by adults. The less 'public' accounts which were told in the more intimate surroundings of the play scheme are different in flavour from those told in the school setting, and may provide insights into how risks and talk about them are actually utilized in everyday social interaction. To provide a forum for more private accounts may be important for research where the aim is to examine the processes by which social knowledge is produced, rather than merely to collect the outcomes of these processes. Allowing participants space to argue (and reflect on their own accounts as they are received by peers) provided access to how ideas are utilized by peer groups. One example was the idea that some accidents 'just happen' and that nothing can be done to prevent them. Although this idea was forwarded by several children, and could thus be reified as an 'opinion', what was of interest here was how that opinion was received. In fact, it was almost always challenged by others in the group, who argued that some kind of preventative action could always be taken. Discussion groups are a particularly useful technique for accessing this kind of information about how ideas are utilized among peer groups, and transcripts from the less formal groups contained more in the way of challenges, argument and interaction between the participants.

One of our groups was held in a play scheme room with constant interruptions from other children and workers, and even though parts of the tape were difficult to transcribe, the data from this particular group suggest that the participants were more relaxed from the beginning and treated the discussion as taking place in 'their space', rather than a formal one created by the researcher. This piece of interaction, for instance, followed an inaudible section of tape where the facilitator had to switch off while she stopped two participants fighting:

Kevin: I used to smoke, yeah, with my cousin Michael, he's sixteen.
Darren: He's seventeen!
Kevin: He's nearly eighteen in June and he smokes. And he used to have a fag and not put it out and Michael put a fag in his hand and it went ssss – and it didn't even hurt Darren, yeah, and he did it to me and it hurt a little bit.
Darren: I'm braver than him! (Group 5)

Such stories may be no more 'true' than those told in the school setting, but perhaps provide insight into how boys, particularly, create risks in their environment as tests of friendship and courage. The structure of what counts as legitimate discussion in a more formal environment might well inhibit such disclosures.

The less explicit rules for conversation in less formal settings are in part an outcome of expectations about the relationship between the researcher and the focus group participants. In schools, facilitators were clearly situated as 'honorary teachers' (being in some cases addressed as 'Miss'), whose role was clearly to 'manage' the discussion, and children were adept at persuading each other to treat them in that way (don't play with the Plasticine, appeals for hand raising to answer questions). In the less formal groups, the facilitator's role was ambiguous, and open to more negotiation. Much discussion about the substantive topic (that is, accident risks) also therefore functions to try to 'place' the facilitator. In this excerpt, for instance, the boys from the Cub Scout group joke about making loud crashing noises as they squash ants which crawl across the table they sit around:

> *Gavin*: Like that was an accident, right, I was just trying to stop Leroy killing an ant, and my hand accidentally went 'crash'! (Group 16)

At one level this is 'data', providing the analyst with information about one use of accident stories, that is, the ironic use of commonsense definitions of 'accident' in a joking relationship with peers. At another level, it is presumably also a way of testing the facilitator: will she restore order to what threatens to become a chaotic exchange? Will they get told off for making a noise, or killing the ants? The most notable example of this ambiguity over the role of the facilitator outside the relatively formal school environment is perhaps one of the play scheme participants telling the facilitator after the session: 'My mate wants to go out with you'. In more long-term research, where the researcher has spent more time in the field negotiating a relationship with the participants, such ambiguity becomes less acute. However, we would argue that it is not necessarily just a disadvantage, as the 'chaotic' nature of the relatively unregulated groups may approximate 'naturalistic' interaction more closely than a more ordered research setting.

Practical considerations of sampling

The foregoing might suggest that the aim of qualitative research is to achieve as naturalistic a setting as possible. If this is an aim, it is one which, as we have already suggested, might need to be balanced with more practical ones. An initial basic consideration is the need for a room which is quiet enough to tape the discussion. This can be difficult to find in a busy school or crowded play scheme, especially in modern 'open plan' primary schools. The school groups were held in rooms including quiet areas of classrooms, resource rooms and public spaces through which other children and teachers walked. Children were on occasion clearly inhibited by staff members entering the room, or even looking through the window. This in part results from difficulties in explaining the research process to school 'gate-keepers', such as head teachers. Had we been more assertive in asking for segregated accommodation for the group discussions, or explained that the groups might become quite rowdy, our access may well have been more limited. However, as we suggested earlier, a 'quiet' room is in itself not necessarily the overriding criterion for a good discussion and it may be worth sacrificing some clarity on the tape for a more relaxed environment.

A second practical consideration is the size of the group. We found five or six to be ideal in terms of balancing audible tape with flowing discussion. Most of the groups had at least one participant who was too shy to contribute, so groups smaller than this risked being little more than interviews between the facilitator and one or more participants. With more children, if the conversation is allowed to develop naturally the tape is too noisy to transcribe, or the children themselves insist on 'turn taking' to make their contribution, and there is no time for interactive discussion. The least useful group (in terms of our subjective assessment of the transcripts) contained 13 children in a school environment, most of whom wanted to contribute. By the time all had answered the introductory question, and had described their last accident, we had to resort to putting hands up to take turns to contribute, and it was not possible to allow participants to react to each other without chaos ensuing (see earlier excerpt, on what to do if a fire broke out in your flat). This number, of course, might work well in a less formal setting when there were fewer pressures to include all children in the discussion. Although schools are most likely to provide more 'formal' institutional settings than other contexts like youth clubs or play schemes, there is no inevitability about the relationship of the setting to the type of interaction in the group. The rural schools in our sample, for instance, were more likely to include friendship groups who played with each other outside school than the urban ones, where children related stories unknown to other participants. One school group in which the discussion flowed with little intervention from the facilitator was a group in which two participants were cousins and the third a close friend. The ethos of the school or other group also influenced styles of participation. Children in the London schools, where equal opportunities were often high on the agenda, made reference to 'fairness' in allowing time for each child to enter the debate. It is impossible to know whether these children make time for each other in the less adult-controlled context of the playground.

In all schools, though, the needs of research inevitably, and properly, are compromised by those of teaching and learning. Although class teachers in general saw educational benefits for the children taking part, such as practising listening and speaking skills, they had to balance these against other needs, such as ensuring children had finished work, or not wanting certain children to feel 'left out'. In practice, then, the facilitators' abilities to control the composition of focus groups was often constrained. This in itself raises a number of more ethical considerations, to which we now turn.

Ethical Issues

Research with children raises particular ethical issues (see Alderson, 1995), in addition to the demands of 'good research practice'. Strategies for addressing the power imbalance between the researcher and the researched, such as 'social matching' for such variables as gender or ethnicity are not possible when researching young children's accounts. Consequently, the researcher has to be constantly aware of possible threats to ethical practice, and how the power imbalance affects the research process.

One issue is ensuring that children are providing their informed consent to participation. We are aware that it may have been difficult for children to say 'no' if asked in schools, particularly if our request for volunteers was made through their class teacher. We were careful, therefore, not to pressurize children into contributing to the discussion once the group was assembled, and also to ask permission to audio-tape their discussion. Schools are one environment where a hierarchy of gate-keepers may influence the sampling process: local education authorities, head teachers, class teachers and parents, for instance, may have unpredictable effects on the group composition. In one school, parents had to 'opt in' to the study, and those who had 'forgotten' to bring their parent consent forms back were not allowed to participate. Although this may formally be 'good' ethical practice, there are ethical implications of non-participation which are rarely addressed. Most children were enthusiastic about taking part (if only as a temporary escape from class!) and their feelings about being 'left out' may be more negative than those of children pressured to take part. Similarly, in another school, only those children who had completed a work assignment were allowed to participate. The exclusion of children still completing work or those who have forgotten a consent form is likely to bias the final sample of participants in a systematic way.

A second ethical issue which has methodological implications is the disclosure of potentially sensitive material. Although it has been argued that group discussions can help shift the balance of power from researcher to participants when researching with children (Mayall, 1993), there are also power imbalances within the children's peer groups to consider. Discussion groups, it could be argued, are potentially a particularly exploitative method, in which participants are not only persuaded by skilled facilitators to disclose intimate views, but also to do this in front of peers with whom they have to interact long after the research has finished. Although accidents may not seem to be a particularly sensitive issue, some of the stories children told in the discussions were potentially disturbing for them, including, for instance, brief accounts of abuse by carers and of violent crimes witnessed. Such contributions were acknowledged with questions such as 'How did you feel about that?' or a comment that the incident must have been distressing. However, we did not follow up such contributions as we did not feel our role was deliberately to explore disturbing experiences, and we did not have the skills to do so. Some of these accounts were of incidents which (in terms of our rather narrowly defined research agenda) were tangential to the study of accidents – such as stories about injuries sustained during gang fights, or of drug taking. In focusing the discussion back to the topic of accidents, facilitators did attempt to limit the potential for disturbing participants. Of course, at the same time such 'focusing' underlines the relative powerlessness of our participants to define the research agenda. What 'accidents' consist of, and what is of interest when examining accounts of accident risks, had already been constructed, and children's accounts, embedded as they are in social interaction about a range of other issues, have little impact on the broader construction of the research question. There is a tension between attempting to recreate 'naturalism' in the research setting, and thus generate disclosure of what might be more private accounts, and at the same time attempting to constrain those accounts within adult-defined research topics.

Following on from this, a third ethical issue which arose in the course of running the groups was dealing with group dynamics. In some groups, for some participants, the peer group setting was potentially threatening at times. Some children, for instance, were 'teased' by peers about being accident-prone, or were challenged robustly about the 'truth' of their accounts by other participants. Similarly, children's views about their peers could be uncomfortable, as in this account of why Tommy (thankfully not present) is accident prone:

Callum: Tommy Stanton has an accident nearly every day . . .
Adam: He's a nut case –
Lauren: – a nutter. (Group 14)

Obtaining 'naturalistic' data from children involves balancing the need to allow such confrontation in their accounts, and not to collude with what could become 'bullying'. We can only hope we achieved a humane balance by acknowledging the contributions of all children and by moving along the discussion if it became uncomfortable for some participants.

The impact of context on the data produced

We would not want to suggest that naturalism becomes a criterion of 'good' discussion groups. Rather, we would suggest that different kinds of stories are told in different contexts, and that it is useful to examine explicitly the impact of context (in terms of physical environment, ownership of the space and the research relationship) on the kinds of data produced. In the different institutional contexts we used, children displayed different ranges of social competencies. For instance, shared stories (which constitute 'collective remembering' of group experiences of accidents) are told in groups where the children have close friendships. Such stories function to reaffirm group boundaries as well as inform the facilitator about views of accident prevention. Here, for instance, Stephanie and Angela collaborate in telling a story which has clearly been told before and which constitutes part of the group's cultural history:

Stephanie:	Angela's bedroom – she has a sort of closet and there's a window there – and there's the garden – Angela says 'd'you want to do it?' Well, we both looked at it and said, 'd'you wanna do it?'
Angela:	No, I didn't!
Stephanie:	Well, we both sort of looked at it thinking the same thing –
Angela:	You said –
Stephanie:	– and we . . . and I said 'have you got a lock on your door?' and she said 'yeah', and we locked the door and opened the window and climbed on to the roof and we looked down and – Oh, God no way! It was fun – there wasn't an accident there, but –
Facilitator:	Did you feel that you were lucky, that there wasn't an accident?
Stephanie:	Yeah . . . and when we came downstairs we thought that we shouldn't do that 'cos we know we got lucky. (Group 3)

Although such stories, which draw on a shared group history, may be less likely to be told in formal settings, the 'public' accounts more likely to be produced in schools or when children are not friends contain stories that may be just as useful in terms of how they illuminate the production of social knowledge. For instance, the children in urban schools (where friendship groups were less likely to be coterminous with classmate groups) told stories that were not known to other participants, and examining how they were received or contested potentially provides useful information for health promoters interested in how their material will be received in schools. Here, for instance, two girls compare notes in explaining why they have listed boiling water as a potential accident risk:

Emma:	[This is about] someone called Imelda, and there was a kettle of boiling water, and she's only a tiny baby, and there was a kettle of water and it just fell off the edge where it had put, and it was boiling and it went all down her chest and she got all this red patch all over here.
Tunde:	I watched this true life film and its like what Emma said but the kid was a bit higher, about 2 or 3 . . . and it poured all over, and she's got scars on her face, like her skin peeled off –

??	Urrgh
Tunde:	– she's all peeled now, she's got scars on her hands, her face and her chest and her legs. (Group 9)

Exchanges like these, and the generally sympathetic reaction of the group to them, who may contribute their own examples as in this excerpt, suggest something about the 'acceptability' of accident prevention messages couched in these ways. Here, Emma's and Tunde's accounts suggest the power of television and 'true life' experiences as important to children's emerging ideas about risks to be avoided, and contribute to an understanding of what is effective in terms of health promotion.

The school based groups were also more likely to reiterate formal safety messages they had learnt at school: such as 'be careful of strangers' or 'look left and right when you cross the road'. The reactions to the introduction of these pieces of knowledge are, again, potentially useful for those developing accident prevention material for schools. Here is one of the many examples in the data of children reciting safety advice, and then discussing why it might not always be appropriate:

Ashley:	Don't ride on the road.
Facilitator:	And do you ride on the road?
Ashley:	Yeah . . . 'cos there's not many cars that come up and down our road. (Group 2)

The more formal rules for conversation in the school setting allowed participants space to consider their reactions to safety messages, such as generalized exhortations to 'be more careful' or more specific advice given by local police or fire officers who had visited their schools. The discussion group provides a forum for testing emerging interpretations of risk behaviour with peers, and the data produced provide the health promoter with useful information about how such interpretations are socially constructed.

Conclusion

This chapter has illustrated some of the ways in which context impacts on the production of data. We have suggested that closer attention to such aspects as sampling strategies, environment, research relationships and language used could be more fruitful than attempting to reproduce 'naturalistic' talk in discussion groups. Using different contexts and compositions (in terms of number of participants, gender, gender mix, friendship and non-friendship groups), enables the researcher to tap different repertoires of knowledge. This is useful for a methodological discussion about the relationships between the process of research and the analysis of data. It is also potentially useful for health promotion practitioners and researchers in such fields as accident prevention who may need to look more closely at how knowledge is locally constructed in different situations.

Acknowledgements

The research which this chapter draws upon was funded by South Bank University, London, where both authors were based when the research was carried out. We would like to thank Ilona Aitsilarbi for help with the data collection, all the teachers and youth group organizers who arranged access and most importantly, the children who took part in discussion groups.

3 Combining focus groups and interviews: telling how it is; telling how it feels

Lynn Michell

This chapter explores the use of focus groups combined with interviews. I used both methods to research young people's experiences of their social worlds. One of the key themes to emerge was the hierarchical nature of peer group structures in school and in the neighbourhood; young people were consistently able to map out their relationships, producing complex accounts of the 'pecking order' and a clear sense of the values and behaviours associated with 'high' and 'low' status. The pre-existing public and shared nature of this knowledge was very obvious in the group discussions. The young people expressed a high level of consensus about this particular aspect of their lives, were able to complete each others' sentences, quickly agreed about the status of diverse individuals and elaborated common ways of understanding the issue. Focus groups were thus a rich and productive way of gaining access to well rehearsed 'public knowledge' and highlighting the way in which social exchange reinforced such hierarchies.

However, some aspects of young people's experiences were excluded from the focus group discussions, in particular, the experiences of the lowest-status girls. These girls were mute and withdrawn in focus groups but, in interview, revealed feelings and personal information which helped to develop a deeper understanding of bullying and victimization. I argue that, although focus groups were a highly productive method for charting the 'pecking order' and examining how it was maintained, it was the interviews which allowed in-depth exploration of the experience of victimization and the identification of some underlying contributory factors.

This chapter thus sounds a warning against using focus groups as the *sole* method of enquiry in all circumstances. Focus groups can facilitate the exploration of mutual experiences and identities (see other chapters in this volume) but this is not necessarily the case. I urge researchers always at least to consider the voices which may be silenced in the particular group research settings they employ, particularly when working with 'captive populations' where research participants have on-going social relations which may be compromised by public disclosure.

Commonalties and differences between the conversation in the focus groups and interviews

The methodological reflections which follow resulted from a longitudinal study of teenage lifestyles. Thirty-six 11-year-olds, and 39 12-year-olds are being monitored over time to find out how changing peer group structures influence health behaviours (Michell and West, 1996; Michell 1997a, 1997b; Michell and Amos, 1997). Pupils took part in both interviews and focus groups at the beginning of the research period. In total 76 interviews and 21 focus groups were conducted at this stage. Ten months later, they chose whether to talk to the researcher alone, or whether to take part in a focus group. This led to a further 23 interviews and 17 focus groups. The following discussion draws on data from both time points. This chapter concentrates on the pecking order between the girls. I do this because it was among the girls that the contrast between what was said in focus groups, and what was revealed in interviews was most marked.[1]

The focus groups typically consisted of three or four pupils, and were made up of people with on-going social relationships. Where the school timetable allowed, pupils came with their chosen friends and peers (this strategy was adopted because pupils said that they were more at ease with this). Although such group compositions made the young people more comfortable about attending the sessions, it also had other implications. Much focus group research relies on bringing members together once or twice for the sole purpose of a one-off research project, so the assumption is that they may not meet again. They are thus afforded some anonymity after the event. For schoolchildren the situation is very different. What pupils disclose during the research session will not only be heard and commented on by their peers during the focus group itself, but may be reported down the line throughout the peer group network, or even beyond. The enclosed social context of the school means that focus group members cannot leave the research encounter behind for their separate lives. This knowledge may impose significant constraints on what young people are willing to disclose, perhaps sharpening the distinction between the 'privacy' of an interview and the 'public' nature of a focus group.

What influence, then, did the different constraints of the focus group and interview have on the accounts which young people offered? In response to open questions, young people presented remarkably consistent accounts of how life was for them, 'telling how it is'. In reply to the question 'So what's happening at the moment?' or 'What's it like being a 13-year-old girl/boy?', pupils introduced the same accounts, using much the same terms of reference whether they were speaking one-to-one to the researcher or engaged in focus group discussion. They talked about school, their friends, the peer group structure in their school year, their families, their interests, as well as (in general terms) more sensitive issues like bullying, drug-use and victimization.

In the focus groups and in the interviews, the young people gave a clear overview of their social world, agreeing that friendships established at primary school began to break up 'at the end of first year and start of second year'. Hierarchies seemed to emerge and consolidate between the ages of 11 and 13. Some of the 11-year-olds denied that there were divisions between peer groups, describing their year as 'all friends together', 'we are all alike', 'one big friendly group' and 'we all just mix'. However, this has changed by the time they settled into secondary school. As one 13-year-old explained: '[At first] the class used to be just one big thing and then towards the end of first year we all started to split up into little groups'. Even at 11, towards the end of the top year of primary school, top girls, for example, were beginning to be defined as a separate group. They looked a lot more mature, wore fashionable clothes and make-up, and appeared more street-wise than many of their peers. Two years later, top girl status was well established.

The 13-year-olds reflected on this process, describing it as a time of settling in, assimilating the attitudes, behaviours and styles of new individuals and groups of pupils, and then slotting in with those similar to themselves, or who accepted them. By the middle of third year at school, new peer groups had formed which pupils consistently described as 'top', 'middle' and 'bottom' and which they labelled and recognized as hierarchical. In one focus group two boys collaborated to draw a social map for me which differentiated 'top', 'middle', 'bottom' and isolated pupils ('they just go around on their own') as well as 'trouble-makers' and pupils who belonged in more than one group or who were in transition between groups (see Figure 3.1). The 13-year-olds were able to describe the characteristics of the different groups in detail including the appearance, attitudes and behaviours of members. They could quickly assign peers to rungs within this hierarchy and clearly articulate the current pecking order. Take, for example, the following extract where 'A', 'N' and 'P' inform me about the status of different girls.

LM: What were you telling me about a sort of pecking order?

P: It's like the top girls have all the looks and that.

A: Nice shapes. . . .

P: Because they're not too fat and not too thin.

LM: Are you saying they're at the top because they're good looking?

N: Aye . . . and they've got all the clothes and that.

P: A great personality . . . like all the boys want to go and talk to them because they are. . . .

N: They've got all the clothes and the trends and that.

P: Say like . . . the top group and the middle group . . . and there was one group of boys . . . they would go right to the top group rather than go to the middle average girls.

LM: So the top group girls . . . they're looked up to because they get the boys?

A: It's because they're popular and everyone wants to talk to them.

P: See like some boys . . . like if they don't get any girlfriends in the top group then they come down to the middle group and that.

The 13-year-olds described top girls as 'loud', 'confident', 'it's if they're good-looking that counts', and 'popular' both with girls and, more significantly, with boys. Their popularity was attributed both to their good looks, and to their spending power which enabled them to wear 'the latest fashion and stuff'. One 'top' 13-year-old girl, animated only by the topic of shopping, did an inventory of what she was wearing that day. This included a £150 jacket, £70 Katerpillar boots and £40 designer jeans. This inventory was displayed to other members of the group to their admiration and approval. Her father was a manual worker and her mother a housewife.

Typically, top girls spent every Saturday in town shopping, and were easily recognizable around the school by their tight black clothing, short skirts and jewellery. Most of them scorned organized out-of-school activities as 'tame' and 'boring', favouring 'hanging about' with older boys in the local park where 'everyone hangs out like 18-year-olds and everyone'.

Top girls were both admired and looked down on by girls lower down the pecking order. Middle girls envied their popularity and looks, but

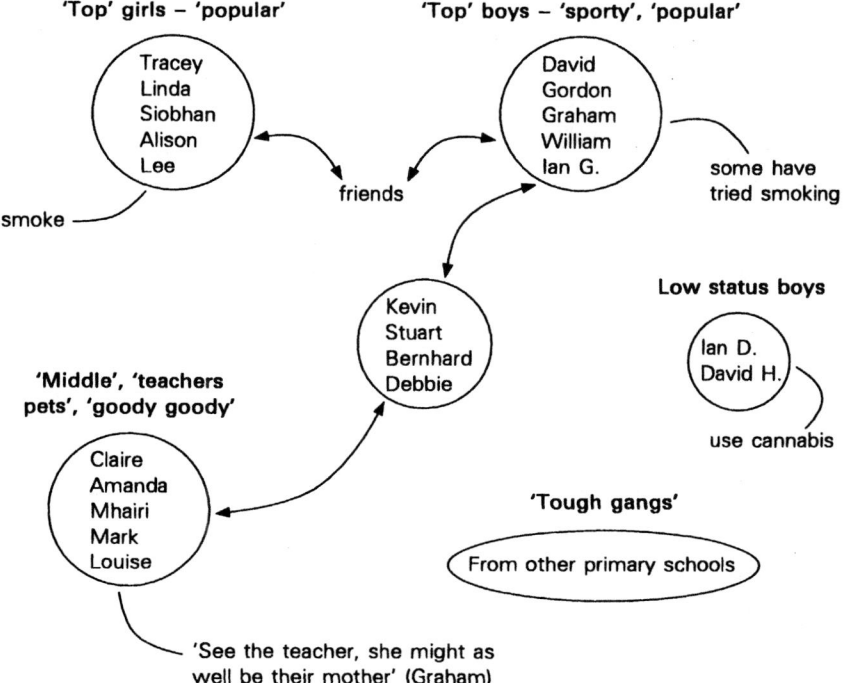

FIGURE 3.1 *Group 6's social map*

disapproved of the way they behaved. They described them as 'girls who think they're big', and 'the wrong crowd' because of their reputation for drinking, smoking, using cannabis, going out with boys and getting into trouble. Top girls down-played their rebellious behaviour, saying they were 'just out for a laugh'. Most had boyfriends, a few had sexual relationships with older boys, and all reported 'boys' to be their main topic of conversation. Some were feeling a conflict between the demands of school and peers, but managed by doing the minimum amount of school work to avoid trouble yet not enough to curtail their social lives.

Middle girls, who made up about 50 percent of the year group, were very different. They gave the impression of having developed some kind of immunity to a set of priorities headed by being attractive to boys and wearing expensive designer clothing. These girls described themselves as 'friendly', 'nice', 'sensible' and, most commonly, 'in the middle'. Top pupils called them 'sad' (meaning pathetic), 'calm', 'posh', 'tame', 'brainy', 'goody-goody' and 'teachers' pets'. They were pupils who 'didn't get into trouble', were doing well at school and had hopes of 'a career' (such as being a vet, a lawyer, a teacher, a dentist). While accepting that they were not the most popular or attractive girls in their year, they were content and satisfied because they had like-minded friends and felt in control. They consistently perceived themselves to be under a lot less pressure than the girls at the top.

Thus in the focus groups, and again in the interviews, top and middle girls not only explained the pecking order, but also volunteered what it was like to be them. Coming together for an informal discussion with chosen friends, they were willing to talk openly about their attitudes, experiences and feelings. If these girls had only taken part in focus groups, I would have gained a fairly full account of their lives in and out of school.

However, conducting interviews alongside the focus groups proved essential to the research questions that I wished to pursue. In particular, it was vital to gaining access to the experiences of the girls at the very 'bottom' of the pecking order. These girls, who were marginalized and even ostracized by their peers, were extremely passive in the focus groups. They 'tagged along' with the girls who would accept their presence in focus groups, seldom said anything and offered mainly verbal and non-verbal agreement with the statements made by others. They revealed nothing about their social status in the group research context, and said nothing about how it felt to be them until they were alone with the interviewer.

Data collected from interviews with these girls varied from that collected in focus groups in several key ways. First, some girls simply did not speak in the focus groups. Second, among those low-status girls who did speak in the groups, it was only in interview that they admitted to their own status within the hierarchy ('top' and 'middle' girls acknowledged their own status in focus groups, pupils of low status did not). Third, the interview process facilitated a shift away from statements and explanations of how life was for all of them, 'telling it how it is', toward talking about 'how it feels' to be subject to the social hierarchies. It was only in interviews that low-status pupils began to talk about what it felt like to be at the bottom of the social ladder. And (with one exception) it was only in interviews that pupils stopped talking about bullying in general terms (explaining where it went on, what happened, and the kinds of young people who were vulnerable), and started to talk about how it felt to be victims. In addition, personal and family problems were talked about by some pupils *exclusively* during the interviews. It was only then that some pupils gave voice to their discomfort, upset and sense of inferiority. In fact, during the course of the interviews, in response to the undivided attention of a sympathetic outsider, layers of meaning and explanation began to be revealed which had been entirely hidden in the focus groups.

From what was said in interviews, it was possible to piece together lives in and outside school which were often troubled and difficult. In interview, the three 11-year-old girls who were marginalized initially explained their low social status in terms of personality traits such as being 'quiet' and 'shy', attributes which were diametrically opposite to the term 'loud' applied most often to the top groups. L described her best friend S as 'She just keeps to herself really and that is what they don't like her for', but she could have been describing herself.

L:	I'm shy
LM:	What difference does that make?
L:	Well . . . they don't like to hang about with you because you are quiet. S and me are quiet most of the time but T, L, J and A and that like they carry on an awful lot.
LM:	And which are the most popular girls?
L:	T and L and that.

But being quiet or shy was not the whole story. A more invidious reason for lack of popularity, voiced by both pupils and teachers, reflected the social attitudes of a society which places a high value on consumerism, personal wealth and fashion. Being poor was a distinct disadvantage in the peer popularity stakes and pupils were very aware of the financial status of their peers' families. Talking about her best friend, L offered two reasons for her lack of status: 'She is quiet and she doesn't afford very much.' Low-status girls of both ages said they were often 'slagged' for having cheap and unfashionable clothes: 'At the age of 13 you like looking for boyfriends and going to discos and that, and if your mum has money problems, you can't go and your friends start to slag you.' They complained that the top girls were 'spoilt' and 'dead rich', and had whatever they wanted. Being popular with boys was also perceived to depend on spending power: 'The boys think T and that is the top because she has got money. They just think that we are nothing really. They just don't bother with us.' These perceptions were echoed by the top girls, who described the 'bottom' girls as 'rubbish', 'smelly', and 'they look like pure tramps'.

Judged against a background of the accounts offered by all the pupils, factors such as being 'quiet' or being 'not rich' may have contributed to the marginalization which the low-status girls suffered. But these girls suffered a lot more than neglect from their peers. All six low-status girls among both the 11- and 13-year-old cohorts admitted during the interviews that they were bullied, and talked at length about their victimization. Here, I am not talking about the general aggression between groups of pupils, particularly the boys, or fights between gangs from different schools or neighbouring territory, which greatly animated so many of the focus groups. Instead, I mean the persistent victimization of an individual pupil. In only one out of the initial 21 focus groups was this kind of bullying made explicit. This was when a 13-year-old boy launched into a long account of how he had been picked on and threatened with a cap gun by an older pupil when he first started at secondary school. The other two boys in the focus group expressed surprise; 'I did not even know that had happened to P!' Obviously this was news to them. From the account of the bullying, this seemed to be a one-off event which was dealt with when P's father reported it to the headteacher. P had friends, was self-assured, and there had been no previous or further incidents. The fact that he felt confident enough to discuss it openly in the focus group further suggested that it was now in the past and something which no longer upset him.

The accounts of bullying given by the low-status girls were very different. What distinguished these accounts was the persistent nature of the taunting and threats these girls had experienced since primary school. They found it very difficult to articulate what it was which led to their being identified as vulnerable. They routinely offered the same kind of explanations as they had given for their lack of popularity, blaming their victimization on being 'quiet' and 'not tough'.

The theme of not being tough was explored in great depth by 13-year-old M, who was not at the very bottom of the social ladder, and did not share other characteristics with the low-status pupils, but who had experienced bullying throughout her school career. Only now was she beginning to be left alone. Her long discussion of victimization is relevant to the experiences of the other girls because of the common threads of explanation which she offers. Eight pages of the interview transcript with M, who is partially sighted, were concerned with the issues of bullying, vulnerability and self-worth. She described the physical and psychological taunting which began at the start of secondary school when pupils would follow her down the corridors 'and come up behind me and walk behind my heels and everything and it was horrible'. Sometimes she would be 'cornered' by a group. Throughout the interview she questioned why she is perceived as easy prey.

I feel less tough than everyone else. They act dead hard and can stick up for themselves. I can stick up for myself but not in the way I would like to.

Everything I say seems to come out the wrong way. People just laugh in my face, you know. It seems to be that everyone is a lot tougher than that. Maybe it's just me.

Sometimes she would ask me for my views, again searching for an answer: 'Is it just that some people are better at disguising their hurt feelings, do you think?' and 'Will there be more people like me at college? I hope so.' Finally, she returned to the theme of pecking order. Top girls, she said, were not bullied because of the image they projected:

> They act smart. They think they know it all. Most of them are dead tall and they look really tough with their short skirts and tights and big boots and all that. You can tell they are a tough group. . . . I'd say it has a lot to do with that.

She also acknowledges somewhat obliquely (and in the context of the topic of boyfriends not friends) that her visual handicap may contribute to her fairly low status: '. . . you really want boys to notice you but in a way they are sort of turned off a little bit I think. You just feel as if the eyes are holding you back, like when you look at a boy, the boy's saying "What's wrong with her?"' What M manages to achieve in her interview is a quite sophisticated understanding of the interrelationship between bullying and pecking order, especially the protective factor of being in the 'top' 'tough' group

While an explanation of victimization in terms of personality traits such as being 'not tough' is relevant, particularly when such traits are linked to peer pecking order, again it is only a partial explanation, and perhaps more an effect than a cause. What the lowest-status girls revealed in their interviews led me to hypothesize that there was another explanation for their failure to thrive socially in school.

It emerged that all six of the girls who were most excluded and marginalized were coping with exceptionally difficult family circumstances, which clearly undermined their confidence. One 13-year-old revealed that both she and her mother had been regularly hit by her father. Another, who had been completely mute during the focus group discussion, described, in interview, how her father had died of cancer three years previously and an older sibling was in a children's home. 'It's hard on my mum', she explained, 'She's the only one that looks after us really. She used to work overnight at the hospital when my dad looked after us, but now she can't do that unless she gets a baby-sitter and that costs money.' Her loneliness was expressed in the following exchange:

> *LM*: So who are you closest to in your family?
> *L*: I talk to the dog.
> *LM*: That's nice you've got her. I think dogs are good to talk to.
> *L*: My mum tells me not to talk to myself.

> *LM:* You're not talking to yourself though, you're talking to the dog. Dogs are good listeners.
>
> *L:* Sometimes I talk to myself as well.

Another girl, 13-year-old P, was truanting regularly and, when in school, was not managing to do any work. In focus groups, she was ridiculed by her peers as 'weird'. At the beginning of every interview, I asked each pupil to ring a number from one to ten on a 'feel good' scale to illustrate how positive they were feeling about themselves. Most ringed seven or eight, P circled one.

Like other low-status girls, P had contributed virtually nothing during the focus group, but had stared into space looking passive, defeated and disconnected. She arrived late for her interview, after I had spotted her from my window sneaking round the school boundary to a side door to avoid the main entrance. When she finally arrived, she sat hunched up at the table, white faced. She then unburdened a family saga of such appalling circumstances that I wondered how she was managing to get through school at all.

What she told me more than explained her truancy, her isolation and her lack of concentration in class. Her mother had been to the school the previous day to inform the girl in the playground, in front of other pupils, that she was leaving and to give her some money to look after herself (an event which had occurred before). Her father, a semi-invalid, had repeatedly tried to commit suicide and was threatening to do so again. Her sister had become pregnant as a teenager and given birth to a brain-damaged child. There were ongoing repeated incidents of violence in the home. The day I interviewed her, P did not know where she would be staying that night, adding at one point: 'If my mum goes and if my dad actually kills himself that's me in the house on my own. Because my mum doesn't want anything to do with me.'

This girl, like her low-status counterparts, did not make explicit the link between her home circumstances and her social behaviour in school. In fact she found it difficult to articulate anything except the bare details of what was happening. However, it would be almost impossible for anyone under this kind of strain to satisfy the social demands of her peers by being 'friendly', 'good fun' and 'out for a laugh'. Asked about the bullying, she said: 'Every time I'm in PE they go like: "Take her out to the shower and do her in".' Asked if she had any support at school, she said 'No', adding, 'It was that bad that I ran away from school on Friday.'

From this girl's interview, and from those of other low-status pupils, it was clear that their position in the pecking order was not simply the result of shyness, which was the account offered in the focus groups and the explanation initially given in interview. This was the public explanation which hid other more private and painful ones. In the interviews, the girls revealed experiences which suggested that behind the 'quiet' fronts they presented to their peers lay family problems which had a momentous impact on their ability to function, and which singled them out as likely victims for bullying. In these cases, lack of 'toughness' which was a recurring motif throughout so many of the transcripts was actually a devastating lack of self-worth. Thus the issues of pecking order, victimization and self-worth were like interlocking rings. Because the girls looked defeated, preoccupied and passive, they were bullied, and so a vicious circle was established in which girls who already had problems out of school were picked on in school. Finally, at 13, these girls' inability to cope was often finding an expression in their truanting. Once they started to truant regularly, they became further disenfranchised. When I returned to school to talk to the pupils nine months after first meeting them, two out of the three low-status 13-year-olds had been expelled.

In conclusion, this research project gained a great deal from using interviews as well as focus groups. It was only in the interviews that pupils revealed certain feelings and experiences which would have remained untold if they had taken part only in focus groups. These experiences were central to understanding very important aspects of their social lives including their position within peer group structures. While in this chapter I have focused on pecking order to illustrate the kind of material which pupils chose not to reveal to their peers, there were many other events and experiences which emerged in the course of the interviews but were not revealed in the preceding focus groups. Two pupils wept as they talked about their parents' recent separation, others spoke about death and illness in their families. One girl revealed that she was being sexually abused.

Of course, this kind of material is not necessarily useful or relevant for other research projects, nor would all studies need to combine focus groups and interviews to achieve their goals. However, since one of my objectives is to document the teenage years from 11 to 15, I would have missed much that was relevant and salient to the young people themselves if I had only recorded their discussions in focus groups.

My experiences conducting this research lead me to caution against a headlong rush into adopting focus groups in an unreflective way if this means further disenfranchising those at the bottom of the social hierarchy. Sensitive group composition; considering the hierarchies within, and social context of, group sessions can certainly help. As other contributors to this volume point out, bringing together people with shared experiences (of illness, oppression, isolation or stigma) can actively facilitate discussion of taboo feelings and address experiences which are otherwise silenced. However, some people will resist, or social structures will mitigate against, such groupings. The lowest-status and bullied girls were isolated from one another. Any association with other stigmatized individuals, indeed any sense of collective identity, would be perceived as dangerous, increasing stigma by association.

For some research purposes parallel interviews will be crucial if the researcher is to reflect the private and isolating experiences which lead some individuals to be silenced and marginalized in group work with their peers.

Note

1 Low-status girls were often silent in focus groups but communicative in interview. Low-status boys, however, responded in both interviews and focus groups in one of two ways. They were either silent or, at best, monosyllabic in both settings, or they were silly, disruptive and related wildly improbable anecdotes about violence and drug use etc.

4 Are focus groups suitable for 'sensitive' topics?

Clare Farquhar (with Rita Das)

How do we decide whether focus groups are appropriate for particular research topics? What happens if sensitive topics are raised? How can researchers ensure the safety of group research participants? And are some topics simply too sensitive to explore in groups?

Sensitive research has traditionally relied on the use of one-to-one interviews (as in the Women Risk and AIDS Project; see, for example, Holland et al., 1994) or questionnaires (Stanley, 1995), and most of the methodological literature has been concerned with ensuring participants' safety in these settings (for example Roberts, 1981). It is only relatively recently that some attention has been paid to participants' safety in focus groups (see, for example, Zeller, 1993).

As focus group methods have grown in popularity, it has become clear that their inappropriateness for research around sensitive topics cannot simply be assumed. Focus group research has shown that people may be more, rather than less, likely to self-disclose or share personal experiences in group rather than dyadic settings (Morgan and Krueger, 1993; O'Brien, 1993; Carey, 1994; Kitzinger, 1994a, 1995). Indeed, Morgan and Krueger (1993) even refer to 'a certain thrill in the open discussion of taboo topics', and the related difficulty of 'overdisclosure'.

To those working from a feminist perspective, the fact that focus groups can facilitate, rather than inhibit, discussion may come as no surprise. By foregrounding inherent power differentials between researchers and research participants, feminist critiques of one-to-one interviews (Oakley, 1981) anticipate the more recent finding that people can feel relatively empowered and supported in a group situation, surrounded by their peers or friends (Fuller et al., 1993; Hoppe et al., 1995). They may also be more likely to share experiences and feelings in the presence of people whom they perceive to be like themselves in some way (such as other HIV positive men: O'Brien, 1993; Carey, 1994; other women with breast cancer: Tritter et al., 1996; Wilkinson, Chapter 5).

Of course, the potential of groups to elicit, rather than stifle, personal disclosure may simply serve to heighten some researchers' anxiety at the idea of using focus group methods. The idea of everybody sharing their

most personal experiences (or 'overdisclosing') may feel even more daunting than the idea of an embarrassed silence! This chapter addresses some of
these concerns, by describing in detail the experience of using focus groups
in two recent projects concerned with lesbian health. It draws on two
separate, though related, projects, one concerned with lesbians and sexual
health conducted by myself (CF) and the other with lesbians and general
health conducted by Rita Das (RD) (see Farquhar and Das, 1995; Das and
Farquhar, 1996; Farquhar, 1996). Unless otherwise stated, illustrations
and extracts used in this chapter are drawn from my own work on the
sexual health project.

The lesbian sexual health project was designed to explore community
narratives or stories. At the time that the fieldwork took place, a number
of heated debates had begun to emerge in this area (for example concerning risks for HIV transmission, and the need for lesbian safer sex; see
Gorna, 1996), and I was interested in exploring the production of these
apparently new 'sexual stories' (Plummer, 1995), and the way in which
lesbian identities were being constructed within and through them.

Both research projects were carried out in 1994/5, and overall 32 focus
group discussions were held (17 on general health and 15 on sexual
health). They were conducted in six different cities across Scotland and
England. All but one of our focus group discussions took place with
existing lesbian groups, identified through listings in the lesbian and gay
press. Some had a relatively open membership (such as lesbian social/
discussion groups). Others were formed around common interests or
characteristics (such as groups for lesbian mothers; groups for younger
lesbians). Initial contact with the groups was made through a joint letter
from both projects. As a result, many groups, and individual women,
participated in both.

The overall aim of this chapter is to use our research experience to
explore a range of ways in which questions of sensitivity may arise when
using focus groups. It begins by exploring what might make particular
topics and research populations sensitive, and the implications this might
have for the use of focus group methods. It goes on to illustrate some of
the particular opportunities and challenges we found in using focus group
methods for our own research, and to suggest guidelines for the ethical
conduct of such group work.

What makes particular topics sensitive?

Before reflecting on the potential sensitivity of a particular research topic,
it is helpful to consider what is meant by 'sensitive' research (Renzetti and
Lee, 1993). In this chapter, the word is not being used to refer to the ability
to measure small changes (as in 'sensitive screening tests'). Rather, it is
used to refer to the potential of some research to raise strong feelings and
opinions, or to pose a threat to those involved, whether researchers or

participants (Lee, 1993). When used this way, 'sensitivity' is a subjective, relative term. What feels sensitive or threatening to one may not to another, and we need to be clear whose judgement, or feelings, we have in mind. Are we thinking of the research participants, and, for example, ethical questions such as informed consent? Are we perhaps anxious about our own feelings as researchers? Or are we more concerned with the reactions of other audiences (such as funders)? In other words, we need to take a step back and consider what exactly is being judged as sensitive and by whom.

For example, reactions to our own research suggest that there is a tendency for all research related to sexuality to be seen as sensitive. Indeed, one of the dangers of choosing to draw on research on lesbian health to explore questions of sensitivity is that, in so doing, we are simply confirming an implicit link between lesbianism and sensitivity. Our intention is, however, the opposite. For it is only in questioning and deconstructing the sensitivity of any given research that we can begin to explore the advantages and disadvantages of particular research methods. So, while it is true that some people (for example, funders) may construct *all* research with lesbians as sensitive, regardless of how, why or by whom it is carried out, for others (for example individual members of the lesbian community) judgements of sensitivity may rest more on the characteristics of the research (and researcher) in question. For example, they may perceive research on lesbian *sexual* health as sensitive, but research on lesbian *general* health as more neutral. So, when considering research design, it is important to assess the extent to which a particular project seems 'sensitive' because of who we want to talk to, who we are or what we want to talk about. Only then is it possible to assess the appropriateness of adopting a particular method, such as focus groups.

Who we want to talk to

Contacting, or sampling, what Kitzinger (1994a) refers to as 'sensitive research populations', presents a challenge, irrespective of the research methods employed (for example individual interviews or focus groups). If the population in question is defined on the basis of a characteristic or behaviour which is not only stigmatized, but also potentially invisible or covert, then coming forward to participate in research may identify an individual as a member of a 'deviant' group, and expose them to oppression, discrimination or even prosecution.

With reference to our own research, for example, we were acutely aware of the potential risks involved in coming out as lesbian in Britain, even in the 1990s. No accurate information is available on the size, distribution or characteristics of the lesbian community. Many women continue to be closeted, due to the risks associated with coming out as lesbian within a homophobic society (for example, loss of custody of children). In this respect, lesbians can rightly be described as a sensitive research population, susceptible to a variety of forms of harm through research participation (James and Platzer, 1996).

Using focus groups with sensitive populations foregrounds issues of participant safety. Focus group methods require participants not only to identify themselves to us, the researchers, as members of the population in question, but also to identify themselves to other group members. Guarantees or reassurances concerning anonymity and confidentiality are therefore key, and the need to provide these may influence not only the appropriateness of adopting focus group methods, but also a number of design decisions, including how participants are contacted, the choice of discussion venue, and the way in which the data are handled and reported.

Who we are

The perceived sensitivity of a given research project may well be influenced by who carries it out. For example, there is now a growing literature on the complex influence of commonality and difference in terms of racial or cultural identity on the dynamics of one-to-one interviews (see, for example, Song and Parker, 1995; Ahmed, 1996; Edwards, R., 1996; Phoenix, 1994). Only recently, however, has attention turned to the impact of commonality or difference on focus group interactions. For example, Kitzinger (1994a) highlights the potential impact of the researcher's gender on group processes, attributing the relative success of focus group research carried out by women with women at least in part to women's well-established tradition of sharing personal information with each other in groups. However, it is also possible that group participants will sometimes feel more comfortable disclosing information to 'outsiders' (see, for example, Spencer et al., 1988 on men preferring female interviewers).

Researcher identities are embedded and implicated in all stages of the research process, and this is no less true for research employing focus group methods than for other approaches. In the case of research which is deemed sensitive, it is important to consider at the outset whether and how its potential sensitivity may be influenced by researcher identities; the appropriateness or otherwise of matching researchers with participants, in terms of particular dimensions of identity (such as race or gender); and how researcher identities can be incorporated into the data analysis.

For example, as lesbian researchers, both I and Rita Das felt that the match between ourselves and our research participants in terms of sexuality and gender was likely to play an important role in how our research would be perceived by participants, and therefore how sensitive it would be. However, although we would both describe ourselves as lesbian feminist researchers, there are also important differences between us, particularly in terms of race and age, and we were uncertain how these differences would affect the research process. This was something that we reflected on throughout the research process, and to which I will return later in the discussion.

What we want to talk about

The overall topic of lesbian sexual health provides scope for discussion of a variety of aspects of sexuality (including, for example, sexual relationships, sexual practice and sexual identity), all of which are topics that are commonly deemed to be sensitive. The assumption that sexuality constitutes a sensitive research topic is not surprising. Sexuality has long been identified by sociologists as an important site of power and resistance (for recent work in this area, see Weeks and Holland, 1996). In addition, specific sexual practices or behaviours are construed as taboo, or forbidden, within a number of cultures and societies. In Britain, individual sexual behaviour is controlled and policed through a variety of practices and institutions. For example, sex between men is commonly defined as deviant, and is subject to regulation and discipline (for example through the privileging of heterosexuality, the implementation of laws against homosexuality, and the operation of homophobia). Similarly, heterosex is powerfully gendered, and particular forms of heterosexual behaviour, including the active pursuit of sexual pleasure by women (see, for example, Segal, 1994) are also commonly defined as deviant or shameful.

While sexual taboos may generate, rather than repress, talk about sex, the form such talk can take is clearly regulated (Foucault, 1990). This regulation of sex talk is an important part of the social context in which sex research takes place. However, the assumption that sexuality is always, and in all circumstances, a sensitive topic to discuss, is open to challenge. From a sociological perspective, sensitivity can be seen as situated and constructed within the context of cultural norms and taboos. As individuals, we belong simultaneously to a range of groups, determined, for example, by our gender, race, religion, culture, age, sexuality, friendship patterns and so on; and we negotiate our life experience not within one, but within several, potentially dissonant, sets of norms or taboos (what may also be described as inhabiting multiple, potentially dissonant, or fractured identities). Our sense of what is sensitive, or taboo, is therefore likely to vary in different contexts, depending on which set of norms is most salient for us in a given situation.

For example, behaviour or topics which feel taboo in mixed-gender groups may feel unproblematic, or even welcome, in single-gender groups. Similarly, a particular sexual behaviour may be defined as taboo – and therefore sensitive – within the context of the wider society (for example sex between women), but this definition may be actively contested by those who practise it.

If we accept that the sensitivity of a given research topic is not fixed, but socially constructed within a complex framework of taboos and norms, then sensitivity can be seen to be not only fluid, but highly unpredictable. This has profound implications for research. Once *all* research topics are understood as having the potential to be sensitive, then the important question is not whether a particular method, such as focus groups, is appropriate for the discussion of sensitive topics but, rather, what implications sensitivity may have for that method and for those involved in its use, including both researchers and participants.

Choosing focus group methods for lesbian health research

The decisions taken by myself and Rita Das to use focus groups were made independently, but in both cases took into account similar issues, including *how* we wanted to work (as feminists), *who* we wanted to talk to (a sensitive research population) and *what* we wanted to talk about (a potentially sensitive topic). In my own case, it was also informed by my particular research focus (the dynamic construction of community stories around lesbian sexual health).

As feminists, we were concerned to give our research participants as much control as possible over not only whether, but how, they participated in the research process (Farquhar and Das, 1995). We anticipated that lesbians would feel less vulnerable in a group than in a one-to-one interview, partly because the sheer weight of participant numbers acts to reduce the relative power of the researcher (Mariampolski, 1989), and partly because of the greater degree of control group participants have, relative to individual interviewees, over how much they feel under pressure to contribute to a discussion (Basch, 1987; Stewart and Shamdasani, 1990). Certainly, we hoped that the power dynamics involved in group, rather than dyadic, interactions would contribute to a greater sense of participant safety, and that focus group discussions with pre-existing groups would be perceived as relatively less threatening than, for example, a group discussion with strangers (Hoppe et al., 1995) or an individual interview with an unknown researcher. We were also encouraged by evidence to suggest that sensitive topics *can* be discussed in groups (Morgan and Krueger, 1993; O'Brien, 1993; Carey, 1994; Kitzinger, 1994a, 1995).

Focus group methods in practice: opportunities and challenges

In practice, the choice of focus group methods for research on lesbian (sexual) health proved highly productive. To illustrate this, I have chosen to look at three aspects of the research process: first, gaining access to a sensitive research population; second, facilitating the discussion of sensitive topics; and, finally, the dynamic nature of the data produced through group interactions around sensitive topics.

Gaining access to a sensitive population

The generally positive response we received to our call for research participants appeared to be influenced not only by our recruitment strategy and our identities (in terms of occupation, gender and sexuality), but also by the nature of focus group methods.

Searching for a recruitment strategy that would maximize participant safety, we decided to work with pre-existing lesbian groups. We were aware that this decision would influence both the form and content of the group discussions. However, by choosing to work with community groups, we were able to negotiate with each group as a collective entity, thus protecting the identity of individual participants. All discussions as to whether a particular group would be included took place between group members, rather than with us, the researchers. If the group decided to participate in the research, individual group members were then free to attend or not on the day, as they chose. At no time was there any requirement for individuals to disclose names (or pseudonyms), or contact addresses/phone numbers (information which is frequently necessary when negotiating appointments with one-to-one interviewees). In addition, the fact that group members were already known to each other meant that at least one of the risks involved in their participation (that is, coming out to each other) was removed. While we recognize that not all sensitive populations have organized community groups, where these do exist focus group methods and group recruitment offer a valuable opportunity for carrying out sensitive research while protecting participant anonymity.

At the same time, recruiting members of a sensitive population through pre-existing groups raised two important challenges: first, the challenge of negotiating informed consent and, second, the challenge of representing diversity within the lesbian community. With respect to consent, it became clear that group consent did not always reflect informed consent at the individual level. The nature of community groups (such as open membership, with voluntary attendance at meetings, and informal communication channels) meant that not all women who attended a focus group discussion had been informed or consulted in advance. Although the research aims and methods were always explained at the beginning of each focus group, surprise or misconceptions about these were sometimes only registered much later in the discussion. Thus, although in theory it was possible for women to leave before the discussion began (that is, to withhold their consent), in practice there may have been pressure to remain (for example lack of alternative space; desire for group approval). In future research we would want to take much greater responsibility for ensuring individual informed consent from focus group participants (for example by producing a brief handout on the research, to be distributed to individuals prior to the group discussion), rather than delegating this responsibility to the community groups themselves, and accepting group consent by proxy.

Our concern to represent diversity within the lesbian community proved to be considerably more challenging. Our decision to be open about our occupations, gender and sexuality when contacting groups appeared to have encouraged participation. For example, by identifying as health care providers, we found that assumptions had been made about our roles (as 'experts'), and about the potential benefits to participants of taking part (for example, getting queries about lesbian health addressed; having an input into service development for lesbians). Similarly, coming out as lesbians appeared to reassure many potential participants about our motives in carrying out the research, and the opportunity for group, as opposed to individual, discussion was welcomed.

However, although the majority of the groups we contacted were happy to take part in our research, we are aware that certain sections of the lesbian community did not participate, and were not involved in the production of the research data (lesbian narratives of general and sexual health). Inevitably, our samples were biased in favour of women who were already 'out' in terms of their sexuality (were attending an existing group targeted at lesbians), and against those who might be expected to have most to lose by coming out (such as married women; women from particular religious, racial or cultural groups; women with children).

Whilst the use of pre-existing groups did provide the opportunity to target a broad range of lesbians, both in terms of geographical location and in terms of group membership (for example, groups for younger lesbians; South Asian lesbians; lesbian mothers; lesbians with disabilities), such targeting was not always successful.

For example, two positive responses were received from groups for lesbians with specific disabilities. However, subsequent letters and phone-calls to one of these went unanswered, and no focus group discussion took place. While some of the difficulties may have been due to practical issues (such as the resignation of the nominated group representative; the informal nature of the group), it is hard to know whether it also reflected some underlying anxiety concerning participation, and if so, how this could have been addressed. The second group opted against a focus group discussion exclusively for its members, instead requesting advance details of focus groups set up with other groups (for example lesbian social groups) that its members could attend. Overall, we made no attempt to collect systematic information on participants' disabilities or special needs. Although we know that a small number of lesbians with physical disabilities (such as wheelchair users) took part in the research, to the best of our knowledge the health and health care experiences of many disabled lesbians (for example those with profound visual or hearing disabilities) were not represented in our discussions.

The participants in our focus group discussions were also more diverse in terms of age (which ranged from 14 to 64) than in terms of race. For example, my lesbian sexual health study failed to include any Asian women. In her study on lesbian general health, RD was able to use personal networks to set up and facilitate a general health discussion with a pre-existing South Asian lesbian group (Das, 1995). However, this group was understandably reluctant to participate in a discussion of lesbian sexual health with me, an unknown White researcher. In an attempt to facilitate the inclusion of Black lesbians in both projects, RD advertised an open meeting for Black[1] lesbians, facilitated by a Black lesbian, to discuss general health and health care issues. The possibility of a later meeting to discuss sexual health was also included in the publicity. However, only one woman attended for the general health discussion, so neither meeting took place.

It is difficult to know to what extent the ethnic bias of the sexual health sample can be attributed to the social structure of the lesbian 'community', my identity as a White lesbian researcher, the discussion topic, the use of focus group methods, or all or none of these. Overall, there is no evidence to suggest that the use of focus groups was a significant factor. First, as a recent review of lesbian health studies shows (Stevens, 1993), such bias is a common feature of research with lesbians. Given the relative lack of racial integration within the lesbian community (see, for example, Mason-John, 1995), it seems reasonable to assume that participants reflected the (predominantly White) membership of my sampling base (groups advertising in the lesbian and gay media).

However, as Platzer and James (1997) and Martin and Dean (1993) illustrate, the underrepresentation of Black and ethnic minority lesbians and gay men in research samples cannot simply be overcome by the use of multiple starting points. Oppressed groups have many reasons to distrust researchers (Lee, 1993). R. Edwards (1996) describes the refusal of Black women to take part in research conducted by a White female researcher as a form of resistance to White institutional power, and to the potential appropriation of material about Black women's lives for oppressive ends. The reluctance of South Asian lesbians to participate in my own research can similarly be understood as a form of resistance to the potential perpetuation of negative sexual images and stereotypes of Black and Asian women produced in the past by White researchers (Marshall, 1994).

Second, the challenge posed by attempts to include and represent 'the other' in research (Wilkinson and Kitzinger, 1996) is not peculiar to focus groups. Similar issues are raised, for example, by White researchers attempting to include Black participants in one-to-one interview samples (see, for example, R. Edwards, 1996). R. Edwards (1996) notes that it is not only *who* the researcher is but also *how* participants are approached (for example through social networks or face-to-face, rather than in writing) that is important. This is confirmed by RD's success in recruiting a group of South Asian lesbians through personal networks, but subsequent failure to recruit a focus group of other Black lesbians through written flyers and advertisements.

Issues of power between researchers and research participants are clearly highly complex, and we would not want to suggest that sensitive focus group research can only *ever* be carried out by researchers of the same gender, racial or sexual identity as their research participants. Indeed, multiple identities and experiences mean that perfect 'matching' between researchers and participants is unrealistic, and power cannot simply be ironed out of the research process. However, if the experiences of people in particular situations are not to be excluded from (focus group) research, the research endeavour and, in particular, the process of participant recruitment, needs to be located and understood within the context and history of oppression, not only in terms of race, but also of sexuality, (dis)ability and so on. For it is within this context that distrust of the researcher (in my case, for example, a white, able-bodied lesbian researcher attempting to access and represent South Asian lesbians and disabled lesbians) is produced.

Clearly, the creation of dialogue between researchers and potential research participants is fundamental if research is to become more collaborative and inclusive. Our research suggests that focus group methods have the potential to facilitate such a dialogue in two ways. First, many lesbians who did come forward to participate commented that they were encouraged to do so by the relatively unthreatening prospect of a group, rather than an individual, discussion. Second, a focus group setting may help to ease, though not erase, the traditional power imbalance found in individual interviews (see also Chapter 5), and facilitate more shifting, fluid power relationships between researchers and participants as different aspects of commonality and difference between us (for example in terms of age, race, class or sexuality) are foregrounded in the group.

Facilitating the discussion of sensitive topics in groups

Hoppe et al. (1995) describe the researcher's role in focus groups on sensitive topics as 'setting the tone and managing the flow of discussion'. Making recommendations for focus group work with children, they suggest that discussion of sensitive topics should be preceded by warm-up activities and the setting of ground rules; that discussion should start with less sensitive topics and then move to more sensitive areas; and that sessions should end with an opportunity for children to ask questions, to clarify any possible confusions or misconceptions.

Some of these techniques also proved effective in our work with adults. For example, I found it helpful not simply to set ground rules at the beginning (such as not to put people down; to try not to talk over each other; to allow people to 'pass'), but also to invite participants to offer their own ground rules that would help them to feel safe in the group, thus enabling them to participate in the creation of safety. It was also important to negotiate with the group how the discussion would be recorded (for example tape-recording; flip-chart records), what would happen to these records (who would listen to/transcribe tapes), and how participant anonymity would be protected, in order to reduce anxiety over self-disclosure. Only one sexual health group (a youth group) declined to have the discussion taped, and none of the participants in other groups took up the offer of having any part of a tape wiped or omitted from the transcript. In general, groups appeared to ignore the tape-recorder once the discussion had started.

However, the use of warm-up activities is more problematic when working with adults than with children. My own previous training experience (for example HIV-awareness training) suggests that, even in a group of strangers, adults are often resistant to warm-up games, particularly if they appear to be unrelated to the main topic. Indeed, when the word 'game' was used to describe a structured activity in one of the pilot focus groups on general health, one participant immediately left the room. On the other hand, introducing broader, less personal topics at the beginning (such as what should a discussion of sexual health include?) did appear to facilitate later discussion of more personal experiences.

While some researchers recommend that focus group facilitators refrain from sharing their own opinions or experiences (for example Murphy et al., 1992), other texts recommend the deliberate use of personal disclosure (that is telling a story drawn from one's own experience) as a strategy for putting people at ease around sensitive topics. Although the use of personal disclosure may sometimes help to increase participants' sense of safety, perhaps by lifting taboos on particular topics or words, using such a strategy in an attempt to bridge differences of, for example, age or gender between the researcher and participants (as in Zeller, 1993) runs the danger of being patronizing.

Disclosure also raises a number of questions concerning the role of the group facilitator. In my own work with lesbians, for example, I was aware that I was constantly having to choose between a number of different, and conflicting, roles. As a lesbian, I was myself a potential focus group participant, and shared many of the experiences that participants described. However, as a researcher I knew that if I decided to share my own experiences, this would inevitably have an influence on the course of the discussion. As a feminist, I wanted the focus group experience to be empowering rather than disempowering for participants, and wanted their experiences and concerns rather than my own to shape the agenda. And as a facilitator, I was aware of the counselling discourse attached to this role, and the stress on 'active listening skills', rather than talking, in eliciting contributions from other people.

In practice, deciding which of these roles was most consistent with my overall research philosophy and research aims was a constant source of tension. Do you, for example, exercise greater power in a focus group discussion by *not* sharing or disclosing your own position or experiences or *by* sharing these and potentially silencing others? On balance, although I was open about my sexuality from the outset, I opted for a non-disclosing, non-interventionist role in the main discussion, in the belief that this would allow participants to have as much control as possible over the agenda. However, although this approach was successful in facilitating discussion, there were times when it also appeared to make some groups uncomfortable. For example, some participants voiced uncertainty as to whether they were giving me what (they thought) I wanted. This suggests that too low a level of input from the researcher may lead to confusion, or even suspicion, about the research agenda, and act to increase rather than decrease participants' discomfort. Similarly, some participants seemed to find strong disagreements between participants uncomfortable, and appeared to want the researcher to intervene or take control.

Although it is important when facilitating sensitive discussions to be aware of the comfort level of the group, and to be alert to any verbal or non-verbal cues of discomfort, this does not mean that such cues should necessarily be used as a sign to change the subject. Rather, acknowledging embarrassment, allowing tension-releasing jokes and yet not avoiding the topic in hand, helps to demonstrate that it is alright to talk about taboo areas. At the same time, it is important to recognize and respect personal boundaries (see Zeller, 1993), and to avoid individuals feeling pressurized to pursue areas that they would rather avoid. (A fuller discussion of 'sensitive moments' in focus groups can be found in Chapter 11.)

Finally, it is important to recognize that the experience of taking part in a focus group may in itself become distressing for some participants. Regardless of research method, discussion of a sensitive topic such as sexual behaviour may raise specific issues for participants. Not only may questions be raised, but painful experiences and memories may also be revived. For example, our discussions highlighted a number of areas where lesbians wanted information (such as the need for cervical smears) or had painful memories (for example homophobic responses from health care providers). Anticipating the need for information, each group was provided with a variety of lesbian sexual health leaflets for distribution after the discussion. Some groups, however, felt this was inadequate, and wanted their questions addressed more directly in the group. Similarly, although we provided participants with information on services and helplines through leaflets, and the chance to talk after the discussion, we made no other provision for supporting them emotionally after they had left. While we have no way of knowing whether such support was necessary, it is an area that we would consider more carefully at the outset of any future research. Similarly, while our collaborative approach provided us as researchers with some degree of mutual support, we recommend that researchers anticipate the need for peer support or supervision when engaged in sensitive research (Holland and Ramazanoglu, 1994; James and Platzer, 1996).

Group interactions around sensitive topics

Concern that the topic of lesbian sexual health might be too sensitive for group discussion proved ill-founded. Indeed, after many of the focus group discussions, participants commented (both face-to-face and in writing) on how much they had valued and enjoyed the opportunity to discuss lesbian sexual health with other lesbians, and how useful and supportive they had found it to share experiences. As one participant said, 'I would have enjoyed even more time to talk in detail about infections and some sexual problems. Where the hell does one go to talk about personal sexual problems?'

The very fact of coming together as lesbians to discuss potentially taboo issues was seen in itself as an empowering experience, which did not merely reproduce, but also actively produced and changed, relationships between group members. As members of one group commented,

- I think a discussion group like this might be quite a helpful experience, because, you know, everyone's been talking about their own individual experiences, and that, but there's a lot of shared experiences there.
- Yes.
- And it sort of makes you realize that you're not the only one who's having this trouble, whenever you try and get information on health.

CF: Mm. So actually having the opportunity to share that? Yes.

- Next time you go to your GP or clinic or wherever else, and they try to tell you, you know, some rubbish, you can just say 'look, you know, I know at least six other women have had the same trouble as well !!'
- Yes. (Laughter)

However, although focus groups were successful in initiating discussions of potentially sensitive topics between lesbians, at times these discussions reflected the way in which talk about sexuality is regulated in Western society (Weeks, 1985; Foucault, 1990). Sometimes discussions appeared to verge on, and then veer away from, explicit descriptions of sexual encounters, and this approach–avoidance process was often repeated several times. The tension between wanting, but not wanting, to talk about sexual practice, was revealed (and diffused) in a number of ways, particularly through laughter. For example,

- What *do* lesbians do in bed? (Laughter)
- This is (Overlap)
- . . . the realization that's been . . .
- I did warn you . . . We're working up to it!

Similarly, the following extract suggests that when discussions appear to be moving towards explicit discussion of sexual practice, this may be accompanied by a certain degree of physical discomfort, or at least the urge to change the subject!

- . . . personally I wasn't envisaging talking about the actual sexual practices of what we do or what we don't do.
- Mm.
- Aren't you hot, this-
- Mm.
- Yes, we are all going to swelter in a minute.
- Is it gas or electric?
- It's erm, it's gas.
- Shall I open a window as well?
- Mm hm. (Pause, window opened)

In Chapter 3, Lynn Michell highlights the distinction between the discourse of focus groups and individual interviews, and suggests that focus group discussions may be particularly constrained where focus group members have on-going social contact outside the research context (such as pupils from the same school). She suggests that the use of focus groups alone would, in her own research with young people, have left untold the 'private and painful' experiences and feelings revealed in individual interviews.

Clearly, the accounts provided in the relatively 'public' arena of a focus group will differ from those provided in the more 'private' context of an individual interview. A key factor in this difference is that of audience. While the primary audience in an individual interview may be the researcher, in focus groups much of what is said may in fact be directed towards other group members, particularly when group members are already known to each other.

For example, in our research with pre-existing lesbian groups, discussions of lesbian (sexual) relationships were clearly affected by past, current and of course potential (sexual) relationships between group members. Doubtless, as Michell suggests, these relationships at times constrained the discussions in particular ways. However, in other ways these relationships were *productive* of discussion, and of the disclosure of particularly sensitive personal behaviour, feelings and anxieties (see the discussion by myself and Jenny Kitzinger in Chapter 11). Given the importance of the group as audience to these disclosures, it is unlikely that these accounts would have been produced within the context of an individual interview.

For example, the acceptability of different forms of lesbian sexual behaviour is actively disputed within the lesbian community, with different behaviours (such as non-monogamy; sex with men; sado-masochistic sex; and so on) constructed as taboo by different sections of the community. Some participants saw their own behaviour as regulated and policed within the context of such taboos, and used the focus group to express their feelings about this. For example,

> I even think in the community [. . .] there's a huge amount of pressure for me to have to find a label, so I sort of say, 'OK, I'll take the label "bisexual" because I need to have something so I can start identifying with others so I can get support and deal with it, and it's like, rather than a sense of me needing to, for myself, identifying . . . others taking that label for you. It actually made me quite angry, thinking of it – because it was a sense of – I don't know – it's like me, as a person, becoming invisible. And this insistence on my sexual activity – like the sort of sex part of me was sort of considered so important. . . .

Others used the group to disclose aspects of their behaviour that other group members were unaware of. For example, one woman used a discussion of cervical cancer to volunteer the following information.

- And I guess my sense is that any irritant, any, I mean I'm quite protective about my cervix, and it's the idea of any . . . I think I have this sort of lay concept of disruption, and invasion, and cells being disturbed and . . . I got really worried about cat hairs recently. . . .
- Oh!
- Don't you like the hairs?
- I didn't know you two had cats.
- No. But I was in bed with a woman who does (laughs). And I've never been in bed with a woman before who had a cat, and who let the cats into the bed! And I found it really disturbing. I started really thinking, 'I'm sure actually cat hairs is the missing link in the cervical cancer thing'.

Group participants were apparently shocked and surprised at this exchange, not because of its surface content (that cervical cancer may be linked to cat hairs), but because of the underlying revelation that the speaker was not, as they had assumed, in a monogamous relationship with her long-term (non-cat-owning) partner. This illustrates how focus groups can provide a relatively safe space for participants to 'let slip', or casually introduce, potentially sensitive information to other group members.

The fear of being judged may not only make it hard for lesbians to be open with each other about their sexual behaviour and relationships, but also constrain their ability to share questions or anxieties about particular sexual practices. However, such questions may be legitimated within the context of a convened focus group discussion of lesbian sexual health. For example, one participant, albeit hesitantly, used the group to voice her uncertainty over the potential internal physical harm that might be caused by particular (unspecified) sexual practices. This enabled others to voice similar (more explicit) concerns, to talk about the difficulties they experienced in getting information, and to pool opinions and knowledge acquired individually (such as through books or leaflets).

Not only did the group negotiate ways of opening up and talking about taboo areas, but they did so with an apparent sense of relief and excitement.

- But in terms of what damage might, you might actually be doing which I think is kind of the sort of issue that you were raising. . . .
- Yeah it is *exactly* the sort of thing that I would like . . . to . . .
- That's in *The Joy of Lesbian Sex*.
- It's an anal chapter.
- That's the one then! (Laughter)
- That's definitely the one!
- There isn't a fist fucking thing, but there's . . . (overlap)
- Yes, that's a first.
- I'll tell you the results!

Most importantly, much of the personal disclosure and relatively explicit discussion of taboo topics that occurred in these focus groups was produced, as here, through the interaction of group members, rather than in response to questions from the researcher.

Conclusions

Whether or not focus group methods are suitable for research into sensitive topics rests to a great extent on the research question that is being asked. Different research methods will inevitably deliver different accounts or perspectives, and it is important to clarify what type of account is most likely to throw light on what it is we want to know.

The aims of research into sensitive topics can be extremely diverse, including, for example, the gathering of statistical data, the in-depth exploration of individual experiences, or the clarification of group norms and values. Traditionally, information that is deemed highly sensitive (such as information on individual sexual practice) has been collected through anonymous self-completion questionnaires (see, for example, Stanley, 1995 on sex surveys), while individual in-depth experiences of sensitive issues have been explored through one-to-one interviews (see, for example, Kelly, 1988; Holland et al., 1991).

However, group methods can make an important contribution to sensitive research. They can be helpful in facilitating access to particularly sensitive research populations, and giving voice to sections of the community who frequently remain unheard. They may create a relatively safe space for the disclosure of experiences or behaviours which in other contexts would be seen as taboo. And, by bringing discussion of sensitive topics into a relatively public arena, they may open up new possibilitites for the analysis of the social construction of sensitivity, and the identification and illumination of such group norms and taboos (see also Chapter 11).

Morgan (1988) suggests that the suitability of any particular research method rests ultimately on its efficacy in answering particular research questions, or at reaching particular populations. We would argue, however, that decisions about suitability must also take account of ethical considerations.

The ethical issues posed by focus group research are only just beginning to emerge. In our own research, for example, we found that the use of group recruitment facilitated the protection of participant anonymity *vis-à-vis* the researcher, but it also impeded the negotiation of individual informed consent. Such consent may be particularly important when research participants are being asked to address sensitive topics. It is also important that group consent to participation is not assumed to represent consent at the individual level, and that initial consent is not assumed to represent process consent (James and Platzer, 1996). Just as in individual interviews (Finch, 1984), the ease with which some people may find themselves sharing personal information or experiences in groups is open to abuse and exploitation, and it is important that at the end of the discussion participants are given the right to take back any or all of what they have said (for example by requesting that part of the discussion be wiped from the tape, or left untranscribed).

Of course, it is possible that some people will find particular topics too sensitive to discuss in a (particular) group context. In our own research, for example, some women admitted that they felt unable to discuss sexual abuse in a group; and the topic of lesbian sexual health appeared to be particularly difficult for women who were in the process of coming out. However, this does not mean that such topics cannot be raised within focus groups, or that they will not be mentioned spontaneously by some group members. It simply means that, as with other research topics, the accounts produced within one context (the 'public' context of the focus group discussion) will differ from accounts produced elsewhere (for example the 'private' context of the individual interview).

Note

1 When publicizing this meeting, Black lesbians were defined as 'lesbians descended through one or both parents from Africa, Asia, Latin America and the original peoples of North America and Australasia'.

5 How useful are focus groups in feminist research?

Sue Wilkinson

Despite the current 'resurgence of interest' (Lunt and Livingstone, 1996: 79) in focus groups, particularly in applied areas, such as communication/ media studies, education and health care, few feminists are yet using the method. Limited use of focus groups by feminists is suggested by the omission of the method from feminist research methods texts: for example, focus groups are not referenced in Miller and Treitel's (1991) annotated bibliography of feminist research methods; Nielsen's (1990) volume of exemplary readings of feminist research methods; or in the recent collection edited by Maynard and Purvis (1994). (A rare exception is Shulamit Reinharz's [1992] text, *Feminist Methods in Social Research*, which includes two paragraphs on focus groups in a chapter on 'original feminist research methods'.) My own literature review reveals only about two dozen published feminist focus group studies to date. In addition, there is my own ongoing research on women's experiences of breast cancer, and two other feminist focus group projects currently in progress at Loughborough University – on young heterosexual women saying 'no' to sex (Hannah Frith); and on feminists criticizing the work of other feminists (Evelyn Kerslake).

In this chapter, I will draw on these studies to show how feminist researchers might use focus groups, and to suggest some ways in which the potential of the method could be realized in the future development of feminist research. The chapter is not primarily oriented towards the focus group researcher who might be interested in feminist research; rather, it is written for the feminist researcher who, in picking up a text on focus groups, might ask, 'What – as a feminist – has this method got to offer me?' This chapter will illustrate how focus groups are particularly useful in offering two key features often suggested as essential in feminist research. First, focus groups are a *contextual* method: that is, they avoid focusing on the individual devoid of social context, or separate from interactions with others. Second, focus groups are a relatively *non-hierarchical* method: that is, they shift the balance of power away from the researcher towards the research participants. Other advantages of focus groups for feminist research include: their use with minority groups; their potential as a tool for action research; and their value as a form of 'consciousness-raising'. I will look at each of these advantages in turn, and then conclude by considering some of the ways in which feminist focus group research might be developed in the future.

Focus groups and key features of feminist research

There is an extensive feminist critique (see, for example, Reinharz, 1983; Jayaratne and Stewart, 1991) of the decontextualized and rigidly hierarchical nature of many traditional research methods. I will summarize the main criticisms briefly here, because it is precisely these problems which, I argue, can be addressed through the use of focus groups.

Critiques of decontextualized methods

Feminists have criticized the 'context-stripping' (Parlee, 1979) nature of traditional methods (such as surveys, questionnaires, psychological tests and experiments, and even interviews), as a result of which, as Janis Bohan (1992: 13) says, 'the reality of human experience – namely that it always occurs in context . . . is lost'. Feminists have consistently emphasized the importance of social context, insisting that feminist methods should be *contextual* – that is, avoid focusing on the individual in isolation, cut off from interactions and relationships with other people. Pioneer feminist psychologist Naomi Weisstein (1993: 200) argued that we must 'turn away from the theory of the causal nature of the inner dynamic and look to the social context within which individuals live'. Relationships with others are an important part of that social context: 'If you really want to know either of us', say Michelle Fine and Susan Gordon, then:

> . . . do not put us in a laboratory, or hand us a survey, or even interview us separately alone in our homes. Watch me (MF) with women friends, my son, his father, my niece, or my mother and you will see what feels most authentic to me. (Fine and Gordon, 1989: 159)

Others suggest that human experience is *constructed* within specific social contexts: collective sense is made, meanings negotiated and identities elaborated, through the processes of social interaction between people (Hare-Mustin and Marecek, 1990; West and Zimmerman, 1991). Feminists have also criticized the individualism which is the legacy of psychology, proposing instead that the individual self may be characterized as 'in connection' or 'relational' (Jordan et al., 1991; Taylor et al., 1996), or seen primarily as a social construction, a cultural product of Western thought (Lykes, 1985, Kitzinger, 1992).

Critiques of rigidly hierarchical methods

Feminists have also criticized traditional research in which people are transformed into 'object-like subjects' (Unger, 1983: 14), with the interests and concerns of research participants completely subordinated to those of the researcher. In traditional research, participants' voices are typically silenced or severely circumscribed by the powerful voice of the researcher, and their experience may be occluded, ironicized, invalidated or even erased (Pollner, 1975; Woolgar, 1983). In feminist research, by contrast, 'respecting the experience and perspective of the other, remains at the heart of contemporary approaches' (Worrell and Etaugh, 1994: 444); with many feminist researchers expressing commitment to 'realizing as fully as possible women's voices in data gathering and preparing an account that transmits those voices' (Olesen, 1994: 167). Feminist researchers have often criticized the traditional 'hierarchy' of power relations between researcher and researched (see Peplau and Conrad, 1989: 386; Campbell and Schram, 1995: 88). They have suggested that feminist research is characterized by '*non-hierarchical* relations' (Seibold et al., 1994: 395, my emphasis), and have called for the 'vertical relationship between researcher and "research object"' (referred to as 'the *view from above*') to be replaced by 'the *view from below*' (Mies, 1983: 123, original emphases). Research methods have sometimes been evaluated in terms of their adequacy in enabling feminist reseachers to engage in 'a more equal and reciprocal relationship with their informants' (Graham, 1984: 113). There has been vigorous debate, in particular, about the effectiveness of interview methods in reducing the power of the researcher (Oakley, 1981; Finch, 1984; Ribbens, 1989; Cotterill, 1992).

These two criticisms – of methods which are decontextualized and rigidly hierarchical – have led feminist researchers frequently to advocate qualitative approaches, even to suggest that these are 'quintessentially feminist' (Maynard and Purvis, 1994: 3). I will not rehearse here the arguments for the use – or particular merits – of qualitative methods in feminist research, as these have been well documented elsewhere (see, for example, Reinharz, 1983; Griffin, 1985; Marshall, 1986; Henwood and Pidgeon, 1995). Rather, I will demonstrate the particular value of focus groups as a qualitative feminist method. I will show how focus groups, in particular, enable the researcher to meet the feminist criticisms of traditional research outlined above: that is, as decontextualized and as rigidly hierarchical. Focus groups meet the charge of decontextualization by being a *contextual* method – by providing an interactive social context within which meaning-making can be observed. Focus groups meet the charge of rigid hierarchy by being a relatively *non-hierarchical* method – by reducing the researcher's power and enabling research participants better to assert their own agendas and points of view. I consider each of these advantages in some detail, before turning to look at how feminist focus group research might be developed.

Focus groups are a contextual method

A focus group participant is not an individual acting in isolation. Rather, participants are members of a social group, all of whom interact with each other. In other words, the focus group is itself a social context. As leading focus group researcher David Morgan emphasizes: 'The hallmark of focus groups is *the explicit use of group interaction to produce data and insights that would be less accessible without the interaction found in a group*' (Morgan, 1988: 12, original emphasis). These social interactions between participants constitute the primary data. The interactive data generated by focus groups are based on the premise that 'all talk through which people generate meaning is contextual' (Dahlgren, 1988: 292). The social context of the focus group provides an opportunity to examine how people engage in such meaning-generation, how opinions are formed, expressed and (sometimes) modified within the context of discussion and debate with others. As Jenny Kitzinger (1994b, see also Chapter 11, this volume) points out, in focus group discussions meanings are constantly negotiated and renegotiated. In the focus group, people take differing individual experiences and attempt to make 'collective sense' of them (Morgan and Spanish, 1984: 259). It is this process of collective sense-making which occurs through the interactions between focus group participants.

In individual interviews, the interaction is between the interviewer and a single interviewee; in focus groups, 'a multitude of interpersonal dynamics occur', through interactions people change their views, and 'the unit of analysis becomes the group' (Crabtree et al., 1993: 144). Not only do focus groups provide a context for the collection of interactive data, they also offer:

> . . . *the opportunity to observe directly the group process*. In the individual interview respondents *tell* how they would or did behave in a particular social situation. In the group interview, respondents react to each other, and their behavior is directly *observed*. (Goldman, 1962: 62, original emphases)

An example of the way in which group processes can become a key part of the analysis is found in Mick Billig's (1992) work on talk about the British Royal Family. One of Billig's concerns is with the way in which people construct others as gullible and uncritical consumers of the media; they are used as 'Contrastive Others' to illustrate the speaker's own critical powers, and thereby enhance his or her own identity. Billig describes a group discussion between four people, aged between 59 and 66 and all related, plus the mother of one of them, aged 87:

> . . . [whose] contributions to the conversation were often interruptions, as she told jokes or reminisced about poverty before the war. She even broke into song once: 'I'm 'Enery the Eighth I am', she sang. For periods, she remained mute, while the not-so-elderly got on with their nimble conversational business. (Billig, 1992: 159)

It is this woman who is constructed as the gullible Other by her relatives, and Billig analyses the interactive mechanisms through which this Othering is achieved. In Billig's presentation of his data, one can see the *process* of Othering at work, and how the elaboration of the speaker's own identity depends on the interactive production of this 'Contrastive Other'. (For a more extended discussion of the way in which Billig's analysis has made full use of the focus group interaction, see Wilkinson, 1998a.) Focus groups, then, offer the researcher the opportunity to observe directly the co-construction of meaning in a social context, via the interactions of group participants.

Those few *feminist* researchers who have used focus groups have similarly taken advantage of the method to illustrate how arguments are developed, and identities elaborated, in a focus group context, typically through challenge and provocation from other members of the group. For example, after viewing a televized reconstruction of the rape and murder of a young female hitchhiker, one participant in Schlesinger et al.'s (1992: 146) research responds to another member of the group (who had expressed the opinion that the hitchhiker 'was leading them on . . . the way she was dancing, and her clothes as well . . . her top, her shirt') with the unequivocal statement: 'Her clothes have got nothing to do with it'. She adds, 'I didn't want to say anything because my views are totally clear on this . . .' – and she then expounds them at some length. The provocation of the earlier speaker ensured that this woman's views were elicited and elaborated. Other examples of this include a (self-identified) 'upper-class' teenage girl, whose remarks imply that the behaviour of the working class is responsible for the problems of the class system, and who is challenged by other group members to defend this view (Frazer, 1988: 349); and female students in an elite law school, who elaborate their experiences of profound alienation (and support each other in so doing) in the context of provocation from a male student who refers to 'making a mountain out of a molehill' (Fine and Addelston, 1996: 80).

In the following extract, two pub landladies (Doris and Fiona) consider the possible role of their profession in causing their breast cancer (another focus group participant – Edith – and the researcher – SW – also contribute to the discussion):

Doris: Well, I erm, like you
Edith: It's not in the family
Doris: Like you I wondered if it was with <u>pulling</u>, you know
Fiona: Yeah
SW: [Explains to Edith] These two were talking about being pub landladies and whether that contributed
Edith: Well that – oh [indistinct]
Fiona: Yeah, you know, yeah
Edith: Is it at the side where . . .?
Doris: Mine's at the side where [indistinct]

Fiona: where you pulled
Doris: Yes
Fiona: and mine's the same side, and I've got two friends who are both pub landladies down south
Doris: And then
Fiona: and they're sisters and both of them have got breast cancer, both on the same side as they pull beer
Doris: And then there's the atmosphere of the smoke in the [stutters] pub
Fiona: Well I, I'm not, I don't know, I'm not so sure about that one
Doris: Well, I think I lean to that more in, what do they call him? The artist, Roy Castle
Fiona: Oh Roy Castle, yeah, with passive smoking
Doris: Mm hm, he said he got his through being in smoke, smoke filled rooms (Wilkinson, 1998b)

Together, these women elaborate a joint theory that pint-pulling is implicated in breast cancer (with Fiona providing additional confirmatory evidence); but they diverge when Doris introduces passive smoking, leading her to draw on a recent television documentary to support her argument that this is a significant factor.

The elaboration of meaning and identity through group interaction is also evident in an over-dinner group, in which 'the text of conversation co-created by we six' (Macpherson and Fine, 1995: 181) is used to elaborate 'racial'/ethnic differences between participants. Janet (described by the authors as 'Korean-American') is challenged by Shermika, when she refers to 'African-Americans' at her school:

Shermika: I don't consider myself no African-American.
Janet: That's the acceptable politically correct . . .
Shermika: I'm full American, I've never been to Africa.
Janet: Are you black or wh[ite] . . . African-American? (Sorry.)
[Janet inadvertently repeated the 'black or white' dichotomy that Shermika had announced was excluding Janet.]
Shermika: I'm neither one.
Michelle: What racial group do you consider yourself?
Shermika: Negro. Not black, not African-American. That's just like saying all white people come from Europe. Why don't you call 'em Europe-American? (Macpherson and Fine, 1995: 188–9)

Here, Shermika is defending and elaborating her identity (as 'full American' and as 'Negro') in the context of a challenge from a group member. Janet's challenge also leads Shermika to explain her reasons for these identity-label choices ('I've never been to Africa'). This exchange then prompts Janet to elaborate her *own* identity, creating her own differences from Shermika.

In sum, then, feminist focus group researchers have shown how the social context of the focus group offers the opportunity to observe the co-construction of meaning and the elaboration of identities through interaction. The interactive nature of focus group data produces insights that would not be available ouside the group context (although there is disappointingly little evidence of sophisticated analyses by feminists of such interactive data). This emphasis on the person in context makes the focus group an ideal method for feminists who see the self as relational, or as socially constructed, and who argue, therefore, that feminist methods should be contextual.

Focus groups are a non-hierarchical method

Compared with most traditional methods, including the one-to-one interview, focus groups inevitably reduce the researcher's power and control. Simply by virtue of the number of research participants simultaneously involved in the research interaction, the balance of power shifts away from the researcher. The researcher's influence is 'diffused by the very fact of being in a group rather than a one-to-one situation' (Frey and Fontana, 1993: 26). As the aim of a focus group is to provide opportunities for a relatively free-flowing and interactive exchange of views, it is less amenable to the researcher's influence, compared with a one-to-one interview. Focus groups place 'control over [the] interaction in the hands of the participants rather than the researcher' (Morgan, 1988: 18).

In direct contrast to the goals of most feminist researchers, the reduced power and control of the researcher is typically identified as a *disadvantage* of the method in the mainstream focus group literature. As leading handbook author Richard Krueger (1988: 46) laments, reduced researcher control 'results in some inefficiencies such as detours in the discussion, and the raising of irrelevant issues . . .'. Other researchers warn that the potential of groups to 'usurp the moderator' (Watts and Ebbutt, 1987: 32) may lead to 'relatively chaotic data collection' (Kvale, 1996: 101). The reassertion of control over focus group participants is seen as an important issue and is addressed by many of the 'how to' books on focus groups (for example Krueger, 1988; Stewart and Shamdasani, 1990; Vaughn et al., 1996). These authors offer advice for dealing with 'problem' participants who do not behave in line with the researcher's requirements. One focus group expert offers detailed instructions for maintaining power over participants in a section headed 'Pest Control' (Wells, 1974).

However, even some mainstream focus group researchers recognize that this reduction in the researcher's influence can also be an *advantage*. David Morgan (1988: 18) points out that 'participants' interaction among themselves replaces their interaction with the interviewer, leading to a greater emphasis on participants' points of view'. Focus groups are sometimes presented as an opportunity for 'listening to local voices' (Murray et al., 1994), for learning the participants' own language instead of imposing the researcher's language upon them (Freimuth and Greenberg, 1986: 39; Bers, 1987: 27; Mays et al., 1992), and for gaining an insight into their conceptual worlds (Broom and Dozier, 1990). Focus groups can allow participants much greater opportunity to set the research agenda, and to 'develop the themes most important to them' (Cooper et al., 1993), which may diverge from those identified by the researcher. Compared with a one-to-one interview, it is much harder for the researcher to impose his or her own agenda in the group context.

Focus group researchers, then, are virtually unanimous that, compared with many other methods of data collection, focus groups reduce the researcher's influence. For some (for example Krueger, 1988), this is a *disadvantage* which (while offset by the numerous advantages of the method) needs careful management. For others (for example Morgan, 1988), it is an *advantage* which enables participants to contribute to setting the research agenda, resulting in better access to their opinions and conceptual worlds. But, whether identified as a problem or as a benefit, researchers concur on the relative lack of power held by the focus group researcher.

Those few *feminists* who have used focus groups have similarly emphasized the shift in the balance of power, and – particularly – the extent to which the method enables research participants to speak in their own voice, to express their own thoughts and feelings, and to determine their own agendas. In their research on date rape, Norris et al. (1996: 129) claim that: 'Within feminist research, focus groups have been used to provide a "voice" to the research participant by giving her an opportunity to define what is relevant and important to understand her experience'. Feminist psychologist Oliva Espin (1995: 228), using focus groups in her exploration of immigrant/ refugee women's understandings of sexuality and their internalization of cultural norms, comments that the method's 'open-ended narratives allow for the expression of thoughts and feelings while inviting participants to introduce their own themes and concepts'. Similarly, in a study of women's reactions to violent episodes on television, Schlesinger et al. (1992: 29) saw the group discussions as an opportunity for women to 'determine their own agendas as much as possible'.

In a group context, it is easier for participants to challenge views with which they disagree, or to reject others' assertions, including those of the researcher. Here are two examples from feminist focus group work in progress at Loughborough University which illustrate such challenges. In the first, feminists are debating whether 'destructive' criticism of other feminists' work has any positive functions. Participant B directly challenges the researcher's suggestion, and strongly asserts her own opposing view:

Researcher: So feminism is now big enough to have disagreements?
A: Umm
B: I'm so sick of that argument . . . I was just going to say that what you were saying – that just struck me that instead of a confidence there is a kind of weakness, where feminism has gone so far there is nothing else to say apart from to attack who ever is saying that.

A:	So it's become irrelevant that – all this kind of post-feminism stuff?
B:	Yeah – there isn't anything different you can say about it because there are so many people spouting off these ideas
A:	Right –
B:	– and there's nothing left to do but attack anybody that says anything of any relevance, so it's kind of not exactly going backwards, but it's kind of degenerated into a kind of personal slanging match. (Kerslake, unpublished data)

Participant B is also able to use participant A's reference to 'post-feminism' to strengthen her own argument that destructive criticism is damaging, and that through such personal attacks feminism has 'degenerated'.

Second, the following exchange arises in response to a (young, female) researcher's request to her focus group participants for examples of the excuses they use to avoid sex. Three young heterosexual women, Lara, Cath and Helen, challenge the researcher's implication that young women have to find excuses to avoid having sex with their male partners:

Cath:	Do you mean like really naff excuses?
Researcher:	Well, anything that you would use.
Lara:	But I mean . . .
Cath:	But it depends how far you've got because that can go completely . . .
Helen:	No, but . . . no, but that just gives you a few days respite doesn't it? – and then I think that after a few days you'd just feel so shitty that you had to rely on that.
Lara:	That's horrible, why should you have to lie on an issue that is just perfectly right and you feel strongly about, why do you have to come up with excuses?
Cath:	That's right.
Lara:	I mean, I would much rather, it would be so nice just to be able to say no, for no particular reason. I don't really know, I haven't felt the need to think about it, I just don't particularly fancy it.
Helen:	I just don't feel like it at the moment.
Lara:	Wouldn't that be nice! (Frith, unpublished data)

Although these young women are evidently able to generate excuses to avoid sex, they reject the idea that this is an appropriate question for the researcher to be asking, or a desirable action in which to be engaged.

Challenges from participants may lead the researcher to alter the way the research is perceived, to rewrite the research questions, or even to change the direction of investigation. In my own research on breast cancer, participants insisted on the 'support group' function of the focus groups, although I consistently emphasized their main purpose as research-oriented. Feminist psychologist Christine Griffin (1986: 180) describes how her participants sometimes 'discuss[ed] particular issues amongst themselves, without waiting for my next question . . . these discussions did not always fall within my list of pre-selected topics, and I was able to amend this list as the research progressed'. Another study involving conversations about gender with teenage girls changed direction because the researcher 'didn't ask questions about class as such, but the public [private] school groups frequently brought it into the discussion' (Frazer 1988: 344).

Shifting the balance of power towards the research participants can also, of course, pose *problems* for feminist researchers, when anti-woman, anti-feminist, racist or other offensive ideas are expressed and elaborated in the group context. Researchers running both interview and focus group studies with men about HIV-related risk behaviours, comment that:

> Harassment was more overt in the public setting of a group discussion. Often, in a group situation men were displaying to other men attempting to humiliate the researcher. Whilst this was unpleasant in itself it also led to anxiety that the badinage might escalate and become out of the researcher's control. (Green et al., 1993: 631)

(One example they cite involves a participant who 'took the microphone off the table, placed it between his legs at an angle of approximately 45 degrees and jerked his hand up and down it'.)

In sum, then, feminist focus group researchers recognize that focus groups shift the balance of power and control towards the research participants, enabling them to assert their own interpretations and agendas. Despite the disadvantages of this in some contexts (particularly when researching powerful – for example male – groups), this reduction in the relative power of the researcher also allows the researcher better to access, understand and take account of the opinions and conceptual worlds of research participants, in line with the suggested principles of feminist research.

Other advantages of focus groups for feminist research

As I have shown, then, the particular advantages of focus groups for feminist research are that they are contextual (they offer a social context for meaning-making); and that they are relatively non-hierarchical (they shift the balance of power away from the researcher towards the research participants). In this way, focus groups meet the concerns of feminist researchers to avoid the problems of decontextualized and rigidly hier-archical research methods. Here, I will draw attention to other ways in which the method may benefit feminist research, before considering how feminist focus group research might be developed in future. I look briefly, in turn, at the method as appropriate for use with underrepresented and severely disadvantaged social groups; as a tool for action reseach; and as a form of 'consciousness raising'.

Work with minority groups

Some focus group researchers suggest that focus groups may be particularly useful for accessing the views of those who have been poorly served by traditional research:

> Social research has not done well in reaching people who are isolated by the daily exhausting struggles for survival, services and dignity – people who will not respond to surveys or whose experiences, insights and feelings lie outside the range of data survey methods. These people are also uncomfortable with individual interviews. We found that almost all elements in the community could be accessed in the safe and familiar context of their own turf, relations and organizations through focus groups. (Plaut et al., 1993: 216)

Focus group participants have included, for example, 'difficult-to-reach, high-risk families' in an inner city (Lengua et al., 1992); 'black gay men' (Mays et al., 1992); 'the elderly' (Chapman and Johnson, 1995); 'village women' in rural counties of China (Wong et al., 1995); 'minority ethnic communities in Britain' (Chapter 7, this volume); and 'street children and refugee children in Nepal' (Chapter 6, this volume). Such use of focus groups is in line with the proposal that feminist research should pay particular attention to the needs of 'those who [have] little or no societal voice' (Rubin and Rubin, 1995: 36) – and feminist focus group researchers have similarly used the method in researching the lives of 'immigrant/refugee' women (Espin, 1995) and 'urban African American preadolescents and young adolescents living in poverty' (Vera et al., 1996).

Action research

Some focus group researchers suggest that the method 'has promise in action research' (Vaughn et al., 1996: 302), that it can facilitate change in organizations (Chapter 8, this volume), even that it can it can be used radically 'to empower and to foster social change' (Johnson, 1996: 536). For example, Padilla (1993) describes a project to overcome barriers to the success of Hispanic students in a US community college, based on the work of Brazilian educator Paulo Friere. He uses focus groups as a 'dialogical method' to empower research subjects to change their own lives as part of 'a larger project of political freedom, cultural autonomy, and liberation from oppressive economic and social conditions' (1993: 154). The intention of the project is that:

> By critically examining through dialogue the problematic aspects of their own lives, the subjects are able to gain the critical understanding that is necessary to identify viable alternatives to existing social arrangements and to take appropriate actions to change and improve their own lives. (Padilla, 1993: 154)

Some feminists have also been concerned that their research should have direct practical effects in women's lives, and have similarly used focus groups in action research projects. For example, Maria Mies, in a project aiming to make practical provision for battered women, insists that, in order to implement a non-hierarchial egalitarian research process, to ensure that research serves the interests of the oppressed, to develop political awareness, and to use her own relative power in the interests of other women, 'interviews of individuals . . . must be shifted towards group discussions, if possible at repeated intervals' (1983: 128). Mies' view is that 'this collectivization of women's experience . . . helps women to overcome their structural isolation in their families and to understand that their individual sufferings have social causes' (1983: 128). Similarly, Jean Orr's project on Well Women Clinics 'encourages members to see that problems are often not caused by personal inadequacy but are based in current social structure' (1992: 32), offering 'support to members in changing aspects of their lives', and enabling them to 'feel confident in asserting their needs to others' (1992: 32) within the Community Health Movement and beyond. (Further examples of the use of focus groups in feminist action research on health issues may be found in the collection edited by de Koning and Martin [1996].)

'Consciousness-raising'

The similarities between focus group discussions and the 'consciousness-raising' sessions common in the early years of second wave feminism have fuelled the interest of several feminist researchers. Noting that it was through consciousness-raising that Farley (1978) came to identify and name the experience of 'sexual harassment', feminist sociologist Carrie Herbert (1989) included group discussions in her work with young women on their experience of sexual harassment. Similarly, Michelle Fine (1992: 173), chronicling a set of group discussions with adolescent girls, claims that, 'through a feminist methodology we call "collective consciousness work", we sculpted . . . a way to theorize consciousness, moving from stridently individualist feminism to a collective sense of women's solidarity among difference'. Feminist researchers using focus groups in this way (see also Mies, 1983; Orr, 1992) hope that through meeting together with others and sharing experience, and through realizing group commonalities in what had previously been considered individual and personal problems, women will develop a clearer sense of the social and political processes through which their experiences are constructed – and perhaps also a desire to organize against them. It has to be said, however, that other researchers using focus groups are less sanguine about their consciousness-raising potential. Jenny Kitzinger's focus groups' discussions of HIV risk offer salutary counter-examples of the alleged 'consciousness raising' benefit of group discussion. In several groups, she says, 'any attempt to address the risks HIV poses to gay men were drowned out by a ritual period of outcry against homosexuality' (Kitzinger, 1994a: 108).

To summarize, the advantages of focus groups for feminist research are that they are a contextual method; that they are a non-hierarchical method; and that they are useful in work with minority groups, in action research, and in 'consciousness-raising'. Given these advantages, it is perhaps surprising that focus groups are not more widely used by feminist researchers.

Developing feminist focus group research

Finally, while it is a pity that there is not *greater* use of focus groups in feminist research, it is also a pity that there is not *better* use of focus groups, capitalizing on their particular advantages as a method. I will highlight here some of the main *problems* in the current use of focus groups (by feminists and others), and indicate the ways in which these could be overcome, in order to maximize the value of the method as a tool for feminist research. These problems are: inappropriate use of focus groups; neglect of group interactions; and insufficient epistemological warranting. I will look briefly at each.

Inappropriate use of focus groups

Although the 'how to' books include advice on 'how not to' (and also 'when not to') use focus groups (for example Morgan and Krueger, 1993; Vaughn et al., 1996), this advice is often disregarded, not least by feminist focus group researchers. For example, although the textbooks caution against using focus groups as a quick and easy way of increasing sample size, indicating that the method is unsuitable for conducting large scale studies, it is not uncommon for researchers to present as their rationale for using focus groups that they are 'effective and economical in terms of both time and money' (Espin, 1995: 228), or that they are 'a means of gathering qualitative data from a relatively large sample' (Lampon, 1995: 171). Similarly, although the handbooks warn against inappropriate quantification of focus group data (see Morgan and Krueger, 1993: 14), this, too, is often apparent: for example, Geraghty (1980) offers a statistical profile of donors to a particular charity, based on four focus groups; while Flexner et al. (1977) present a graph comparing three focus groups ('consumers', 'potential consumers' and 'providers' of abortion services) in terms of the average ranks given by members of each group to features of an abortion service. More recently, an article included in a special issue of *Qualitative Health Research* on 'Issues and Applications of Focus Groups' (Carey, 1995), categorizes the social services concerns of HIV-positive women and tabulates the number of responses coded under each category (Seals et al., 1995) – this is despite at least two injunctions elsewhere in this Special Issue *not* to quantify focus group data.

Neglect of group interactions

Although interaction between group participants is supposed to be a defining characteristic of focus group methods, one review of over 40 published reports of focus group studies 'could not find a single one concentrating on the conversation between participants and very few that even included any quotations from more than one participant at a time' (Kitzinger, 1994a: 104). For this chapter, I reviewed almost 200 focus group studies ranging in date of publication from 1946–96, with the same result. Focus group data are most commonly presented as if they were one-to-one interview data, with interactions between group participants rarely reported, let alone analysed. This is despite clear statements in the focus group literature that 'researchers who use focus groups and do not attend to the impact of the group setting will incompletely or inappropriately analyse their data' (Carey and Smith, 1994: 125). The extracts quoted in this chapter are not typical of the way in which these data are normally reported. I have deliberately sought out (rare) published examples of interactive data in order to make the best possible case for the use of focus groups. In presenting these data extracts, I have often drawn attention to interactional features which are *not* commented upon by the authors themselves. More commonly, the focus is on the *content*, rather than the *process*, of interaction. One wishes feminist focus group researchers were producing analyses of interactions approaching the sophistication of that offered by Billig (1992), quoted earlier.

Insufficient epistemological warranting

In common with other types of qualitative data, data from focus groups are open either to essentialist or to social constructionist interpretations (Guba and Lincoln, 1994; see also Kitzinger and Powell, 1995). For feminist researchers working within an essentialist frame, it may be the voices of individual women (speaking with, or in contradiction to, other women) that they wish to hear, and for them focus groups offer a valuable route to 'the individual in social context' (Goldman, 1962; Rubin and Rubin, 1995: 95). These researchers may well argue that focus group data are more 'authentic', or 'closer to the essential meanings of women's lives', than are data elicited by other methods. Within a social constructionist (or postmodernist, or discursive) frame, however, focus group data are just as constructed – albeit differently – as (say) responses to an opinion poll. Viewed within this frame, the method offers access to 'the patterns of talk and interaction through which the members of any group constitute a shared reality' (Devault, 1990: 97) – the analytic emphasis is on the construction and negotiation of persons and events; the functions served by different discourses; and – for feminists – the ways in which social inequalities are produced and perpetuated through talk (see Wilkinson and Kitzinger, 1995, for further examples of this approach). However, focus group researchers rarely offer a clear epistemological warrant for the interpretation of their data, and there is a great deal of slippage between essentialist and social constructionist frames.

In conclusion, this chapter has argued that focus groups offer considerable potential for the future development of feminist research, in a way which is congruent with feminist research principles and feminist goals. I do not embrace the 'orthodoxy' that qualitative methods are 'quintessentially feminist' (Maynard and Purvis, 1994: 3); nor believe that any particular method can be designated 'feminist' *per se* (see Wilkinson, 1986: 14). Indeed, as Peplau and Conrad (1989: 379) say, 'no method comes with a feminist guarantee'. Following Peplau and Conrad, I do not seek to define feminist research primarily at the methodological level, but rather to evaluate a particular method – focus groups – in terms of its usefulness in the pursuit of feminist goals. However, in order fully to recognize the potential of focus groups as a research method, some developmental work is needed. Feminist researchers could develop a better awareness of the appropriate uses of focus groups, and of the functions they can – and cannot – serve. Feminist researchers could also usefully pay more attention to the interactive nature of focus groups, reporting and analysing interactions between group participants in ways which do justice to their role in meaning-making. Finally, feminist researchers could more clearly identify the epistemological frameworks which inform their interpretations of focus group data, in order more sufficiently to warrant the particular analyses they present. Given these caveats, I consider that focus groups have much to offer the interested feminist researcher. I also believe that focus groups offer considerable potential for the future development of feminist research, in a way which is congruent with key feminist principles and central feminist goals.

Acknowledgements

With thanks to Hannah Frith and Evelyn Kerslake for data extracts and discussion. Some of the material in this chapter first appeared in Wilkinson (1998b).

6 Do focus groups facilitate meaningful participation in social research?

Rachel Baker and Rachel Hinton

What does 'participation' mean in a research context? Although widely used, the term remains ill-defined and researchers have only recently begun to examine the means of achieving participation (for example Nelson and Wright, 1995). This chapter attempts to define participation and investigates the potential of focus groups to satisfy the primary aims of participatory research: to produce a valid set of results and to enable a partnership between researchers and the informant community.

Participatory research is not a discrete activity, rather it is a cycle followed by researchers and participants that begins and ends in shared activities and understanding. This article examines each stage of the research process and identifies components that may enable completion of the cycle to the satisfaction of all involved. These measures challenge the traditional dichotomy between 'researcher' and 'researched'. We are concerned with focus groups as a component of the overall research process. We evaluate the contribution made by focus groups to two pieces of anthropological research in Nepal. The case material used provides concrete examples of researchers' and participants' experiences of focus group work. Bearing in mind the cultural specificity of the material presented, we do not intend to prescribe how best to use focus groups in research. Rather, our aim is to discuss the decisions that researchers and participants make in preparing, implementing, analysing and reporting focus group work. The term 'focus group' refers here to any group-based research activity that is grounded in regular interaction among the participants such that it becomes a social and political forum in its own right. Thus the term encompasses focused discussions in natural groupings, structured group exercises with targeted participants and debate or activities facilitated by community members.

In the light of reported misuse of focus groups (Barbour and Kitzinger, this volume), our particular concern is that the technique is often assumed to be inherently participatory. Little attention is given to relations of power and control that are brought into the research forum of focus groups. Each individual, whether researcher or participant, has their own expectations and personal agenda. Researchers may aim to involve informants on a voluntary basis, to minimize their own input and to value the views of all group members equally. Yet their requirements for specific information may restrict the degree of control given to participants. Our discussion raises questions about the nature of informant participation during the process of focus group work with regard to the knowledge or action generated by these activities.

Participation in research

Participation is one means to uphold an ethical principle that individuals and groups under investigation should retain control over their lives. Clearly all research is born into and develops within a web of social and political relationships. Research will therefore either reinforce or change existing power differentials among participants and their wider community.

A general definition of participation provokes researchers to consider the scope of their particular project: 'Participation is a way of working and a way of relating to people that can be used in any situation. It is about shared responsibility, power and knowledge. It is a democratic way of getting things done' (cited in Kefyalew, 1996: 208).

Participation in development may be viewed as a means to an end, where community members are viewed as the implementors rather than the decision-makers in the programmes. This approach has been criticized for tokenism because the control remains in the hands of the outsiders. In recent years development practitioners cite community participation as an end in itself. Yet can researchers realistically build this level of participation into their objectives?

The legacy of 'participation' stems from development programmes which aim to enable beneficiaries to control improvements in their well-being. As stated by Oxfam, it 'follows that women and men have the right to organize together, in order to bring about equitable change, and to shape the decisions which affect their lives' (Eade and Williams, 1995: 10). Because the agenda is participatory, challenges to pervasive power relations are anticipated by programme workers. To this end, development organizations have devised frameworks to address differences in power within the community and between community members and those implementing programmes. For example, four levels of increasing participation are identified by Paul (1987) – information sharing, consultation, decision-making and initiating action. More recently, the 'ladder of participation' has been adapted for use with children (cited in Ennew, 1994: 34). It details eight rungs ranging from non-participation (for example manipulation and tokenism), through stages of increasing involvement and power of subjects, to child-initiated participation in which decisions are shared with adults. The assumption is that greater participation will heighten the effectiveness and sustainability of a development programme.

Researchers working alongside development practitioners and guided by these frameworks have found them incompatible with their own aims. While development initiatives are concerned primarily with direct action, research aims to generate knowledge that may or may not be purposefully linked to action. Correspondingly, development work and research have different means of achieving their goals. The linear models correlating increased participation with higher research validity need to be re-evaluated in the light of the current findings that show the complexities of group interaction to impede as well as enable valid research results.

Cornwall (1992) highlights the potential for exploitation during the research itself and in relation to how others are represented in anthropologists' texts. Here, the recurring issue is the potential exploitation of research participants which may easily undermine notions of 'partnership'. Beginning at a project's planning stages, researchers must grapple with the precise nature and means of ensuring informed consent plus their responsibilities to protect participants. Morrow and Richards (1996: 94) rightly point out that these two objectives are particularly problematic in research with children. In addition, much of their discussion and suggestions — both methodological and practical — are relevant to researchers working with other groups who lack power through illiteracy, economic dependence or lack of political autonomy. Within the anthropological discourse the final stage of representation has received much debate including the issue of co-authored texts. 'However much multiple authorship is acknowledged, using people's experiences to make statements about matters of anthropological interest in the end subordinates them to the uses of the discipline' (Strathern, 1987: 289).

Guidelines for ethical practice in anthropological research written by the (British based) Association of Social Anthropologists state that 'as far as is possible anthropologists should try and involve the people being studied in the planning and execution of research projects' (ASA, 1987: 6). The achievement of such subject participation poses a challenge to the researchers if they are to follow earlier advice to 'minimize disturbances both to the subjects themselves and to the subjects' relationships with their environment' (ASA, 1987: 2). Here the researcher is sensitized to the potential effects of their research presence. In addition, attention is drawn to possible differences in opinion among subjects and researchers regarding any resulting action for change.

Research in Nepal

This chapter draws on two recent anthropological research projects carried out in Nepal. Baker conducted research among street children living in Kathmandu, the capital city, over an 18-month period (Baker et al., 1996) and Hinton spent one year living with refugee families from Bhutan in camps in Eastern Nepal with follow-up research seven months later (Hinton, 1995).

The street children are predominately male but from a wide variety of ethnic and caste groups. The local term '*khate*' (rag-picker) embraces all who live and work independently from their families on a daily basis. Legally children are those under 16 years of age, however the popular term *khate* includes older street youth. The refugees are a community comprising families with variance in ethnicity and socioeconomic status. Many of the Bhutanese refugees have moved in family units comprising several generations. Though primarily of Nepali ethnic origin, the principles of Buddhism influence their codes of daily life. Both *khate* and refugees are marginalized within the wider society. They share the experience of subordination to more powerful members of society who define their needs and make decisions about appropriate provisioning on their behalf. In Nepal, where the majority of the population live in extreme poverty, these two groups are deemed especially vulnerable because they are disconnected from their home supports. For this reason they receive particular attention from the state and non-governmental organizations (NGOs). It should also be noted that the presence of refugees and street children is problematic for the state, and to some extent, the local communities.

Both research projects took an anthropological perspective that sought 'an understanding of the needs and priorities of the community with knowledge of the communities' existing skills and emerging structures' (Hinton, 1996: 24). In addition, we were concerned to explore differentiation of status within the community that might have an impact on lifestyle and well-being. With the support of research assistants, we preceded our focus group work with ethnographic investigation of daily activities, social relationships and concerns about well-being.

The research projects were undertaken in consultation with organizations that are respected by the majority of the informant community. Although neither researcher was employed by an organization, Hinton was affiliated to Oxfam and Baker worked closely with Child Workers in Nepal (CWIN), the Child Welfare Society (CWS) and Children-at-Risk Network Group (CAR-NG). CWIN and CWS each runs a drop-in centre for street children that offers basic food, shelter, games, medical facilities, non-formal education and support towards moving off the streets. CAR-NG is an umbrella organization to which the majority of NGOs working with children in Kathmandu belong. The collaboration of staff in these organizations provided us with increased access to our informants and the opportunity to share research findings. We benefited considerably from their vast knowledge accumulated over several years. Our associations also carried obligations of a practical and political nature. A common aim to our two research projects was to explore problematic areas of health and well-being as defined by both community members and service providers. Thus, in line with such jointly constructed agendas, focus groups were used for two purposes. First, they were an exploratory tool to illuminate issues of concern within the community and to generate hypotheses. Their second function was to verify (or challenge) problems identified by the organizations, the community and the researchers' prior findings. Hence triangulation was sought with other methods including interviews, demographic surveys, Participatory Rural Appraisal (PRA), NGO clinic data and participant observation.

Baker used focus groups to explore particular social topics among existing groupings of street children in their everyday environments. The resulting knowledge and rapport facilitated more structured focus group exercises that specifically investigated health issues. Here, Baker used a Participatory Rural Appraisal (PRA) approach to elicit information about ill-health and health seeking behaviour by making schematic drawings. PRA is a 'growing family of approaches and methods to enable local people to share, enhance and analyse their knowledge of life conditions, to plan and act' (Chambers, 1994: 953). Although developed for use in agricultural development, the techniques are now widely used in researching health and gender issues. Hinton's initial entry into the field was as a participant observer and once living in the refugee camps she used a variety of group-based PRA techniques to enquire into the cultural influences on health service utilization. Through engaging with specific sectors of the refugee community, it was possible to build an understanding of the heterogeneity and complexity of refugee health seeking behaviour and disease aetiology. In an overall attempt to increase participation, focus group work in both projects was frequently conducted by informants themselves. The benefits and problematics of bridging the traditional divide between researcher and researched are discussed later in this chapter.

Focus groups within a framework for participatory research

The framework proposed maps four stages of participatory research, the last of which initiates a new cycle of research or action (see Figure 6.1). Our concern is to examine the factors that affect researchers' and participants' progression through each stage. These impinging factors include constraints of the wider socio-political environment and decisions about practical issues made by the research team. In practice, can researchers and participants undertake focus groups that will produce mutually satisfactory outcomes?

We approach this question by discussing four stages of the research process in the sections to follow. In this way the reader is introduced to the elements of focus group work that are both beneficial and problematic to the objectives within participatory research.

Rooting the research

Given the priority for data collection, what are the preconditions necessary for researchers and their subjects to work in partnership? Anthropologists

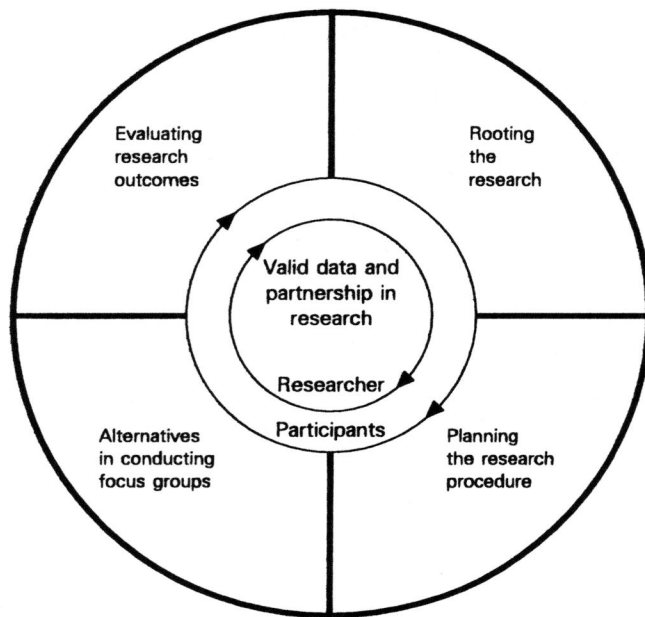

FIGURE 6.1 *The four stages of participatory research*

insist that engaging in participants' daily activities is of utmost importance for effective communication and trusting relationships. They have also long acknowledged the need to understand the composition of 'the community' before the research question is finalized. The way in which groups are defined by outsiders may differ from the affinities expressed by informants. It is only through participation with the community that local definitions may be fully comprehended and this was clearly demonstrated through the Nepal case studies. Although all termed *khate* by the media, children who rag-picked for a living differentiated themselves on certain grounds from those who begged in the tourist areas of Kathmandu. Similarly, journalists tended to amalgamate all refugees into one category or saw differences within the group primarily in terms of caste. The refugees themselves, however, classified themselves in far more complex ways that related additionally to their history and birthplace.

The daily routines of community members, the practices of relevance to the research question and, most importantly, the culture of group activities, can be understood by maximizing the time spent in participant observation. Knowledge of the precedents set by previous research or programme activities with the community in question will shed light on informant expectations. We briefly illustrate how perceptions of the researcher were influenced by historical, socio-political and practical factors in our respective research settings.

Long-term involvement in CWIN's activities legitimized Baker's role in the programme and enabled her to build personal relationships with the children who used the centre. Four comparable settings were chosen to represent different street lifestyles (beggars, rag-pickers and NGO-based children) within which participants were self-selecting. Her personal background and the purpose of her activities were questioned, often indirectly, by the children in the centre. Over time she established relations with independent rag-picker children and was invited to spend time in the junkyard where they sold the recyclable plastic and metals collected on the streets. There her role was under constant negotiation by both the children and the owner. Initially, the children expected her to buy tea, then to facilitate medical treatment when required and latterly to convey their concerns to service providers. Hinton's work drafting the Nepal group of NGOs' position paper for the Partnership in Action enterprise with the United Nations led to increased involvement with the NGO community, while living with the refugee community enabled integration within it. Hinton established two long-term focus groups in the refugee camps. The first was a group of self-selected secondary school pupils. The second were a random selection of 9–11 year-olds who were invited to participate in discussion and drawings.

Observation of the refugees' daily routines showed Hinton that, in the absence of the opportunity to pursue traditional livelihoods, some refugees had time to participate in focus groups and other research activities. The boundedness of living in a refugee camp created frustration and time to reflect on their loss of homeland. Thus the chance for communal research activity and engagement outside the home was often welcomed. This contrasts with many research contexts where the time that is invested in research is diverted from essential subsistence tasks.

It was particularly important that trust was developed with the wider refugee community and that they too understood the aims of the research. Gossip thrived among refugees in close physical proximity whose strong internal networks provided channels for rapid transmission of information. In this manner, single individuals could easily sway or unnerve those with whom rapport was being built. Hence, in the refugee context it was not only private localized relationships that were important, but the opinions of the wider community who also influenced the decisions. Community members have longer-term considerations beyond participation in a single research project. Refugees have to consider the implications of supporting 'outsiders', who may not be allies of those who control their lives. The fact that Hinton was initially feared to be a spy sent from Bhutan showed the complexity of perceptions of outsiders and the difficulty of ensuring 'transparency'. Community members often desire the exchange of cultural information and researchers' social histories. If researchers do not state their positions, they may expect gaps to be filled with stories and rumours that are detrimental to both parties. Allowing participants time to ask questions of the incoming researcher increases their opportunities to evaluate the proposed activities and negotiate the terms on which they might participate.

Yet, despite such efforts, Hinton found that 'transparency' was frequently insufficient. The refugees categorized her with other expatriates associated with those in authority and therefore as someone who could bring about beneficial change. In this context no degree of transparency could alter the expectations that contributing to the research might indeed be advantageous at a practical level.

In research with children, the issue of 'informed consent' is complicated by issues of parental rights and biological maturity that vary cross-culturally. These affect adult attitudes towards children's ability to participate and whether their opinions are treated seriously. Children are often identified as being in need of particular attention due to their vulnerable and powerless position. They have been classified as presenting significant barriers for community participation (Kalnins et al., 1992). In contrast to the argument that such special sub-groups require more active encouragement, the majority of children in the camps were often the most vocal in the refugee context. The acceptance by the local community of the contribution children had to make became visually evident during PRA discussions, where children were often actively encouraged to sit at the front and to contribute to the information being generated.

In addition to age, gender roles varied cross-culturally and proved influential in the wider social dynamic and at the level of group interaction. Such intercultural variations are often overlooked by researchers. In Hinton's case, she observed that Bhutanese women were often the ones who spoke out during discussions of health with the men being asked their opinion by the women. In contrast, the Nepali women in the host community, who were regularly facilitators in the PRA process, would often subsume the articulation of their ideas to the Nepali men who were seen as more authoritative. A prior appreciation of such cultural difference is essential to understand the dynamics of focus group discussions and to interpret the data.

Planning the research procedure

This section addresses the decisions that are made before focus group work begins. We include determining where the investigation should take place, what are appropriate questions to ask and how the groups should be conducted. We investigate ways in which a partnership between researchers and participants can be realized and the factors that operate against it.

The kind of rapport engendered in close, day-to-day living in communities creates a deeper level of understanding about people's lives and the relationships between them. It does not however guarantee that participants and researchers can easily work in partnership to facilitate the second stage of research, that in which the research procedure is determined:

A group of camp leaders gathered in the privacy of the camp committee room for discussions on caste. I had assumed that this room was suitably private. However, during discussions other refugees in authority wandered in. What had been an appropriate discussion with friends in my room was inappropriate in this more public arena.

Introductions and pre-PRA discussion began in a lively atmosphere of trust. The topic of caste was raised and immediately an onlooker who had joined the group objected. His status meant that no one spoke out. I was unknown to him. My motive, gathering knowledge for academic purposes, was questioned. A hidden agenda was feared. The session was redirected to mapping the districts from which people originated to diffuse tension. (Hinton, fieldnotes)

The recent course of events meant that a discussion on caste in the presence of refugee leaders was perceived as more threatening than usual. Bilateral government talks had concluded with a decision to reclassify the refugees into distinct groups, only some of whom would be eligible for repatriation. Thus in all spheres they wanted to be portrayed as the single group: 'the Bhutanese'. This wider context explained why participants were wary of being seen to give confidential information to 'outside officials'. This PRA activity was too close to the process of government classification. Group size, location, time and the personalities involved all determine the acceptability of a topic for discussion. In addition, knowledge of the local political climate is critical. It is the rule of a single objector not the majority that dominates. Disclosure may be governed more by rules of hierarchy than the desire to inform. The recounted incident not only raises issues of context, appropriateness and local power relations, but it also highlights the responsibilities of the researcher toward individual informants.

Where to conduct focus groups?

The way in which particular settings for focus group work influence the nature and content of members interaction is well documented by Green and Hart (Chapter 2, this volume). Interestingly, although they found that the formal school environment constrained children's behaviour and input in discussions, in the refugee camps school was viewed as the most appropriate context for focus group work by participants, researchers and other community members. In the refugee environment, Westerners were associated with the provision of services and paid employment. By locating the research in schools, participation was viewed as an educational process and this reduced material expectations that often arose from Western involvement in external group activities. Hinton also reports that, for certain topics, the refugees found open conversation in public space easier than in the 'private' forum of their own crowded home. In contrast, respondents showed discomfort and lack of engagement in survey interviews within the home which ultimately yielded results of low validity.

> It was often not until later that I realized the extent that women didn't like to speak openly at home. 'Politeness' demanded a response. If a response to the question is not within their knowledge the respondent doesn't feel confident. They feel the same way when they really have an opinion but they are worried that they should tell the 'refugee rules' and not the reality. In the camp, someone is always listening (Jamuna Nepal, refugee interviewer).

A further practical advantage to debates in public arenas was that women could delegate childcare and domestic responsibilities to relations and thereby join in discussions freely. With regard to participants' control over the information sharing process, refugees preferred to use 'private' group space (such as the camp committee office where other refugees would not enter to observe, but was not an individual's home). There they could talk about a generalized other, rather than about themselves. In contrast, information given in the private home space was immediately personal.

What to ask and how?

Our introduction drew attention to the fact that research agendas are primarily determined outside the community in question. The remit of applied researchers is often to answer certain questions within a short time period. Despite such constraints on exploratory work, an anthropological approach lends itself to pursuing issues defined by the community. Indeed, the fact that researchers identify pertinent topics during social interaction in the field validates their accounts. Given that they meet the practical and analytical scope of the research agenda, focus groups can be successfully used by community members to identify relevant questions.

Where irrelevant questions are brought in from outside, the responses have minimal validity and participants are effectively excluded from the research process. In Nepal, many of the refugees had been interviewed on several occasions by different NGO workers. Where refugees felt that the questions had no relevance to their lives, they rarely clarified or elaborated their answers but instead said what they thought the interviewer wanted to hear. NGO workers were perceived to have a 'busy schedule' and 'no time to talk'. This belief commonly resulted in feelings of exclusion and resentment. Bishnu Maya, who was interviewed, later admitted: 'It's two years now, people come into my house and ask so many questions. But nothing ever happens. So now I just give a quick answer to let them go away'.

Once they were involved in the process of research, the refugees were able to show the significance of their history and culture. They felt in control of what was being 'sought'. Participatory groups provided a forum in which people had the confidence to speak their mind without presenting the 'NGO appeasing' or 'intellectually acceptable' view.

Given community heterogeneity and the political climate of the research setting there are likely to be varying perceptions of what constitutes a relevant research topic. In the context of applied research, the challenge is often to marry issues pertinent to service providers and to the 'target community'. In an investigation of street children's experiences of ill-health carried out by Baker and the CWIN health worker, there were two key perspectives. The critical issue differed for each. The children were concerned with the impact of illness on their ability to earn and with access to treatment. In contrast, CWIN's focus was on ways of promoting better health practices and changes of lifestyle.

An understanding of both perspectives was achieved using simple visual representations adapted from PRA techniques. Each session began with a group brainstorming of member's experiences of 'ill health'. An elected scribe drew these in as 'legs' on a 'spider diagram' where the living environment (for example the home village, the street) was the spider's body. Using a table drawn on large pieces of paper, the ill-health experiences identified by participants were then scored according to criteria deemed relevant to the children and the CWIN health worker. These were frequency of occurrence, degree of pain and effect on ability to earn. Thus, an important component of this group exercise was to draw on children's ideas of what constitutes 'ill-health' and their vocabulary in a forum that included a service provider and a researcher.

Participatory activities were quick and also actively engaged people in the process. The close working relationships between members of the group allowed for an honest exchange of opinion about both the content of the questions and the manner in which they should be asked. As Sunkeshra, a refugee facilitator, observed, 'the questionnaires consist only of questioning and answering so it is not enjoyable like PRA'.

However, focus groups do not always revolve around local issues or give rise to local categories. Hinton, working with the focus group of older school students who were themselves designing and conducting research, observed the effective communication between group members and the development of interesting research questions. With community members participating actively in the decision-making process it was tempting to believe that such a forum would give rise to appropriate questions for use in the wider community. However, the uniform nature of the group members, their similar age, backgrounds and level of education meant that they were only representing a small sector of the community. Moreover, in the early stages they were unaware of the complexities of informant disclosure and the heterogeneity of the population they were studying. They utilized the categories that they, as a schooled group, were familiar with and thus filtered the data collected.

Early in the training of the students one group returned with a neatly copied chart of their work. They were proud to claim that they had listened to a group of illiterate women who were not part of any of the formal programmes in the camp, and whose voice they felt was often lost. Yet, when they displayed the diagram, not only was it in neat bar chart form, but the categories outlined were those of the Western calendar. We discussed the issue and it materialized that the women had spoken of wet and dry seasons with no relation to months of either the Nepali or the European year. The students in drawing up their work had reinterpreted it into the 'school style' table that held prestige (Hinton, fieldnotes).

Alternatives in conducting focus groups

This chapter is primarily concerned with the overall research process in which the focus groups are embedded. Hence we have chosen to limit our discussion of the actual sessions to two options open to researchers that may increase participant ownership. The first is group production of a video and the second is facilitation by an 'insider'.

Baker and Onta jointly facilitated a video project that aimed to maximize participation of the street boys living in the CWIN centre. Previously, some boys had taken part in and/or watched films about street children (produced by journalists and the police). They were familiar with video-recording and aware of the opportunity to convey their own experiences and opinions. Most boys elected to participate and decided to show the differences between their daily lives in the centre and on the streets. Although filmed by an adult, the children participating chose which of their daily activities to include and enacted sketches showing rag-picking, selling scrap, spending money and sleeping on the streets.

As a medium of communication, video holds great potential among illiterate groups or those who are inexperienced in formal discussions or interviews. The visual dimension allows people to use movement and 'those not in a position of power often find expression in the non-verbal' (James, 1995). The use of the video among the refugees following training of two camera people brought much scope for expression; 'we can film our history in the way we wish, without others filtering out the parts they do not wish us to tell' (Birkha, refugee cameraman). The use of video by the refugees led to several films being subsequently produced for both internal and external audiences (Oxfam, 1996).

Two practical issues arise regarding the analysis of videos and the transferability of results. First, the atmosphere created by acting and story-telling frames data pertaining to children's experiences in an entirely different way to conventional interviews or discussions. It is much closer to the informal interactions witnessed during participant observation. Hence, in order to use the data, researchers must be able to distinguish normative expressions and 'acting for effect' from direct expressions of experience and feeling. Second, an advantage to video work is that information is not constrained by translation and externally defined formulae for results. However these pose a great challenge to researchers in making the data accessible to policy makers and triangulating the visual material with findings from other methods.

Focus groups conducted by an 'insider'

As newcomers, outside researchers are often aware of their lack of knowledge of community practice or pertinent issues. When researchers experienced difficulties in facilitating a debate, they may opt to employ an 'insider' for this role. Drawing on Baker's experiences, we point out potential effects on data validity and the research partnership between 'insiders' and 'outsiders'.

At his own request, Kisan, a 15-year-old ex-street boy, joined Baker in interviewing current street children and leading discussions on their daily lifestyles and social relations. He contributed to data validity by asking relevant and sophisticated questions with a sensitivity resulting from his own experiences of street living. His youth and understanding enabled a rapport with street children unachievable by outsiders and those who represent the 'correct childhood' as advocated by wider society and NGOs. Thus he elicited frank responses to questions that, had they been posed by an outsider, may have been answered normatively. It is in the interest of children who beg for a living to maintain public perception of their vulnerability.

Kisan:	If someone approached you and offered you a place in school, would you take it?
Boys 1 and 2:	No
Kisan:	What about if they offered you a job?
Boy 1:	Yes, well, if it was a good one.
Kisan:	Have you ever helped someone get a job?
Boy 2:	Yes, once I helped a boy find work in a restaurant near my house. (. . .)
Kisan:	So what would you do if you had no money?
Boy 1:	Go home, my parents would give me money . . . 400 rupees if I asked.

Did this boy really believe that his parents would give him 400 rupees? In this case, further information about his home supported his assertion. Kisan was subject to peer pressure among his acquaintances on the street and there are potential costs to validity of the data thus collected. Baker was in danger of misinterpreting comments that were designed to impress Kisan because she cast him as an expert in the 'street' arena.

Kisan's status as neither fully 'insider' nor 'outsider' influenced the content and format of discussions. As an 'insider' he had his own views about the lifestyles of the children participating. Some of his questions were value laden and conveyed a negativity with regard to street living. For example, he frequently asked whether boys felt shame about begging or rag-picking. As was natural in his everyday interaction, he gave advice to street children about improving their quality of life that was based on his own experience. (Although researchers are normally encouraged not to intervene at this level, we point out that in the case of informed advice from an ex-street child there is a lesser power differential between adviser and recipient than when advice is given by adults in authority.) Kisan's current schooling and association with Baker and her research placed him outside present street life. There were therefore limits on what his involvement could achieve in terms of access to sensitive topics. For example, organized crime, drug-taking and sexual behaviour were not discussed by or with Kisan and hence Baker did not pursue these topics in their joint work.

Evaluating research outcomes: achieving valid data

A retrospective analysis of focus group interaction highlights two areas of consideration regarding the status of the data generated. The first concerns the overall scope and limitations of the focus group method in answering research questions. The second issue is how communication within the focus group affects the status of the data and the feasibility of a partnership between facilitator and group members.

Hinton's research revealed that the refugee community could represent trends of population and behaviour using diagrams generated in focus group discussion. PRA activities offered insights beyond 'official statistics' and exposed the low validity of data gathered by questionnaires alone. For example, while the official surveys illustrated the illnesses that people took to the health centres, PRA revealed the prevalence of deficiency diseases that the community treated in the private domain. This process produced enough data to highlight and address beri-beri as a serious health problem months before official action was taken.

Nevertheless, there were some aspects of people's lives that neither focus groups nor surveys could adequately make sense of. It was only through participant observation that Hinton could begin to understand the processes people followed when seeking a cure for their illness. No verbal or visual 'reason' was available. In such instances data validity is higher when using multiple approaches.

When the facilitator is well-known to participants, and focus groups take place in the context of normal social interaction, a dilemma may arise. The facilitator must choose whether to ask to be educated by the focus group members or to reveal what she knows about a particular issue. The former strategy would seem to produce more information of high validity. Yet a facilitator who is apparently ignorant even after working in the participants' community for considerable time, is likely to be seen as disinterested.

For example, Baker conducted a focus group in the CWIN centre about the differences in working careers between girls and boys. The agreed objective was to inform British people about Nepali children's lifestyles. Those who wished to participate joined the group sitting around the tape-recorder. Questions were posed by Baker to stimulate discussion such as 'Why are there very few girls living on the streets?' and the group members asked her about British cities and children's activities. Looking over the transcript, Baker identified an apparent weakness in her technique because some of her questions assumed certain 'facts' about girls' and boys' lifestyles. Yet, the boys participating knew that she had considerable understanding of Nepali children's lifestyles. On reflection, this context demanded that Baker made her own knowledge apparent. For participants, the credibility of the proposed task depended on Baker learning about their concerns. Without proof of her ability to do this, they saw little point in pursuing issues to any depth.

This example may appear to be a case of compromising validity in order to achieve partnership in research. However, we assert that careful consideration of the context of verbal exchange in focus group work can alert the researcher to the particular type of data generated. It is important that facilitators are able to understand particular modes of exchange as they occur within focus group discussions.

The following extract is one of the many jokes interspersed in a vibrant discussion with street boys. Clearly the boys are not giving their serious opinions about health but are taking the opportunity to joke about popular notions of *khate*. The performative nature of this interchange is therefore central to its meaning, and like much of group generated data, cannot be taken at face value.

Baker: Have you heard of children's rights about health?
Boy 1: I'll say something about health! '*khate* don't become ill!'
Boy 2: Yes, that is right (laughs)
Boy 3: They get meat out of the rubbish tip and don't become ill. Hey, we could get some and cook it for you!
Baker: Sounds great! Those raw beans you gave me the other day were tasty . . .

Participants may tell jokes and lies in order to test the facilitator's reactions. The facilitator's response will indicate how much they know and, if there are moral implications involved, whose side they are taking. In general, overt lies are less common in discussions conducted within friendship groups because peers are quick to question (see Green and Hart, this volume). However, it is possible that the group will collude against the facilitator. When such a strategy is suspected, we found that replicating participants' jokes or 'lies' was successful. Thus in the above extract, Baker responded to the boys' quips in a similar manner. Obviously spurious remarks – or blatant lies – can be similarly treated. Without making it explicit or personalized, there is mutual understanding between the facilitator and participants as to the status of the information given.

A continuing partnership?

In general, relatively little attention is paid to the products of the research process other than the data generated. Questions are seldom asked about how the methods employed have supported or altered existing power relations. The issues that we raise in this section relate to the effects of the research process on participants, their community and those conducting it.

We begin by identifying some of the ethical issues arising out of focus group work that is facilitated by a community member. Kisan's case is enlightening because his involvement altered the power balance between 'the researcher' (Baker) and the children participating. In certain respects, his role challenged his (legal) status as a child. Thus we highlight the potential consequences of Kisan's involvement for himself as an individual and to the partnership between Baker and the street children participating in the research.

Kisan's immediate objectives, namely to gain experience of interviewing and knowledge of current concerns of street children, were compatible with Baker's research aims. Thus joint decisions were made regarding the timing, location and content of focus groups. However, Baker's intention that she and Kisan should play an equal role in facilitating focus groups proved unrealistic. At first, Kisan rarely added to discussions with the street children, presumably because he viewed Baker as authoritative and may initially have doubted his own role and ability. In due course he took the lead and suggested that they both might hold a discussion in a junkyard situated in another town where he used to sell scrap. On this occasion the fact that Kisan was accompanied by Baker and was familiar with the setting enabled him to secure agreement from participants as to the aims and practical arrangements of the discussion. He took advantage of a natural setting and his previous experiences to pursue topics that concerned the junkyard owners and the boys presently rag-picking.

Regardless of the extent to which Kisan was able to control the focus group activity, it was Baker's responsibility to protect him from negative consequences of the research process. He was taunted by a number of his peers on the streets for what they viewed as special treatment by Baker. Although Kisan himself did not perceive any risks, Baker was mindful of the concern expressed by the school staff that his friends currently on the streets would encourage him to return.

From the participants' perspective, Kisan's facilitation changed the balance of power and enabled them to express views about their own lives and the lifestyles at variance with those advocated by their parents, NGOs or wider society. The fact that Kisan had 'made good' and was now at school may have created a sense of inferiority among those children who had not succeeded in the opportunities given to them. Unlike that of the street boys, Kisan's lifestyle is socially acceptable. He is an outsider and his presence cannot equalize power relations between researchers and the street children.

Nevertheless, did the children participating consider it appropriate that Kisan was inquiring about their personal histories and relations with the NGO centre? There was no evidence to the contrary. Nor was there evidence to suggest that Kisan was passing on personal information (for example to school friends or NGO staff). Yet Baker could not guarantee confidentiality to the children participating. These observations raise the issue of protecting participants in a research partnership when responsibility is shared. For, even given Kisan's own view of his personal responsibility, his status as a minor under supervision made Baker accountable in the eyes of the wider community.

Participant expectations and unanticipated consequences

A research partnership continues after the required data have been collected. Furthermore the group dynamic cultivated during focus group work is likely to produce expectations for action. Both authors were acutely aware of the dependency relations that arise out of long-term and in-depth involvement in peoples' lives, particularly among those who to some extent rely on the state or NGO services. In an attempt to relieve the immediate situation, researchers may initiate action upon which communities become dependent. Rather than increasing participant control, such action may disempower by reinforcing ideas about 'providers' and 'beneficiaries'. We give short accounts of some of the outcomes to our research that provoke questions about the scope of a project that starts out as 'participatory'.

Clearly, no researcher is able to fulfil the myriad expectations of all participants. Nevertheless, shared expectations may arise from the subject matter and personnel present during a focus group that cannot be realized by the researcher. During the PRA exercises about ill-health and health seeking behaviour among the street children, Baker and the CWIN health worker explained the purpose and scope of these activities. Yet they were often asked whether a full medical examination would be carried out and appropriate treatment provided.

Although rarely anticipated by researchers, the effects of the interactive dynamic created within a group setting are potentially very significant for the researcher and the wider community. Group members' perceptions of each other and of the group as an entity are likely to evolve as research progresses (Kitzinger, this volume). The facilitator is included within this process which does not end once he or she has stopped collecting information. In some cases, participants and researchers are able to work towards the objective of the group. For example, after spending several months researching in the junkyard, five key participants asked Baker to facilitate skill training so that they could leave rag-picking. Their determination and the time available to Baker prompted a joint endeavour to secure apprenticeships in motorcycle maintenance workshops using funding provided by CAR-NG. Here the primary objective was to improve well-being. Second to this, with the agreement of the participants, was to improve Baker's understanding of the transition from 'street living' to a regular job. The ends were clear, shared and practical. Thus, although fraught with operational difficulties, the scheme was participatory in that knowledge, power and responsibility were shared by participants and facilitators.

Interestingly, group consciousness in the same setting gave rise to problems for the wider community and researcher. One discussion that began about migration into the city was quickly turned into a debate about the 'failures' of NGO service provision. Two days later, several of the older boys were verbally abusive to the staff of one NGO and threw stones at the office windows. Although a number of contributory factors can be identified, this incident depicts the strength of feeling that can arise in a group debate and particularly if dominant individuals want to push their agenda in competition with established authority. The incident prompted discussion between Baker and the NGO director about her role in interaction between these young people and the NGO centre. It also highlighted a researcher's responsibilities not only to the participants of focus groups, but to other members of their community and those who work on their behalf.

Participatory research can act as a catalyst in ways that the researcher hadn't anticipated. The reaction that giving the community a voice incites from those with authority may be against the participants, the researchers or both. While the researcher has the power to walk away, participants do not. Individuals vary in their ability to deal with the situation. How then do the researchers carry out their responsibility to those with less power to remove themselves or constructively deal with the situation?

Remaining an outsider: the benefits and constraints to a research partnership

Researchers may never know whether the measures they have taken to enable participation are beneficial or detrimental to the community in the long term. Here we point out some of the advantages to being an outsider in research among marginalized communities. We then draw attention to the relative lack of control that researchers have within the wider social arena.

An outside researcher can bring two important assets to group-based research. An external facilitator's degree of detachment from local political relations can reduce subjectivity in participants' responses and complex obligations felt by the community towards the researcher. Moreover, inquiry from an outsider emphasizes that disclosure of personal experiences is in order to explore a general issue. In this light, individuals are not targeted as 'problem cases'. The second factor relates to feeding participants' views and experiences into the appropriate channels. Here a researcher who is trained in various research techniques can implement focus groups, analyse the data with respect to results from other sources and share their skills with participants. Hinton found that even where group members formed the theoretical ideas and a logical argument, agencies consistently wanted information presented to them in a 'formal' format. This excluded the participation of the majority since they rarely possessed the skills in English and computing to take total control and organize the information in a form acceptable to the service providers. Compounding this is the additional issue of research dissemination. Once 'translated' into a form suitable to funders, it is often made inaccessible to the very people who were partners in its creation. This issue is rarely addressed in traditional focus group research. PRA, however, places great emphasis on the appropriate dissemination of findings, ideally retaining ownership with the community itself.

Researchers affiliated with an organization are frequently required to produce information to a time scale and in a format incompatible with a truly participatory approach (as shown above by refugees' non-participation in the presentation of results). Ultimately, funders are in control of whether money is available for research and in this way control the selection of research topics. Fulfilling the requirements of those in power determines the extent to which both the initial and the final stages are participatory. Thus, completing the cycle of participatory research depends first, on the commitment of the researcher and, second, on the support of those to whom researchers are accountable.

Michael Edwards describes the problems of implementing participatory research and programming with children within the context of an organization working directly for children (1996: 47). He describes the effects of entrenched attitudes about children's immaturity, irrationality, their non-productive role in society and the ability of adults to make decisions in children's best interests. Such attitudes within institutions that commission research can impede the practice of children's participation because they are not attuned to listen to results generated. To address this problem, Edwards stresses the importance of demonstrating the benefits and constraints of participation at field level and sharing these in forums attended by researchers and policy makers. His own experience suggests that 'practice rarely changes unless those involved see tangible benefits from new innovations which repay the time and effort involved' (Edwards, 1996: 50).

Conclusion

We have illustrated various factors that shape participation throughout the research process. At issue is the degree of control accorded to participants in decisions concerning methods, means of evaluation and use of findings. For the researcher, the new knowledge generated in focus groups comprises 'data'. For participants the outcomes may be future action and altered perceptions of self, peers or others involved in the research project. Participation involves sharing these forms of knowledge and finding ways in which they can be channelled towards ends as defined by informants and researchers.

Evidently the limitations to achieving full participation arise from power hierarchies in the particular research setting and the controlling influence of external factors. Researchers bring an agenda that prioritizes the collection of knowledge. Participants can gain significantly from their increased engagement in the research process. However, a research partnership must account for its long-term intentions regarding its individual involvement and the overall outcome of the exercise. The consequences of group-based research move beyond the group itself into the community, often raising issues of controversy. Significantly, the group dynamic in focus groups can change participants' expectations of discussions and lead to unanticipated consequences during and after research.

Given a commitment on the part of the researcher, we propose that steps can be taken to facilitate meaningful participation of research subjects. However, there are serious ethical implications to writing evaluations of research techniques, such as focus groups, without due attention to the difficulties encountered and extent to which objectives were met. In line with ethical responsibilities to the discipline of anthropology and colleagues, there are long-term consequences of misrepresenting the degree of participation achieved and indeed the actual data yielded during group-based research.

Implementing a research partnership requires changing the balance of power within the social arena. We have outlined the problems that might occur in placing control (and therefore responsibility) entirely in the hands of participants. Unlike models of participation advocated in the development arena, more is not necessarily better in the research context.

Acknowledgements

The authors are grateful for the collaboration and support of their assistants J.B. Shrestha and J. Nepal, their colleagues Lazima Onta, Deepa Dhital, Rita Dhakal, Gita Rai and Damini Vaidya and the NGOs in the field, namely CWIN, CWS and CAR-NG in Kathmandu and Oxfam, LWS, SCF and UNHCR in Jhapa. Baker's research was funded by a Durham University Studentship and Hinton's by Trinity Hall Studentship and Williamson Award, Cambridge University. Both researchers would like to thank colleagues at CNAS (Centre for Nepali and Asian Studies), Tribhuvan University, Kathmandu. Sincere thanks to those who commented on earlier drafts in particular Dr V. Morrow and Dr G. Williams.

7 How useful are focus groups for obtaining the views of minority groups?

Lai-Fong Chiu and Deborah Knight

The purpose of this chapter is to share with readers our experiences in facilitating focus groups as part of two separate projects (one on breast screening and one on cervical screening) funded by the National Health Service's Breast and Cervical Screening Programme. It provides the background to our adoption and adaptation of the focus group method as a vehicle for Participatory Action Research (PAR). In tackling the methodological problems generated by orthodox research in the area of minority women and cancer screening, our experience has given us valuable insights into the key issues of cultural diversity, researchers' racial identity, and the conscientization process in the production of health knowledge.

Background

Studies in the past decade have attributed low uptake of cervical screening among minority women to their lack of basic information, and to their cultural beliefs and attitudes (McAvoy and Raza, 1988; Doyle, 1991; Naish et al., 1994). The Health Education Authority's report on the health and lifestyles survey of black and minority ethnic groups in England (Rudat, 1994) has also identified lack of information as the major reason for low uptake of cervical screening among minority groups.

A brief review of the above literature suggested that research in minority women and cancer screening suffers from many theoretical and methodological problems. In this limited space, we can only highlight those problems which motivated us to adopt an alternative paradigm, and which we sought to address in our research. We found that common to both quantitative and qualitative studies in this area, 'ethnicity' as a category is ill-defined and is often used interchangeably with 'culture' (Bhopal et al., 1991; Sheldon and Parker, 1992). Moreover, beliefs and behaviours are frequently assumed from ethnicity (Pfeffer and Moynihan, 1996). In over-objectifying these categories, much of the research has failed to acknowledge the diversity and fluidity of minority groups in the contemporary

British context. Far from highlighting the racism and inequalities experienced by minority women within the health services (Bowler, 1993), the uncritical interpretation of results from this type of research can easily lead to generalization and stereotyping.

The unexamined assumption about the meaning of 'ethnicity' has not only led many researchers to recruit, group and comment on their 'ethnic subjects' uncritically, but has also created another common problem in qualitative studies in this area. In spite of the fact that the researchers who undertake qualitative studies are instruments of their own research (Patton, 1990), their ascribed status – such as race, ethnicity – has seldom been discussed. Researchers' racial identity matters, in that it determines what they see and do not see, as well as their ability to analyse data and disseminate knowledge adequately (Ahmed, 1993; Standfield, 1994). The lack of self-awareness of racial identity has led often to Eurocentric views of research methods imposed in cross-cultural settings. Yelland and Gifford's (1995) criticisms of their bilingual moderators' behaviours in the focus group discussions exemplified this. These problems will impede not only the continuing development of qualitative methods in general, but also the advancement of innovative practices of focus group methods in minority health research in particular.

However, the most common of all problems has been the assumed causal relationship between information and uptake. Although this health education model is generally recognized as far too simplistic (French and Adams, 1986), it can be found to be the common underpinning of many intervention studies concerning minority women and cancer screening (McAvoy and Raza, 1991; Hoare et al., 1994; Kernohan, 1996, ScanLink Report, 1996). This is compounded with the overemphasis on the language and culture of minority groups to imply a 'deficit' model, where 'problems' such as low uptake of cancer screening are seen as internally generated by minority groups themselves (Stubbs, 1993). Research conducted in a contextual vacuum leads to minority women's health being marginalized, exploited and pathologized in the process of health services research (Ahmed, 1993; Standfield, 1994).

We view the screening of minority women as essentially in the realm of intercultural care, in which professionals and clients bring potentially conflicting sets of beliefs, expectations and practices to each encounter (Geist, 1994). Intercultural communication, as a theoretical framework, helps to contextualize relationships between health professionals and minority women in relation to cancer screening. Once we put human actions into social context, the problem takes on a different emphasis. The biomedical model of uptake rate becomes an issue of access, and paying attention to the perceptions and experiences of both health professionals and minority women about the screening event begins to shed light on how existing 'knowledge' from different perspectives has been constructed, and how it serves to shape experiences of minority women in their contact with the cancer screening services.

Having taken an alternative view of the problem, we felt that an alternative approach was required to understand and to tackle it. Participatory Action Research offered us a way in which many traditional barriers between communities and institutions, and between researchers and 'subjects', could be broken down. Using primarily focus group methods, participants were involved in the various stages of problem identification, solution generation, practical action and reflection. The conscious and creative use of a variety of focus group methods throughout all these stages allowed us to go beyond understanding and documenting the issue of minority women and cancer screening: it provided an opportunity to create new knowledge through a process of conscientization among all parties involved.

In adopting PAR, we made explicit the intercultural setting within which we operated, and designed our research to take account of the differing perspectives that emerged. Participants were encouraged to explore Western medical concepts within the context of their own language and culture and to reconstruct and reproduce their own knowledge in the process (Jegede, 1996). As Reason (1994: 325) has rightly asked, 'Who owns the knowledge, and thus who can define the reality?'

The two projects

Research designs

It would be churlish to proffer the practice of PAR without acknowledging the influence of the funder (National Health Services Breast and Cervical Screening Programme). The funder has the power to set the agenda and define the 'problem' at the outset. In these projects, the funder played an active part in negotiating which minority groups should be involved. We were also aware that the political environment was ripe for the import of PAR into health services research, since PAR mirrors the iterative processes of needs assessment, intervention, and evaluation demanded by current NHS practice (Hart and Bond, 1995).

Both projects share a similar research framework within which it was expected that three key stages would develop: (a) problem identification; (b) solution generation; and (c) fieldwork and evaluation.

People involved

Bilingual minority women belonging to seven linguistic communities in Leeds were recruited in order to obtain the views of minority women towards breast cancer screening. The languages involved were: African-Caribbean, Bengali, Cantonese, Gujariti, Hindi, Punjabi (Sikh) and Urdu. The Cervical Screening Project involved bilingual and non-English speaking minority women, as well as smear takers from six general practices across South Yorkshire. The decision as to which language groups to involve in the cervical screening project was partly constrained by the funder's brief and partly by the availability of language groups in the locality. This second project involved Arabic, African-Caribbean, Bengali, Cantonese, Vietnamese and Urdu/Punjabi (Muslim) language groups.

Lai-Fong Chiu was a Health Promotion Officer in Leeds (1990–94), and in Rotherham (1994–98). She is of Chinese ethnic origin, and speaks English and Mandarin. Cantonese is her mother-tongue. She was the principal researcher who had the main responsibility for the design and execution of both research projects at all stages. She collaborated with Deborah Knight who was a Regional Health Promotion Officer on the Breast Screening Project, and with Jan Povey, another Health Promotion Officer in Doncaster, on the Cervical Screening Project. Deborah and Jan are both white, and neither speaks languages other than English. Deborah's main input was to assist the focus group data collection at Stage I in the Breast Screening Project, while Jan assisted in the smear takers' focus group discussion as a co-moderator. Both Deborah and Jan assisted in facilitating in the solutions generation in Stage II in the light of the views obtained from Stage I of their respective projects.

The characteristics of minority women involved in the two Projects

All the minority women were systematically recruited and involved in the projects as focus group participants, and in the cervical screening project minority women were initially involved as bilingual focus group moderators. A variety of focus group methods were used as vehicles for participation in the whole research process. Because of the combination of various groups of participants and focus group methods, these experiences have been rich and have provided us with further insights into the use of focus group methods in an intercultural setting.

In the following discussion, we reflect on lessons learnt in practising focus group methods in the context of PAR, with particular reference to the three main issues raised by the orthodox methods, that is, cultural diversity, researchers' cultural and racial identity, and the problem of health knowledge.

Linguistic diversity and research strategies

Language has the potential to express thought and to acknowledge experience (Lago and Thompson, 1996). For qualitative researchers, linguistic and cultural skills are crucial in the access to and accurate interpretation of experiences of members of minority groups. Additional challenges are presented by the linguistic diversity that exists within and between communities. Much research, however, either fails to include those who do not

Breast Screening Project	Cervical Screening Project
Minority women from seven language groups: African-Caribbean, Bengali, Cantonese, Gujarati, Hindi, Punjabi (Sikh), Urdu	Minority women from six language groups: African-Caribbean, Arabic, Bengali, Cantonese, Urdu (Mirpuri) and Vietnamese
High competence bilingual and biliterate in English and their own mother tongue	Poor English ability
High educational level	Unspecified educational level
35–50 years	20–65 years

FIGURE 7.1 *Selection criteria for focus group participants involved in the Breast Screening Project (1990–3), and Cervical Screening Project (1995–7)*

speak/read English and/or is focused on a particular linguistic minority through a bilingual researcher who speaks a specific minority language.

The two projects reported here adopted a different approach in that both tried to access the experiences of non-English-speaking women and, within this brief, to work with a wider range of linguistic minority groups as described earlier (Figure 7.1).

The purpose of the focus groups for the Breast Screening Project was to explore health beliefs of different language groups and their receptivity to the new breast screening programme. The majority of the focus group members across all the language groups described earlier were highly educated and many were community workers, nurses or ESL (English as second language) teachers. All groups except the Afro-Caribbeans were both bilingual and biliterate

In contrast, the Cervical Screening Project sought specifically to recruit women with poor language ability in English, as lack of English is believed to be a crucial factor in minority women's isolation. The Project also sought to recruit women with a wide range of ages. These choices were made in an effort to address the findings of the 1994 HEA survey (Rudat, 1994), which suggested that uptake of cervical screening was low at the two extreme ends of the age spectrum, and of McAvoy and Raza's study (1991), which indirectly suggested that health education on cervical screening should target more isolated minority women.

The advantages and disadvantages of bilingual research participants

In the case of the Breast Screening Project, a full command of English on the part of the participants minimized the possible distortion resulting from the need for and delays arising from the interpretation process and, by avoiding an obvious language barrier, offered the prospect of good group dynamics and interaction between participants and the researcher or moderator. However, this strategy requires highly selected and educated participants and provides the researcher with only indirect access to the views of those members of the communities who lack the linguistic abilities and education to participate in focus groups conducted in English. Selection of participants in this way introduces subtle linguistic and cultural filters that may potentially influence the data generated.

To limit this distortion, the researcher attempted to raise the cultural awareness of the participants through frequent reminders that they should attempt to distinguish between their own views (those of educated bicultural and bilingual women) from those of their communities. Prompts were used, such as 'Was this the view of the community or of yourselves?' and 'What do you think would be the view of the community if they are asked the same question?'

Although participants articulated the health beliefs of their respective communities, they appeared to distinguish between their own and their communities' beliefs by making analytical statements. For example, on the effect of breast cancer on body image:

> [Older] Chinese women do not put great emphasis on the body as an expression of femininity. Their [social] activities are different [from Western women]. The way they dress. . . . Therefore, it is not so damaging as others might think. (Member of the Chinese focus group, 38 years of age, Breast Screening Project)

> Well, everybody is concerned about their body image, but [the] over 50s, they are not so worried about it. The family is most important for older women, not sex. (Member of the Hindi focus group, 45 years of age, Breast Screening Project)

An interesting aspect of our observations is that participants of all groups arrived at their consensus statements on cultural beliefs almost without any initial disagreement. This consensus should not, however, be assumed to reflect the accuracy of the description, only the prevalence of this way of characterizing 'the community' or 'older women'. It is also important to note that focus groups involve the negotiation of identity (in relation to the researcher and the 'others' not included in the focus group). This point is discussed in more detail by Waterton and Wynne in Chapter 9.

We have to be aware of the distortion that we are liable to introduce by overemphasizing the differences between the 'traditional' beliefs of 'uneducated', possibly 'rural' women *vis-à-vis* 'educated' participants. Careful interpretation of data in the light of these differences is necessary, to avoid legitimating Western medicalization at the expense of a truly empathetic understanding of a particular world view (Stubbs, 1993).

Given that cultural heterogeneity and diversity exist within all minority groups, the researcher must be aware that the selection of participants will mean that views expressed in focus groups discussions will be a sub-set of those that exist in the community at large.

The advantages and disadvantages of bilingual moderators

In the case of the Cervical Screening Project, the data collected were filtered through bilingual moderators. This introduces at least two possible types of distortion, arising from: (a) a moderator who has an inadequate command of the community language or who doesn't share precisely the same dialect or culture as the focus group participants; and (b) a moderator who does not fully understand the research framework.

For example, an Arabic-speaking individual, who had worked with the Yemeni community for many years, was recruited and trained to act as a bilingual moderator. However, it became apparent that she came from Bahrain whereas the focus group participants – and the Arabic-speaking community in Rotherham – came from Yemen. In addition to speaking a dialect of Arabic which was different from that of the Yemeni women, the bilingual moderator was unable to achieve a good grasp of the research method. This mismatch had serious implications for the focus group session. Participants felt constrained, were reluctant to interact with the moderator and a strenuous effort had to be made directly by the researcher to elicit experiences from the participants. Although some personal stories were told, the discussion was prosaic, and interactions between participants themselves were limited. Although mutual comprehensibility between the bilingual moderator and the women was not in question, the infelicitous discussion limited the potential richness of the data generated.

The Mirpuri/Urdu language group provided a stark contrast. There was an immediate rapport between the bilingual moderator, who had been born in the local Mirpuri community, and the women she invited to the discussion group. Women interacted as though the researcher was not there, exchanging experiences, only pausing occasionally in their discussion to allow for interpretation. The researcher's intervention in the process was minimal, and she was able to observe expression of feelings, emotions and other non-verbal communication during the session.

The use of bilingual moderators in conducting the focus group discussions influenced both the group dynamics and the ways in which data were recorded. Apart from the Afro-Caribbean (English), Chinese (Cantonese) and Vietnamese (Cantonese) groups, the researcher had no direct access to the discussion, as the other groups, that is the Bengali, Urdu and Arabic groups, were conducted in languages which the researcher does not possess. There were noticeable differences in group dynamics between group discussions that were interrupted by interpreting and those that were not. Indirect access through bilingual moderators produced much more matter-of-fact and prosaic responses from participants. Emotions and feelings were edited out in a majority of cases through the process of interpretation. The fact that both situations were experienced directly by the main author, leads her with some certainty to the conclusion that linguistic ability and the persona and the skills of the bilingual moderator need to be taken into account in the formulation of research strategy.

In addition, there are inter- and intra-language differences among minority languages. For instance, someone who is a Pakistani from the City of Lahore, who speaks Urdu and Punjabi, may not be able to converse comfortably in a focus group whose members are drawn from the rural communities of Mirpur, Pakistan, where a distinct dialect of Punjabi is spoken. Even when a linguistic match between focus group members and bilingual moderator is available, the bilingual moderator may be unable to facilitate a discussion around an unprepared and unfamiliar domain, such as medical and health services terminology. The researcher needs to have an acute understanding of the nature of bilingualism and the process of translation. Symmetrical bilingualism is a rare phenomenon. The researcher needs to be able to devise methods to assess and select suitable bilingual candidates for appropriate training before the focus group discussion takes place.

Obviously, appropriate language matching is crucial; but, in addition, the class and cultural match between bilingual moderator and focus group members is a significant factor in achieving rapport. Incongruity in culture and class may impair interactions, thus affecting the quality of data generated. However, if a good match for these attributes cannot be found, the researcher has to judge whether such shortcomings can be remedied by the competent use of interpersonal skills on the part of the bilingual moderator.

The boundaries between the researcher and the bilingual moderator became blurred and roles became interchangeable when participants share a common language with both the bilingual moderator and the researcher. Participants in the Cantonese, Vietnamese and Afro-Caribbean groups tended to draw the researcher (Lai-Fong Chiu in this case) into the conversation. Participants frequently sought to explore personal health problems with the researcher. For example, in the Vietnamese group, while discussion centred around women's general health problems, a few women started to query the researcher as to whether use of coitus interruptus as a contraceptive method would harm their husbands. One woman told the story of a friend whose mother-in-law blamed her for the husband's ill-health when she discovered that the couple were using this contraceptive method. The researcher has to be mindful that, in the absence of language and cultural barriers with participants, her identity and her presence provides an unusual opportunity for women to bring forth many health issues which they find impossible to discuss with other health professionals. The prospect of obtaining rich peripheral data has to be balanced with the needs of the agenda and objectives of the research programme.

Strategies adopted to address the linguistic diversity that exists in minority communities and to obtain views from minority women in Stage I of both projects have raised many complex issues. Research design must acknowledge the trade-off between the ease of communication that can be achieved with bilingual participants, versus the direct access to those members of the minority communities most at need that can be achieved through the use of bilingual moderators. Gaining direct access to non-English-speaking minority women can undoubtedly reduce the forms of distortion mentioned at the beginning of this section. However, other potential problems generated by bilingual moderators' class identity and other technical and interpersonal skills cannot be ignored. Above all, the researcher has to be mindful of her own racial and linguistic identity as she interacts with participants, and it is to this issue that we now turn.

'Black' and 'white' identities

The debate of 'insider' and 'outsider' in qualitative research is not new. Ethnographers have long recognized the impact of the ethnic identity and nationality of the researcher on the behaviour of their subjects (Standfield, 1994). Black researchers have also documented the ways in which a good racial and cultural match between ethnographer and subjects can create interesting interactions (Sudarkasa, 1986; Whitehead and Conaway, 1986).

As Farquhar and Das have pointed out in Chapter 4, the gender and ethnic identity of the researcher conducting the focus group can have an important influence on its success, particularly where 'sensitive topics' are being discussed. This is supported by our experience in both the Breast Screening and Cervical Screening Projects. Some focus group discussions were led by both of us – a 'black' and a 'white' researcher. Although English was used as the medium for discussion, participants were very conscious of the 'white' researcher's presence. One of the participants preceded her comments on a sensitive issue with the following:

> Well, I'm sorry Debbie [the researcher] you are 'white', but I have to say this . . . many of our people die early usually at their 50s, because of racism, because they had to work very hard as immigrants in this country. (Member of the Community Health Educators' focus group, Breast Screening Project)

A researcher having the same, or 'near same', racial identity, may facilitate the expression of feelings of racial discrimination. The following exchange illustrates this point:

> *PN:* For ethnic people, one thing I do know though is that if you go to the doctor or anybody in the surgery, they don't explain, or give black people as much information as they should.
> *Researcher:* Do you think that they give white people more information?
> *SB:* Yes, because when I had my daughter, the doctor's nurse asked about what colour my daughter's father was, then when I went to

> hospital, they gave me an extra needle for Sickle Cell, and I even knew no nothing about it. She said 'Looks as if though you need another needle'. I said, 'What is this needle for?' She said, 'For Sickle Cell for black people'. That was the first time I have ever heard of it. First time, they never said nowt. And I went back to ask Jane [a friend], and Jane had to have one because of Jimmy [Jane's partner] being half-caste. And Margaret, they just gave her the needle, never explained anything. (Members of the Afro-Caribbean focus group, Cervical Screening Project)

Racial identity does seem to be significant in influencing disclosure of participants' feelings toward race issues. We found not only that minority participants were more ready to talk about racism with Lai Fong present, but that 'white' smear takers on the Cervical Screening Project were also more ready to disclose their displeasure about an Asian facilitator to a 'white' colleague after a focus group session. In this case, the Asian facilitator's physical appearance is European, but she was dressed in her traditional clothes when conducting the session. When the session ended, one of the white smear takers told the white co-facilitator, in private, that she was very angry as she thought that the facilitator was 'a white girl dressed in a Sari to trick us'.

Similarly, bilingual participants in the Cervical Screening Project reported to Lai-Fong Chiu their dissatisfaction with the attitudes of a white co-facilitator after focus group sessions involving mainly bilingual minority women. Remarks such as 'I don't think she is aware of the issue [racism] . . . it's a waste of time', reflected participants' frustration in finding little resonance from the 'white' co-facilitator when they tried to express their views about racism in the health services.

These examples illustrate the racial tensions that can arise within a cross-cultural focus group. Apart from paying attention to what is said inside the focus group, what is said outside the group, by and to whom, is also significant. Focus group sessions are embedded in the ongoing lives of participants and can also lead to changes in the perceptions of those who have taken part.

Conscientization and the participatory action research approach

The focus group experience with the two PAR projects has helped us to recognize the potential in this method for engaging participants in the process of conscientization, a term popularized by Paulo Freire in the 1970s and adopted by PAR researchers to mean a process in which participants identify 'concepts' through language and, through owning these self-defined concepts, achieve a greater understanding of their predicament (Freire, 1972). The process of conscientization was observed throughout the two projects. The focus group method can facilitate dialogue and interaction among participants, and thereby bring about the active construction of meanings in the context of the 'problem' that they face. It is impossible to illustrate the whole process in this limited space, but the following extracts from some of the focus group discussions indicate the dawning of the conscientization process.

CYL: I feel that there is not enough communication going on to make women aware of the consequences of not attending smear tests regularly. Although we can find out something about the 'test' itself, we don't understand why we need it, and what happens if we don't go. [Turns to researcher] Could you tell me whether they [the English] had a better health promotion campaign about this? As we don't understand English, might we have missed this information completely?

YWK: I think nowadays many women in the country are more open about these things. They would quite often discuss their problems amongst each other. I think that we need more information about women's health. (Members of the Chinese focus group, Cervical Screening Project)

NYK: It was an accident that I went to the Doctor, there was a nurse who wanted to give me a check up because I was newly registered there. I think they have to keep some kind of record, don't they?

LVH: I never had any check ups. My periods became abnormal, so I started to have a check up every three years.

Researcher: Yes, many people don't know when they begin to have smear tests regularly. The programme is offered to women between 20 to 64.

LVH: Oh, so it is not just after you have a baby then.

Facilitator: No, usually, after you start to have relationships with a man, you'll need to have check ups.

NYK: Is this a new programme, because I don't think I've heard of this test in the past. Why didn't we know anything about it before?

Facilitator: Would it be because we have very little information?

NYK: But Doctors should be telling us, if this check up is necessary, why don't they? (Dialogue extracted from the Vietnamese focus group discussion, Cervical Screening Project)

In the Urdu group, discussion of the negative experiences of women with the health services went further. As the bilingual moderator was very much part of the community, she momentarily lost herself in the recollection of her interpreting experience with her invited participants and said:

Bilingual moderator: When she went for the smear, there was a lady doctor. She said that she was embarrassed even with a lady doctor. I was there with her at that time. They didn't explain to her what the test was, and I didn't explain to her either. Because they didn't explain to me. I know what a smear is,

	but nobody sat me down, and said to me 'Well, could you explain to this lady'. All they said was 'Could you ask her to take off her trousers and get on the couch'.
Researcher to SF:	How did it make you feel when things were not explained to you?
SF:	We do mind that they don't explain things to us. Maybe because we are Asian. That's why they do it. Because they might have thought we would not be able to understand anyway. (Dialogue extracted from the Urdu focus group discussion, Cervical Screening Project)

It is clear that through this interaction, the participant became conscious of her own ascribed racial status *vis-à-vis* the smear taker. Paulo Freire would have described this as people's critical awareness of the relational phenomenon between those of the 'culture of silence' and those of the 'culture that has a voice' (Freire, 1985).

During the focus group discussions in the Cervical Screening Project, a demonstration of cervical screening equipment was arranged after probing into participants' existing knowledge and experiences of the smear test. The purpose of this demonstration was twofold: while offering the participants an opportunity to relate their own direct experience to the technical account of the smear testing procedure, it also served to elicit participants' responses to the clinical concept of smear testing.

In fact the majority of women in focus groups displayed a similar response to the speculum at first sight. Many were amazed at and perturbed by the appearance of the speculum, but seemed to be familiar with the spatula. All women watched the demonstration of the mock procedure assiduously, and with exclamations such as 'Ah, that's how they do it!'. Some would burst into embarrassed laughter. Some cried 'Yes, that metal thing, it's cold'. The researcher then asked the women if they would like to handle the speculum. First, many were reluctant. However, this inhibition was soon overcome when other members in the group took the lead in handling the speculum. The demonstration had the dual effect of validating women's personal experiences of smear testing and, at the same time, serving as a common reference for women to bridge from that experience to the medical knowledge provided (Cornwall, 1996).

Within the Participatory Action Research framework we used focus groups to define and to understand the 'problem' and employed the method as a vehicle for community participation. Unlike pure 'research', Participatory Action Research committed us to a course of action for change. Women who participated in the initial stage of the Breast Screening Project were invited to be trained as Community Health Educators and thus became actively engaged in the construction and delivery of health education messages about the breast screening programme to their own communities. The Community Health Educators from different communities were brought together in learning and in supporting each other in their fieldwork. The nature of this multicultural group evolved throughout the project as it responded to different research tasks.

Similarly, the cervical screening project has also taken participation as its central philosophy and the bilingual moderators were recruited as Community Health Educators for the respective communities involved. Through a series of workshops with smear takers and Community Health Educators, gaps in perceptions between women from the communities and health professionals were identified and solutions to the 'problem' – of uptake among minority women – were generated. Both health professionals and Community Health Educators were actively involved in constructing the communication strategy for enhancing minority women's experience of cervical screening, and were involved in the dissemination of this knowledge among other members of their professional group and communities.

Practising PAR work in the minority communities is satisfying. It addresses the lack of 'committed action' so desperately needed in the communities (Pearson, 1983; NAHA, 1988). It pays attention to people's lived experience (Reason, 1994) without running the danger of cultural stereotyping. Using focus group methods to help minority women to construct their own experiences of the health services in general and to become critically aware of the nature of their encounters with the screening services is a valuable tool in the 'process of self-awareness through collective self-inquiry and reflection' (Fals-Borda and Rahman, 1991).

Conclusion

Focus groups conducted among a range of minority groups are likely to involve an intercultural encounter, with unequal power relationships. Their usefulness depends on the recognition of the potential creativity that is available on the one hand, and the complexity inherent in that encounter on the other.

Since the reclaiming of the focus group method by social science (Morgan, 1988, 1993), much of the usage of this method in health services research in the cross-cultural setting remains on the needs assessment level (Naish et al., 1994; Henning et al., 1996). Adopting the focus group as a strategy in Participatory Action Research has meant that we could experiment with a number of variations on the basic method, drawing on techniques from both social and marketing research practice (Secker et al., 1995). As a result, we have gained much insight into the flexibility of the focus group method in intercultural settings. We recognize that there are still challenges facing us in conducting focus groups in a diverse linguistic and cultural environment. The development of the bilingual moderators, and of the working relationship between the moderators and the researcher at all stages of the research, are important factors for success (Knodel, quoted in Yelland and Gifford, 1995: 258). It is also important for the researchers to be critically aware of the impact of their own racial identities, and of the influence of the tensions potentially created by racial and cultural differences upon the collection, generation and interpretation of data.

The overall advantage of using focus groups in the context of PAR is that women from minority communities can be brought together to create changes that are appropriate and relevant to themselves. The cyclical spiralling process of changing and refining practice starts with dialogue with and among participants about the problem. Possible solutions for change are then generated collectively. Through reflection on and evaluation of changes in practice, lessons can be learnt and better solutions can be generated for new practice. Through these collaborative processes women can motivate and empower each other, and thus enhance self-esteem and develop solidarity (Reason, 1994). The focus group method in both the Breast Screening and Cervical Screening Projects also provided opportunities for participants to engage in the production and dissemination of health knowledge which is sensitive to the language and culture of their respective communities (Chiu, 1993; Chiu et al., 1993). A further aspect of the focus group method in both projects was the unanticipated benefits to the researchers involved, both in terms of their own conscientization process and professional development.

8 Are focus groups an appropriate tool for studying organizational change?

Rosaline S. Barbour

This chapter assesses the potential of focus groups to enhance our understanding of organizational change. It examines the degree to which it is possible to separate the monitoring and effecting of change. Finally, it asks whether we, as researchers, can employ focus group methods within the organizational context without being co-opted by the concerns of management or professional groups.

I argue that focus groups can bridge the gap between 'traditional' organizational research and 'new' organizational theory, which draws on the models of social constructionism and negotiated order. The inherent flexibility of the method means that, with appropriate modifications, focus groups can be used either as a stand-alone method or in conjunction with ethnographic methods or structured research instruments to both monitor and implement change.

The following observations about the potential role of focus groups in studying organizational change are based mainly on the author's experience of using focus groups to examine the impact of a pilot project involving changed management arrangements for community nurses. Focus groups formed part of a multi-method strategy, and were used alongside individual interviews, observational fieldwork and analysis of computerized workload data to chart change as experienced by 14 general practice teams. These teams were all participating in the pilot project introduced in one Health Board area, with the research component funded by the Scottish Office Home and Health Department. My observations are also based on group discussions carried out in the course of previous research projects. In common with many other researchers, I found that I had already used variants of focus groups, although I had not explicitly labelled them as such.

Models of organizational research

Organizational research in general, and research into organizational change in particular, has been shaped by a constellation of factors, some historical and others reflecting the more recent preoccupations of the 1990s. The most important have been the 'new managerialism' (as discussed by Sarah Cunningham-Burley et al. in Chapter 13) and the attendant view of change being effected via management strategies within a consensus model of organizations. It has also been shaped by the focus on the 'consumer' (Popay and Williams, 1994) and the associated transformation of clients into consumers. There has also been a continuing reliance on individualistic notions of change and the dominance of the positivist paradigm has been maintained in determining how change is measured. Dingwall and Strong thus describe organization theory as 'a discipline that retains a touching faith in the rationality of human actions' (1997: 153).

Managerialism and consultancy

Mirroring the situation regarding marketing research, much organizational research has been conducted under the auspices of the consultancy model. Within this approach group methods have an established pedigree, dating from their application in the USA in the early 1940s and, in Britain, from the late 1940s, with the approach developed by the Tavistock Institute (Hart and Bond, 1995). The 'Tavistock model' reflected traditional management consultancy in that the focus was on the client's problems, and action researchers were engaged in 'organizational problem-solving'. This approach is summed up by Hart and Bond (1995: 24) as enabling an organization 'to work through conflict by a therapeutic process underpinned by action research'.

Much organizational research can thus be described as involving action research, where the intention has been to work within organizations to facilitate or engender change. This, however, has important consequences for the development of both theory and method, since researchers are admitted to organizations at the invitation of key individuals, can be dependent upon the organization for payment and for definition of problems/issues meriting study, and may even be engaged as employees of the host organization. The focus has been on problem-solving and providing solutions.

Consensus and conflict models

Anderson argues that traditional organizational research has been based on the 'illusion of manageability', relying on a consensus view of organizational life which, according to Anderson, results in 'the reification of managerial dominance' (Anderson, 1992). This approach has led to a concentration on solving technical problems as defined by management. Thus, the capacity of lower-grade employees to resist or even subvert the actions and intentions of their superiors (Mechanic, 1962) has been overlooked. The 'Tavistock model', which much organizational consultancy work continues to emulate, was based on the psychotherapeutic approach (Hart and Bond, 1995). It is, thus, open to the same criticisms as were levelled against social work's individualistic casework approach (Bailey and

Brake, 1975) for failing to raise fundamental structural issues, relating to power relations and external constraints on individual behaviour.

As Hart and Bond (1995) also point out, it is probably no accident that those independently-funded researchers from the London School of Economics who were, thus, relatively free to determine the nature and content of their work, were able to serve a wider constituency of interests. Such work notwithstanding, it is psychologists who have assumed the mantle of organizational researchers, while the discipline of organizational sociology – which, with its understanding of social structure (Popay and Williams, 1994) might have acted to counter the implicit bias towards an individualistic and consensus model – has remained relatively underdeveloped.

The positivist model

The psychology of organizations, and thus the bulk of research into organizations and organizational change – in common with many areas of scholarly endeavour – has been dominated by the positivist tradition, relying on structured research instruments and concentrating on the measurement of outcome rather than process. Pettigrew (1990) comments:

> There are remarkably few studies of change that actually allow the change process to reveal itself in any kind of substantially temporal or contextual manner. Where the change is treated as the unit of analysis the focus is on a single event or a set of discrete episodes somehow separate from the immediate and more distant antecedents that give those events form, meaning and substance. Such episodic views of change not only treat innovations as if they had a clear beginning and a clear end but also, where they limit themselves to snapshot time-series data, fail to provide data on *the mechanisms and processes through which changes are created*. Studies of transformation are, therefore, often preoccupied with the intricacies of narrow changes rather than the holistic and dynamic analysis of changing. (1990: 269, my emphasis)

The uncritical adoption of the perspectives of management, together with the reliance on the positivist model of research, has deflected attention away from the study of decision-making and innovation processes at the level of the work group. Anderson (1992: 149) comments: 'Paradoxically, the implementation of many innovations necessarily involves group discussions, negotiations, and reaching consensus over plans to implement modified work practices or procedures'.

The interactionist model

While there is a strand within organizational research which recognizes the importance of culture and, hence, social interaction within organizations, it has been argued that the view of culture employed has been too static. '[I]n focusing on what is stable and permanent about organizations, we have lost sight of the precariousness of organizational life' (Gray et al., 1985: 83). Similarly, as Dingwall and Strong (1997) point out, ethnomethodologists, who have focused on the categorization employed by individuals seeking to find an order in social action, have overemphasized the constraining nature of rules.

Dingwall and Strong argue for attention to be focused on the symbolic aspect of organizations, which is often dismissed by organizational researchers as being irrelevant – or viewed as immutable and fixed (Gray et al., 1985). Both Rosen (1991) and Dingwall and Strong stress the importance of studying official ceremonies and Dingwall and Strong (1997: 151) add to this list public relations events, formal policy-making events, interdepartmental transactions, assessments, and routine handling of complaints.

Michael Rosen advocates an approach based on the ethnographic study of organizational culture, grounded in a social constructionist understanding of science (Berger and Luckmann, 1966; Schutz and Luckmann, 1974; Geertz, 1983). 'By definition, ethnography is a longitudinal method, geared towards a process-based understanding of organizational life. As such, when properly reported, ethnographic data does not provide a snapshot-like view of behaviour and action, but instead focuses on their flow and interrelationships' (Rosen, 1991: 12). According to this approach, pieces and set-pieces of organizational interaction can be studied as 'social drama; instruments through which the social order is reinforced and political control sustained' (Rosen, 1991: 11).

A specific strand of interactionist theory – the 'negotiated order' approach to the study of organizations, as developed by Anselm Strauss (1978), takes this further, highlighting that 'any change arising within or imposed on the order will require *renegotiation* to occur' (Dingwall and Strong, 1997: 143). This formulation is able to transcend the criticism often levelled against interactionism that it fails to take account of structural factors which influence and constrain the production of social or, in this case, organizational life.

Addressing the limitations of interactionist approaches

Interactionist approaches attempt to bring theory to bear on describing and explaining organizational behaviour, but there are limits, both in terms of the potential for rendering findings accessible to sponsors and participants and in terms of using such analyses to develop and refine theoretical perspectives.

Of ethnographic description, Rosen says that it:

> . . . is not to be confused with the recounting that would be provided by the actors themselves in a social setting. It is, instead, a construction cast in the theory and language of the describer and his or her audience. It is a second-order recounting. (Rosen, 1991: 12)

To the extent that such approaches emulate traditional ethnography, with the researcher withdrawing from the field to make his/her analyses, this results in researchers' subordinating of our respondents' experiences and perspectives to the uses of our own disciplines (Strathern, 1987). Such analyses may also fail to address the issues which concern those who have commissioned the research. Even where findings have been written up specifically for organizational clients, respondents' voices may be lost in the oversimplification which can arise when brevity is a prime consideration. There are parallels here with market research, where focus group data tend to be subjected to a very broad content analysis and the findings summarized for clients. However, there are signs that this may be changing in organizational research, with Cassell and Symon (1994) reporting that several clients have recently indicated a preference for detailed qualitative reports.

Despite their advocacy of ethnographic approaches to organizational research, Dingwall and Strong are critical of such approaches for their failure to adequately display the inferential processes involved in the analysis of members' interactions in organizational settings. Both Ritchie and Spencer (1994) and Dingwall and Strong (1997) highlight the difficulty of making qualitative research findings intelligible to both participants in and commissioners of research.

Focus groups offer several interesting possibilities in terms of responding to these challenges. We might, for example, consider presenting our findings in the interactive setting of a further focus group, which has the added advantage that it enables the collection of further data. A focus group discussion around a dissemination exercise can be particularly fruitful. Lundberg (1990) provides an account of organizational development practitioners 'surfacing' (or making explicit) organizational culture – in this case collecting and analysing data through a workshop format – rather than traditional ethnography. The active participation of members of the organization in question also counters the criticism of the way in which ethnographic findings tend to be packaged and reported to commissioning organizations. Steyaert and Bouwen (1994) describe a group intervention where a summary of discussion was provided halfway through the session and then a further question was raised. This can be a useful strategy for use in focus groups, provided the researcher is able to process discussion on the spot and formulate other questions.

Dingwall and Strong continue their critique of ethnographic data analysis and presentation, commenting:

> Members' language remains relatively neglected, except where talk has an exotic character. . . . If the ethnographic study of organizations is to advance, then, as Goffman (1981, 1983) came to emphasize, it must respond to developments in the sociology of language, making the detailed examination of members' talk, from transcripts or near verbatim notes, its hard ground for analytical inference. (Dingwall and Strong, 1997: 143)

This undoubtedly applies to some uses of focus group data – most notably the more superficial analyses which characterize market research reports. However, focus groups, as structured eavesdropping, can make a distinctive contribution, allowing the researcher to study naturalistic talk elicited in relation to specific topics. Moreover, the approaches to analysis advocated and explained elsewhere in this volume (Chapters 10, 11 and 12) render possible a theoretically sophisticated understanding of interaction and language.

The potential of focus groups for research into organizational change

Focus groups have been identified as especially useful for studying the success or failure of particular programmes (Morgan and Krueger, 1993). They are well suited for use in pilot projects, such as the one under discussion here, as they provide unique access to the range of perspectives and experiences of participants in a situation where individuals are involved in defending, explaining or even constructing their views through the interactive process, as they respond to change. Using a longitudinal research design, focus groups can tease out shifts in perspectives and invite participants to comment on these as they unfold.

Although, in theory, focus groups can simply reflect or monitor change, there is always the potential for the focus group process itself to initiate changes in participants' thinking or understanding, merely through exposure to the interactive process. This is what Johnson (1996) is referring to in his paper entitled '"It's good to talk": the focus group and the sociological imagination'. This is not, however, a foregone conclusion when using focus groups (see Sarah Cunningham-Burley et al., Chapter 13). Research may be positioned anywhere along a continuum spanning purely descriptive research through to dialogic action research (Freire, 1970; Padilla, 1993), which builds on community development approaches in seeking to empower the disenfranchised, or those whose voices have been muted.

Working within a health services evaluation model, we viewed our study as veering towards the descriptive end of this continuum, although some of the nurse managers who formed our steering group tended to view the research as located further along this continuum, towards the consultancy or action-research end of the continuum. Their somewhat different view is probably attributable to their involvement in conceptualizing and setting up the pilot project (involving different management arrangements) which the research component was designed to study. In hindsight, it might have been profitable to have explored further this discrepancy in views. At the very least, such discussions might ensure that those who commission research are less likely to be disappointed with the results. We had assumed it to be important that the researchers were seen as independent of nurse management and that this necessitated a somewhat detached research role. While we viewed our focus groups essentially as a method for collecting data, we could, perhaps, have worked more creatively with the liaison nurse (appointed to provide advice to general practices throughout the pilot project) to harness the potential of focus groups for identifying and addressing problems.

Located at a mid-point on the descriptive-action research continuum, focus groups, within the context of pilot projects or ongoing work with groups, can be used to facilitate the identification of barriers to change while allowing potential solutions to be weighed up. Perhaps because focus groups have so often been used for the exploratory phase of research, the potential for using focus groups in longitudinal studies has tended to have been overlooked. They are likely, however, to enjoy greater popularity among action researchers and those involved in pilot projects as their use, generally, becomes more widespread. However, as Krueger (1993) has warned, there are potential dangers for dilution in the quality of any method as it gains in popularity. It is, therefore, essential that we retain a critical perspective in developing the use of focus groups: innovation must not occur at the expense of strengthening rigour.

The inherent flexibility of focus groups means that they can include different exercises as appropriate at different stages of a research – or action research – project. In the case of the research into community nursing described here, an initial focus group discussion explored individuals' and teams' expectations and concerns about impending management changes while also allowing for the collection of baseline data on the functioning of teams and the way in which work was allocated within them. A later focus group, with each of the 14 general practices, took the form of a dissemination session, where preliminary findings were presented for discussion. Although this did offer the opportunity for discussion of problems and potential solutions, the report was based on aggregated and anonymized data and there was, consequently, less opportunity for each team to address the specific issues which engaged them as a work group.

Focus groups can be used as a stand-alone method to study the process of organizational change and are certainly better suited to capturing the dynamic nature of change than are approaches which rely on repeat measures or snapshot pictures gained through administering questionnaires or interviews at specific points during the process. They are less demanding of the researcher's time than is participant observation and, by focusing discussion, they are more economical in terms of ensuring that the research agenda is addressed. However, they can also be used in combination with other methods to provide a broader picture of organizational change. The responses elicited using focus groups alongside other methods can best be conceived of as parallel data (see Chapter 3), giving an insight into group perspectives as opposed to individual perspectives. For example, focus group comments about other professionals – notably social workers – were much more critical than those elicited in one-to-one interviews, where respondents were much more likely to acknowledge the difficulties faced by other professionals.

In addition to the qualitative – and, indeed quantitative – toolbox available to us as social science researchers, there is also potential to draw on all of the models outlined in this chapter in further developing focus group approaches. Figure 8.1 gives an indication of both the differences between standard approaches using these models and the implications and possibilities afforded for focus group applications.

Model	Main focus	Implications and possibilities for focus groups
Consultancy	Organizational problem-solving	Action research (identifying barriers to change and facilitating the development of solutions) Adopting or adapting exercises used by management consultants/analysts
Consensus	Addressing technical problems	Not applicable
Conflict	Empirical or theoretical study of industrial conflict/ professional rivalry	Implications for sampling strategies
Positivist	Measuring of change (using questionnaires/scales as repeat measures)	Incorporation of scales[1] alongside other focus group exercises or discussion
Interactionist	Observation/ethnographies of interaction in a range of settings (e.g. those with symbolic significance)	Structured eavesdropping (using a set of of naturally-occurring questions and/or exercises in a group setting convened for research purposes)

[1] With due attention to problems of representativeness (see Chapter 1)

FIGURE 8.1 *Potential of focus groups for research into organizational change*

Politics and practicalities

When working in the organizational context, researchers are often there at the invitation of managers. In the case of the present research, the pilot project was instigated by the Director of Community Nursing in collaboration with the Director of a Research Unit. In common with many projects thus initiated, access was via a top–down approach, with nurse managers and senior partners being the next line of contact. A system was set up whereby researchers had to report back to a Steering Group comprised of nurse managers drawn from throughout the Health Board.

Carrying out research with professionals within organizations means that we are more likely to come into contact with people who know – or think they know – about research. 'Reflective pracititioners' (Schon, 1991) have generally undergone some research training, although Schon himself laments the dominant approach to using academic research techniques to address the instrumental problems of professional work (cited by Lyon, 1995). Both practitioners and managers may wish to be included in detailed discussion about the precise research methods to be used or may wish to oversee the construction of research instruments.

The issue of timing is central to the study of organizational change and here, too, those who commission research may wish to stipulate – or the amount of funding available may dictate – when research should take place and for how long. However, this question is not as straightforward as it might appear. A host of factors impinge on the decision as to when to administer repeat measures or for how long to track a process. Pettigrew (1990: 271) asks, 'Is time just events and chronology or is time a socially constructed phenomenon which influences behaviour?' How do we, as researchers, ensure that we are brought in at the most appropriate point? In the case of our study of community nursing management arrangements, we were not party to the negotiations involved in recruiting general practices to join the scheme, and were, thus, reliant on nurse managers' retrospective accounts of this process.

There is a tension between managerial and research timetables, with managers and organizations seeking 'usable, speedy answers' while social science researchers are more concerned with providing 'well-substantiated' answers (Lyon, 1995: 534). Initially, it took some time for the effect of management changes to become apparent, and the same system of management worked rather differently in different general practices, so that we were involved in trying to understand the complex effects on team functioning of practice styles as well as management arrangements. As researchers, our involvement started as the pilot project commenced, which compromised our ability to distinguish changes brought about by the new management arrangements and differences between the 14 general practice teams involved in the study. Had we had the opportunity of working with practices for, say, a three-month period prior to the introduction of the pilot, it may have been easier to have produced preliminary findings at the stage required by commissioners of the research. As with all pilot projects, participants were aware from the outset that the new management arrangements would be in place for a relatively short period and towards the end of this time everyone became more relaxed, knowing that things were soon to revert to normal, there was much less talk of problems and difficulties, and individuals began making preparations for returning to their previous management conditions.

Although the pilot project which we were studying lasted for 12 months, decisions about contracting for the following year had to be made relatively early in the progress of the pilot and the researchers were not in a position to provide conclusive answers or, indeed, much in the way of detailed guidance. However, given that managers have, in any case, to make such decisions, with or without the benefit of our preliminary research findings, perhaps we should be less squeamish about providing summaries and recommendations at an early stage. Alternatively, there may be a role for an individual with management training on the research team, and focus groups (or exercises within focus groups) could provide a useful avenue for pursuing questions related to contracting, budgeting and forward planning, should this be an expectation of the research.

The researchers and one of the grant-holders had an initial meeting regarding research access with the lead general practitioner (GP) in each practice which had agreed to participate in the pilot project. On one occasion a GP expressed strong reservations about our proposed research design: 'I know about research and your research protocol is not at all well-thought out. This is so wishy-washy and vague. How do you propose to match the general practices? How are you going to measure change?' This individual was clearly referring to a different model of research: the positivist approach which he would have been exposed to as a medical student. Another GP, who was reluctant to allocate us time to carry out a focus group discussion, said, 'If you want some answers from us send us a questionnaire. We're used to those and they make sense. Just give us your questions and we'll fill them in.' The necessity of having to defend qualitative methods in the face of such challenges can, however, act as a useful spur to strengthening their rigour.

In response to the criticisms of the study made by these GPs, the researcher attempted to explain the need for flexibility in an exploratory project such as this one. By the end of the 12-month pilot period, however, both of these two initially rather hostile GPs had turned into advocates of at least some aspects of qualitative methods. Their 'conversion' was probably influenced by their experience of participating in semi-structured interviews and focus group discussions, both of which they apparently found to be enjoyable – and, perhaps, also insightful. This unintended consequence of involvement in the research process suggests that there may be considerable potential for providing research training opportunities in the course of ongoing projects, and focus groups afford a setting conducive to experiential learning while simultaneously providing an opportunity for more structured training input.

In the case of this particular research project we met with considerable resistance to the idea of using focus groups from nurse managers, who were concerned that bringing teams together for discussion would lead to conflict or that certain members of the team (notably GPs) were likely to dominate discussion to the exclusion of other categories of staff (particularly junior nurses). In response to these concerns, we opted for a combination of written exercises and tape-recorded discussions, which gave individuals an opportunity to record individual thoughts, while choosing which of these to share with the wider group.

However, practice managers were more positive, since we emphasized the potential of focus groups for efficient use of team members' time (Barbour, 1995). The climate may well have changed since the study was carried out (1993–4), given the media attention recently accorded focus groups (see Chapter 1), and it is possible that both steering groups and organizations are now likely to be more amenable to focus group research.

When moving into any new research setting we are necessarily dependent on the detailed knowledge of key respondents or contacts. Managers' or professionals' help may be invaluable in determining selection strategies and their advice on focus group composition can be helpful. However, there is also considerable potential for them to unwittingly – or intentionally – manipulate selection strategies. They may suggest the inclusion of individuals who share their own partisan views or who are viewed by the group as a whole as 'opinion leaders'. Such individuals may be particularly forceful and dominant during discussions, and may limit the extent to which other participants are willing to reveal their own views. One nurse manager participated in a focus group session with the one general practice team within her area of geographical responsibility. In market research it is fairly common practice for a client to sit in on some focus group discussions but, in this case, there was the additional issue of this individual being the respondents' direct line manager. This focus group, however, passed without incident, although discussion was rather more inhibited than in some of the other sessions. The provision of booklets, fortunately, allowed us to collect comments from individual respondents which were not shared with the group as a whole.

There is considerable potential for researchers to be co-opted by managers or certain factions within organizations. Particularly in the case of organizationally-commissioned research, the purpose may be to usher in particular changes which may be unpopular. Focus groups themselves are sometimes seen as a way of rendering palatable such changes and they can also be presented as evidence that consultation has taken place. Thus, several members of the general practice teams involved in our study viewed the researchers – at least at the outset of the study period – as having been employed by the Health Board to impose the new management arrangements and convince staff of their viability. As I have argued earlier, we may, in seeking to emphasize the separation between the researchers and nurse management, have missed out on opportunities for working *with* practices to address their concerns. Such negotiations, however, are very delicate and time consuming and to have entered into discussion at the start of the study might well have led to research access being denied. Perhaps such innovative approaches are, after all, better-suited to situations where a researcher or a research institution has a long-standing relationship with an organization – as, indeed, happens with the consultancy model.

Focus groups within organizations generally involve pre-existing groups or teams. This raises important ethical issues as groups have a life beyond the research encounter and interaction in the research setting may have far-reaching consequences. (It is, of course, precisely this aspect of focus groups which makes them so useful in action research.) Some of the more serious implications of sharing views within work groups can be avoided by recruiting across rather than within organizations, where appropriate, but the nature of the research may mean that such a strategy is not feasible. Researchers faced with this situation can compromise by identifying where conflicts are likely to occur and splitting up work groups into different grades or categories of staff. Thus separate focus groups might be held with GPs, district nurses, and health visitors, or with full- and part-time staff. As with sampling strategies, generally, other potentially illuminating comparisons may suggest themselves in the course of a research project (see Chapter 1) and individuals might be invited to participate in more than one group. Alternatively, the researcher may recognize the limitations of group composition, but seek to redress the balance by careful ordering of questions or exercises (Morgan and Krueger, 1993; Barbour, 1995).

Within organizations and work groups there are likely to be routine and/ or tacit agreements between participants – and particularly between managers and managed – as to what is or is not said. Bringing people together and stretching the bounds of such informal practices, either by encouraging discussion around topics normally avoided or by prolonging discussion to explore issues in greater depth, can lead either to very stilted discussion or to a situation where participants later regret having revealed their views. However, participants – particularly where they already work closely together – can be very skilled in dealing with the requirements of a supposedly open discussion forum. In one focus group session, a GP insisted that participants share the comments which they had written down in booklets provided with the assurance, from the researcher, that they need not share these comments with the group as a whole. However, the other team members present showed themselves to be adept in dealing with this individual and his somewhat confrontational style and unhesitatingly responded by providing only some of the less contentious comments which they had written down.

However, the banter between individuals who have a history of working together can illuminate underlying concerns. For example, in one focus group discussion around a vignette (depicting a 'typical' patient referral scenario), the commentary revealed participants' ambivalence towards management protocols:

> *GP1*: I think the GP, health visitor, practice nurse, dietician, social worker, chiropodist would all be involved. What we are going to do is to treat his leg and assess his needs and deliver appropriate resources to the level of the patient's agreement.

GP2: That sounds like management speak. Correct, basically what we do is take a swab from the thing to start with . . .

GP1: The practice nurse . . .

GP3: The main problem is not the man's leg, unless it's a different sort of ulcer . . .

GP2: You treat his leg and you've got to assess. Until you assess his needs you can't be . . . say anything more specific other than that you will deliver the appropriate resources with the review.

With their detailed knowledge of each others' work practices, team members can also challenge each other's responses to the researcher's questions, as did the district nurse who commented to a GP, 'That's interesting, I seem to remember that's not exactly what you did with Mrs McCormack [another patient]!'

In any organizational setting, focus groups are unlikely to be the only form of group activity to which participants are exposed. We opted to use pre-existing team-meeting slots. There are both advantages and disadvantages to such 'piggybacking' (Krueger, 1993). Much has been made in the focus group literature of the problems of the alleged 'artificiality' of the focus group format. However, the similarities between focus groups and other group situations are equally important, and consideration of participants' preconceptions arising from either the usual function of the meeting slot or space used is crucial in terms of contextualizing and thus understanding their response (see the discussion in Chapter 2 on the impact of context on data elicited). In such situations the ever-present potential for conflict between the needs of researcher and researched is heightened. (This issue is also discussed by Sue Wilkinson, Chapter 5.)

Within organizations there is a plethora of 'group activities', all of which may be similar in some respects to focus groups, hence clouding participants' appreciation of the specifically research-driven focus group. Brainstorming groups, consensus groups, groupwork sessions, strategy groups, team-building exercises, retreats and office outings all share some features with focus groups, and the atmosphere within a focus group discussion can shift to approximate that associated with a variety of group activities in the course of even one session. Certainly, there was a noticeable change in the tenor and content of focus groups held at the beginning and end of the study in question.

Action-research focus groups occupy a somewhat problematic position, located midway between 'pure' research use of focus groups and more overt professional or management exercises. The distinctions between such activities are also somewhat blurred: although introduced for different purposes, exercises may be very similar in content – and, indeed, in consequence. Just as one-to-one interviews may provide therapeutic encounters, so too can focus groups achieve management objectives. Particularly where researchers act as consultants, activities such as professional consensus panels may employ techniques more usually favoured by academic researchers. An example of this is the exercise in developing consensus guidelines for the management of the menopause reported by Fardy and Jeffs (1994), where the 'expert panel' was recruited by purposive sampling, the discussion was fully transcribed and participants kept diaries between sessions. Researchers might also usefully adopt or adapt tools such as cognitive mapping techniques developed by management analysts. Gray et al. argue:

> [An] extension of cognitive mapping techniques to study processes of meaning construction over time is needed to shed new light on socialization, training, and experiential learning and decision-making processes in organizations. (1985: 94)

Thus there is considerable potential for multidisciplinary collaboration. Francescato and Tancredi (1992) describe an approach to carrying out organizational research involving both a work/community psychologist and an organizational consultant (a systems engineer/economist). They advocate the development of a participatory approach 'with intervention, consultancy and training likely to become more integrated'. Ernecq (1992), for example, recounts how a research case study was rewritten for use in training sessions on decision-making.

Conclusion

Focus groups are a useful and versatile tool for studying organizational change. They enable detailed study of social interaction, during which changes in attitudes and understanding can be observed, even, sometimes, as they are constructed. They allow for the study of organizations as dynamic phenomena with symbolic components and for the study of social interaction itself as involving a delicate and precarious balance.

The inherent flexibility of the method means that it can render the research process more accessible both to research participants and commissioners, while its analytic potential promises to enhance our understanding of the processes involved in organizational change and to enrich our theoretical frameworks. Focus groups can be used to carry out descriptive research, to evaluate programmes, to explore the adequacy of theoretical models, or to carry out action research.

Using focus groups within organizations also opens up the possibility of working in collaboration with professionals with group work skills rather different from our own (management consultants, teamwork facilitators or information specialists). Perhaps one of the most interesting challenges facing us is how to work effectively alongside such individuals. However, we must remain cognizant of our limitations as well as our skills as social researchers and recognize where our expertise ends – particularly if we are not to be co-opted by management or other constituencies within organizations.

9   Can focus groups access community views?

Claire Waterton and Brian Wynne

This chapter considers whether focus groups can contribute to an understanding of community attitudes to risks. We look at this question on two different levels. The first level appraises the use of focus groups, in contrast to opinion polls, as a methodology for ascertaining community attitudes. The second level considers the challenges of interpretation of focus group data. Using an example of an attitude poll held near Sellafield, West Cumbria, in contrast to our own research using focus groups in the same area, we demonstrate that focus groups can certainly uncover a far richer sense of community views on nuclear risks than that ascertained through the poll. We argue that opinion polls have constructed a misleadingly simple and impoverished view of locals' feelings about the nuclear industry in West Cumbria. They have achieved this by assuming that 'attitudes' and 'risks' are objects whose basic meanings are stable and universally accepted.

Through the use of focus groups we have challenged this assumption. Our focus group research provides much counter-evidence, suggesting that, when people talk about risks from the nuclear industry, they do so in a highly complex way that requires careful interpretation. The focus group transcripts illustrated that when people express attitudes about risks they do so: (a) in relation to their relevant social context (seen in example 1); (b) interactively – that is, they actively form attitudes through the opportunity of discussing issues that are not often addressed (seen in example 2); and (c) as a process of negotiation of trust between themselves as participants and ourselves as researchers (seen in example 3).

We have called these various ways in which people talk about risks the 'relational construction of beliefs'. We make a general point here that, in conjunction with various theoretical perspectives (in the areas of risk, social psychology and rhetorical analysis), we believe that people express themselves in this relational manner most of the time – including when they are responding to opinion poll surveys. This has implications for the interpretation (and use) of survey as well as focus group data, which brings us to the second 'level' dealt with in this chapter, the complicated process of distilling focus group transcripts to find valid meaning.

The relational element of people's talk means that data are complex, requiring a lot of unravelling, sometimes leading to counter-intuitive conclusions about their meaning. Research participants' frequent use of ironic humour, 'black' humour and paradox in our focus groups, for example, sharpened our role as interpreters. We were forced to try to see what people *meant* when they said what they said. While we sought to identify people's feelings and beliefs through the discussions, an important point is that such feelings and beliefs were not 'ready-made' (unlike the supposed 'attitudes' reported in polls): they had to be interpreted from a wealth of data. Therefore, the *way* we interpret focus group data is of vital importance. In this chapter we make the point that such insights are dependent on deployment of relevant interpretative skills. In our case, these are totally qualitative. In our examples, we underline the importance of looking at the *interactive* nature of the discussions that take part in focus groups, relying on ourselves as researchers (interpreters) to draw out meanings through detailed textual analysis.

With the increasing popularity of focus group techniques, there have been various calls for a kind of standard setting of the use and interpretation of focus groups. There is considerable diversity of interpretative techniques for analysing focus group data (ranging from quantitative computer analysis to a practice more akin to literary analysis), yet we reject the idea that limits need to be set on this plurality. This chapter stresses the importance of looking at the interactive nature of the discussions that take place in focus groups, thus giving normative value to a particular way of analysing focus groups for our own particular purpose. In our view, however, validation can only come from a kind of open-ended peer review in which our conclusions have to stand up to scrutiny by other researchers, by the community under study, and by others who read the research results. This process is less to do with 'quality control' than it is to do with trust in the research. We suggest, therefore, that accounts of focus group work should include description of the *context* of the work, including why, and how, the work was carried out. By creating open debate and encouraging judgements to be made as to the trustworthiness and accuracy of the research reporting, the social science community can create a far more valid quality control mechanism than any suppression of variation in methodological approach or analytical technique.

We deal specifically with this last point first by outlining the context of the research study that forms the basis of this chapter.

Perceptions of risk: locals' views about the nuclear industry in West Cumbria

The case study presented here derives from research carried out in 1992/3 in West Cumbria (see Wynne et al., 1993). In this relatively remote part of north-west England, many quantitative studies have been conducted over the years to gauge local attitudes to the nuclear industry at Sellafield, especially in the light of possible developments and expansion of the plant around the Sellafield site. Taken together, the picture of 'support' for, or 'concerns about', the nuclear industry in West Cumbria is mixed. However, many of the polls carried out in the area local to Sellafield claim to indicate a higher measure of support for the industry in the local area, than that measured in the county, or in Britain as a whole (ICM 1991a, 1991b, 1994a, 1994b; North East Market Surveys, 1995).

The research we conducted in 1992/9 came about in the context of a planning application made by Nirex UK plc to the local authority (Cumbria County Council) for permission to build a nuclear waste repository at Sellafield for the nation's low and intermediate level waste. At the time, the methodology of focus groups was relatively undeveloped in the sphere of the academic social sciences (at least in areas like risk perception), although it had been used for years for market research purposes by commercial companies in the UK. The established approach to testing public opinion to a proposed development was through opinion polling and the County Council had commissioned several polls.

Through a series of meetings and discussions in 1992, a research project simultaneously meeting the interests of Cumbria County Council and the research team at the Centre for the Study of Environmental Change, Lancaster University, began to emerge. The researchers, Brian Wynne, Claire Waterton and Robin Grove-White considered that by using an empirical focus group approach in academic social science research, the more subtle aspects of people's feelings about risks that had been theorized in risk perceptions research could be accessed.

Why focus groups?

The decision to use focus groups as a method was made explicitly to complement existing quantitative survey analyses, which the research team felt were an inadequate representation of locals' views. Our hypothesis was that focus groups could potentially illuminate things about local perceptions of risk that were elusive to survey techniques, since focus group methodologies have the capability of throwing some of the assumptions made in polls into question. Focus groups, if treated in an appropriate way, permit us to open up epistemological assumptions about the subject matter (for example, how, or more accurately, *in what ways*, do people 'know' what health risks are?) as well as about the research process (how do researchers gain 'access' to other people's knowledge, their views and attitudes?). Potentially, therefore, focus groups offer a more critical or reflexive framework for research on the very nature of attitudes, on the construction of the issue at hand, as well as on the constructive role of the social scientist as interpreter or part-constructor of such views.

A second (and related) reason for the use of focus groups related to current sociological understandings of risk, and perceptions – or *definitions* – of risk. The idea that risks exist 'out there', independent of human meaning and interpretive commitments, and that they can be measured and quantified, has come under considerable criticism in recent years (Royal Society, 1992: chaps 5 and 6; Krimsky and Golding, 1992; Wynne 1995; Irwin and Wynne, 1996). Current sociological understandings of risk suggest that people's understandings of risks (to health, for example) cannot be divorced from the institutional context (who is supposed to be controlling such risks?); the historical context (what has been people's experience of risks?); contextual issues, such as dependency (are risks being weighed up in terms of employment or lifestyle benefits?); self-esteem and identity (are risks being considered against individual or community self-worth?); and a sense of agency or power (are risks being considered against the likelihood of being able to improve or control a given 'risky' situation?). Since sociological understandings of risk underline the crucial importance of the context in which risks are set, focus groups can be viewed as a particularly apt methodological tool since they, in turn, expose such contingencies, and reveal all of the messy context found in conversations that is cut out in opinion poll surveys.

We consider briefly one such poll, to highlight the assumptions that focus groups can provide an alternative, or complementary, method of understanding community views on risk.

Focus groups in contrast to opinion polls

The perceived advantage of polls is that they represent objective knowledge pertaining to a representative sample of the population. However, developments in social psychology, rhetorical analysis and linguistic theories have challenged the assumption made in polls that attitudes or beliefs can be taken to be coherent self-sufficient and discrete entities. For example, the idea that whenever we talk we perform a perlocutionary 'speech act'. The theory of speech acts offers us a highly *social* view of language overall, in which people use langauge not only to state things, but to do things (Potter and Wetherall, 1987: 18). Speech or conversation might not only be a means of communication but might have the effect of forging a sense of trust between two people, for example (Austin, 1962; Searle, 1969).

Equally, we would agree with the observation that a personal expression or 'attitude' should not be interpreted as a stable internalized belief, but rather a stance or position, which can only be understood by reference to wider societal debates (Billig, 1987; 1991). Since debates are usually controversial, and change over time, Billig claims that it is often through argumentation that people express their views. As Macnaghten and Urry

(1998: 94) note, this suggests that 'individual responses to survey questions will reflect context, a certain understanding of the cultural significance of the question and its broader argument located in time and space'.

The implication of these theoretical points for the use of polling methodologies is that responses given may, in fact, reveal as much about the particular situation, or context, in which the attitudes have been elicited as they do about the attitudes expressed. The 'situation' or context on a macro scale – for example, the status of nuclear power in national and media-led debates – is not taken into account in the analysis of polls. Nor is it possible at 'micro' level to consider the relationship and dynamics between researcher and participant in a poll. The lack of opportunity to accommodate these contextual issues within a polling or survey methodology, in turn, places limits on the researcher's capacity to understand how he/she or the research method itself is shaping responses.

A poll we refer to carried out in 1995 in the Sellafield area, and used as evidence in the public enquiry held that year to establish whether Sellafield ought to be the site of an international nuclear waste repository, shared many of the following questionable assumptions: (a) attitudes exist as stable objects identifiable to populations in specific locations; (b) such attitudes are focused on separately existing objects (health risks; 'safety' etc.); (c) methods to elucidate responses through surveys do not themselves shape the responses observed; and (d) the poll's framing of the issues covers the reality of the situation and does not impose assumptions on the respondents.

In this poll, risks identified as those causing concern were 'health risks' (14 percent of the total sample); 'radiation leaks' (10 percent); 'safety risks' (7 percent) ('unprompted responses', North East Market Surveys 1995). At the end of the survey, respondents were asked to say how much they agreed or disagreed with certain statements, ranking their responses from 'Agree strongly', 'Agree', 'Disagree strongly' to 'Disagree'. The first four statements concerned risk and are reported in Table 9.1.

From the perspective of risk perceptions research, it is notable that attitudes are presented as stable and unambiguous representations of residents' concerns. The concepts of safety and risks to health are implicitly assumed to have a straightforward, universally comprehensive meaning. The poll cannot illuminate what is meant by people when they agree or disagree with the statement 'it is safe living near Sellafield', or, for example, what being 'concerned about the health risks' might mean to people answering the poll. As our later examples show, negotiation around issues of risk and trust taking place in focus groups is an intrinsically on-going process, 'an endlessly revised narrative' (Wynne, 1996) in tandem with shifting beliefs and values within the group. Sociological work on risk perceptions suggests that, not only does such a poll omit social dimensions that ordinary people include in their evaluation and responses to such statements, it also tacitly constructs a misleadingly simple and superficial view of participants and their recorded attitudes.

TABLE 9.1   *Ways in which risk is framed through opinion poll techniques*

	Agree strongly /agree	Disagree /disagree strongly
I think it is safe living near Sellafield (*particularly by residents in Seascale and those working in the industry*)	79%	17%
I believe the nuclear industry is a safe industry (*particularly by residents in Seascale and those working in the industry*)	71%	23%
I am apprehensive about the safety assurances given by the nuclear industry (*significantly lower in Seascale*)	41%	55%
I am concerned about the health risks posed by the activities of the nuclear industry at Sellafield (*significantly lower in Seascale and those working in the industry*)[1]	40%	58%

'Lay people' generally have an often unacknowledged 'reflexive capability' in articulating responses to scientific surveys and the like (Wynne, 1996: 43). This means that people are consciously thinking not only of the poll itself and the questions posed, but about their own social context in relation to the poll: who is the poll for? What will my answer be *taken* to mean if I agree or disagree? What will the poll be used for? Their responses are likely to reflect a much more sophisticated view of 'safety' and 'risks' than the poll's relatively naïve construction. First, the trustworthiness and credibility of the social institutions concerned are basic to people's definitions of risks. Second, trust and credibility are tied into social relations and 'identity negotiation'. So, for example, when people in our focus groups expressed faith in the nuclear industry's safety assurances, as in the statement, 'we *have* to believe them', we interpreted this as more a statement of a necessary condition for satisfactory existence in the area, rather than as something authentically felt. It also reveals the extent of dependency on the industry for information. The desire to trust the industry is combined with anxiety at the reality of being forced to trust them.

A relational perspective

A defining characteristic of focus group research has been identified as 'the explicit use of the group interaction to produce data and insights that would be less accessible without the interaction found in a group' (Morgan, 1988: 12). Our interest in adopting focus groups as a methodological tool was to identify and explore the more explicitly 'relational' aspects of the way that a local community perceives or feels about risks in ways consistent with current perspectives on risk; to explore the connections between how people experience, define, think, feel and represent risks *in relation to* wider debates (for example in national and local media), as well as to their feelings and conversations about work, families and friends, the community in which they live and other morally significant units (such as 'the nation').

As other contributions in this volume point out, an important part of the debate surrounding the use of focus groups in social science research revolves around the discussion of how much of that context is actually carried explicitly through to the analysis. In our consideration of focus group data (transcripts, audio- and video-tapes), we have found that paying attention to different ways of talking (using irony, humour, telling stories and anecdotes, accommodating others' opinions in the group, and even apparently contradicting and shifting argumentative positions or stances) opens a wealth of information. It allows us to consider the ways that people accommodate risk both in their discourse and in the fabric of their lives; and, as a corollary, how the meaning of risk is constructed in a collectivity. Through looking at the way that people in West Cumbria talk to each other about risks we were able to observe a level of ambivalence and fluidity in the meaning attached to various health and other related risks that would have been impossible to capture through questionnaire methods. Critical factors in this more 'relational' picture of risk perceptions are the social ties of trust, of dependency, of stigma, and of loyalty and pride in the local community around Sellafield.

Trying to identify the way that people talk often involves looking back at focus groups through written transcripts (or, often even better, through audio- or video- tapes) as pieces of interactive talk, rather than as a background in which 'themes' arise. The focus group is seen not simply as a fertile setting for the emergence of salient ideas or themes. Rather, it may be viewed as a site of constant negotiation, involving elements of the participants' and the researchers' identities, and an iterative shifting and resettling of positions within the group around the issues that arise in the discussion. Thus, in direct contrast to analysis software such as NUD•IST or Ethnograph (although for many needs we acknowledge their usefulness), the kind of analysis we need does not 'sieve', or distil a transcript for associations between key words or phrases, or even sets of ideas. It looks, in contrast, at the associations between *people* in the group. It follows that what might seem to some analysts as a high degree of *noise* in the data (such as that part of the transcript where everyone is laughing and half of the group is making fun of the other half, or where no one single issue emerges and the conversation seems to be 'all over the place') is in some cases precisely that part of the discussion that can reveal most about the issues being investigated.

We give three examples of this type of analytical approach in the following sections, the first relating to a group where joking between participants gave us many clues about the way that locals experienced and handled risk. The second example relates to the way that attitudes are constructed and change even within the time-period of a focus group. The third example addresses the issue of the constant negotiation of the relationships and identities of the 'researched' (focus group participants) in relation to the researchers conducting the focus group. All three examples provide a *relational* (therefore fairly open-ended and messy, or 'noisy') sense of what is at issue.

Joking about risks

Given that West Cumbria has a strong 'rural' component, as well as being an area where the primary industries of farming and fishing have historically (and up to the present day) formed an important part of the local economy, two out of twelve focus groups in the Sellafield area comprised farmers and fishermen in approximately equal numbers. In the context of the methodological debate as to whether or not recruit for homogeneity within a group (Morgan, 1988; Kitzinger, 1994a), this mixture of farmers and fishermen could be seen as a relatively 'safe' group combination, in that the group consisted entirely of men who had some common understanding. They were all involved in skilled manual work, working in a primary industry and currently operating under very similar pressures (increasing international regulation, bureaucratic procedures, economic insecurity, subsidies and quotas and so on). In recognition of these pressures, one could anticipate some feeling of a common identity among them. On the other hand, these fishing and farming groups sustain a particular dynamic in relation to one another – consisting of a certain degree of respect, but tinged with a hint of antagonism.

In the discussions there was ample recognition of the risks and uncertainties around nuclear power, and of an 'outside' view of the area around Sellafield as downtrodden and dependent. However, there were many examples of the sheer resilience of ordinary people when confronted with such pressures. Joking provided one such mechanism of resilience, as has long been recognized in social research (for example Mulkay and Gilbert, 1984). The following joke that these two groups shared could easily be seen as providing distraction from the 'real' issues being researched, born as it is partly in response to the relationship between farmers and fishermen. Yet it expresses precisely the nature of local realism and ways of living with and relating to risks. The exchange is between a fisherman and a farmer and is about compensation due to the 1957 fire at the Windscale (Sellafield) works. The site chosen in 1947 for the production pile of the UK atomic industry was 'Sellafield', an ex-Royal Ordnance factory on the West Cumbrian Coast. This site was re-named 'Windscale', or the 'Windscale Works', to avoid confusion with another nuclear factory at Springfields in Lancashire. The name 'Sellafield' always remained in local use, however, and was re-adopted officially by the industry in 1981. This latest change in the site's name has come to be seen as a PR-inspired move, although we have no direct evidence to this effect.

Fisherman:	Tell me something. You know when you had to throw all that milk away when it got contaminated, did you get paid for that?
Farmer:	Yes, yes. It was just exactly the same amount of gallonage we sent in . . .
Fisherman:	Well, on the same scale, when our fish were labeled Irish Sea and nobody wanted to buy them, we never got a cent.
Farmer:	What did you do with your fish then?
Fisherman:	But you'd give over catching them. Here, even more important, what did you do with your milk?
Farmer:	We poured it down the drain.
Fisherman:	Went down the drain and then where did it go to?
Farmer:	To your fish! (general laughter)
Fisherman:	We're only fishermen so it doesn't matter!

The joking between the farmers and the fishermen shows that there was obvious recognition of the risks and uncertainties about nuclear power, but it also highlights a self-awareness and consciousness of the low social status of farmers and (especially) fishermen, coupled with a typical stoicism ('We're only fishermen so it doesn't matter!'). The participants' ironic humour is underlain by a powerful feeling of marginality. In other communities, too, the use of irony has been described as a rhetorical strategy heard from the margins of power (Traweek, 1992: 446). Mueke (1970: 69) also recognizes that it can be an expression of helplessness, resignation, melancholy, or even despair, bitterness and indignation. Hence, we might infer that statements that actually downplay risks – to health, or to the local population in more general terms – may actually reflect the perceived social status of participants, or their ability to affect change (their power) rather than representing any objective view on the likelihood of health, accident, safety risks or other subjects brought into consideration.

A further point is that the light-heartedness, and even the apparent flippancy of views, in this exchange would never be found in opinion poll data, and could easily have been overlooked as irrelevant in focus group data. Analysis of complicated interactions involving irony or 'black' humour also brings the researchers' role as interpreters much more explicitly to the fore in the analysis which has its own complications (for example, how to 'read' irony – see the debate set out in Fish [1983] as to whether irony can have stable meaning or whether the interpretation of irony is inherently unstable and uncertain).

Relational construction of beliefs

One of the most deeply-ingrained assumptions in conventional approaches to public attitudes is that they are intrinsic to the individual respondent being questioned. However, meanings may be objectively open to negotiation, and attitudes or values associated with them likewise may betray shifts, ambivalence and openness to negotiation with others (Harding, 1986; Billig, 1991; Singleton, 1993). This general insight has implications for the way in which the quality of community interactions is recognized and treated. Such interactions are not just a neutral medium through which intrinsic preferences and values are expressed, but are themselves a substantive part of the *formation* of values and attitudes; they themselves have moral and social 'weight', as ends and not just means.

For example, a typical progression of group discussion moves from safety and the ability of 'the experts' to identify levels of risk, to the relative sovereignty of 'experts' or political-economic interests in deciding whether a nuclear plant like THORP[2] is allowed to run. It then shifts to the (perceived lack of) democratic accountability of political elites, and on to economic determinism (*'I don't think they can afford not to open it [THORP] to be quite honest'*) (mothers in Seascale; Group 2):

> *A*: It's so complicated, you just can't answer it straight away. I mean you were talking about plute plutonium: bombs before and I mean we all know the Cold War, you know, the Russians are talking now, the . . . Yugoslavia, you know, they don't need the weapons like they used to. Plus the fact that we've got America's Trident missiles and everything. It's such a complicated issue, you can't just say, well . . .
>
> *B*: You could go on for ever more couldn't you?
>
> *A*: Yeah, we could sit here all day and we still wouldn't come to a conclusion . . .
>
> *C*: What about that . . . it might be that other energy sources take over, like you know, they might open the pits again, or they might discover a way of using solar power, or they might . . .
>
> *B*: I don't think they –
>
> *D*: I can't ever see that happening . . .
>
> *B*: Plus they're not on as big a scale I don't think, I mean as you say, if nuclear power gets the go-ahead to open up in new areas, it's such a big expanding field isn't it?
>
> *A*: It's all politics as well. Why do they want miners got rid of? Why?

Not only does this typical kind of interaction illustrate the inseparably tangled nature of the issues; it also indicates the way in which stances are developed and defined *interactively*, in relation to the responses of others. This often exposes ambivalences and contradiction, but rather than viewing these as weaknesses or lapses from rational maturity, they can be seen as authentic expression of conflicts and multivalency in the issues themselves, and people's experience of them.

As in the exchange quoted, many of the responses show statements tailing off, being left almost deliberately hanging 'in mid air' (a point also commented upon by Frankland and Bloor in Chapter 10), available for someone else to develop further in a collaborative mode. Such interchanges collectively express a powerful feeling of stigma attached to West Cumbria as a site – or 'dumping ground' – for the entire country's nuclear waste:

C:	In other words Britain's going to become the dumping ground for the rest of the world . . . isn't it?
A:	I think we already are . . .
C:	Getting that way aren't we? We're heading that way, that's what it's going to be in the future, I can sum that up in one.
Interviewer:	What about other people?
D:	Well, I can see that we're being used obviously. I mean on the other hand you've got to think of . . .
C:	Work for the area isn't it?
D:	Jobs, yeah.
C:	But what's the use of a job if you're dead?
A:	I know. And then on the other hand if it don't go ahead we don't have a life anyway because there's nothing here, so . . .
C:	What's the point of being alive? . . . If you're depressed and unemployed and . . . on the scrap heap
A:	The odd ones'll have jobs but most people would have to leave the area and you can't really leave the area because there's no jobs anywhere else anyway, so. . . you wouldn't sell your house anyway, you'd be stuck . . .
C:	Looking down the country we're not so bad compared with some of the others . . .
A:	But we wouldn't sell the houses and that'd be it. If they didn't go ahead we'd be stuck in the houses we're in . . .
C:	. . . Still stuck . . .
A:	Well, yeah, that's right, but I mean if it didn't go ahead well that's different then isn't it.
C:	You've got to sell your house to get your money to go somewhere else . . . plus I mean it's going to affect the shopkeepers and everything. I mean, some of them, you know, we don't work at Sellafield, it won't affect us, but it does, it will, because I mean if everybody moves away . . .
Interviewer:	Right. Can I pick up on what you were saying . . . your immediate reaction to this was that it means that . . . Britain's going to become a dumping ground, or Sellafield?
A:	No, Britain, because I feel that more of these nuclear power stations are going to be sprouting up all over. I mean we've got a few now in Britain including. . . . They're going to be sprouting up all over – I really feel in the near future, I mean you are looking in the future, it is going to become a nuclear dumping ground for the rest of the world.
Interviewer:	How? I don't follow exactly how you see that happening.
A:	Well, it's just erm . . . it's expanding such as Sellafield's expanding now. I just feel this is going to happen . . . shifting all the waste over here now, and they're reprocessing it now.
Interviewer:	What about you Barbara? That was quite close to your initial reaction as well.
B:	I feel that we're already – that anyway – we've got everyone else's – I mean the Japanese are supposed to be starting aren't they?
A:	I mean if THORP goes ahead they're going to bring a lot more into the country aren't they?

C:	I don't know. The Japanese are talking about reprocessing their own waste . . . so are the Germans . . . the French are already doing it . . . the French are already dumping into the Channel. Nobody goes on about them though do they? You know, I mean Guernsey, they're sounding off about it because they're right beside it.
A:	They're talking about bringing it here though aren't they? Nobody knows though . . . at least we don't.
C:	It's just in the wind at the moment.
Interviewer:	Yeah. There are two things you're saying here – on the one hand this means jobs, yeah, therefore good; and on the other hand it might mean that . . . we might have more stations like Sellafield in other parts of Britain as well? (mothers in Seascale, Group 2)

Here we can see two individuals, A and C, both initially quite negative about expansion because of the 'dump' stigma, shifting their positions through the interaction as the balance of considerations develops. Their 'final' positions are not necessarily altered by the exchange, although C seems more positive and hopeful; but it shows that the very notion of a 'final' coherent position may itself not do justice to the open-endedness of either's view, and may obscure the continuity between an 'attitude' and the social relations within which it is constituted. This was a recurrent factor in the focus group fieldwork.

Interestingly enough, there were suggestions of gender differences on this relational aspect, with women showing themselves typically to be more fluent than men in expressing the conflicts and ambivalence they experienced with respect to living near Sellafield; the men tended more to take a definite position, and then work hard to rationalize it by eradicating contradiction. This was hinted at, for example, in the occasional profusion of clichés, and difficulty in acknowledging uncomfortable aspects of life in this area. This interpretation would be consistent with MacGill's (1987) study in the same area, and with other work on gender differences concerning control and ambivalence (for example Harding, 1986; Singleton, 1993). At the same time, the quote shows that, whatever their shifts in position, the two women talking are supporting each other in the difficult situation of discussing a sensitive issue in front of two complete strangers (that is, the researchers). This solidarity may be a combination of reaction to the focus group situation, but perhaps also blended with local ways of coping with risks and danger in everyday life. As Marion Bowman writes:

Solidarity has usually been a characteristic of West Cumbria because the work of West Cumbria has always been dangerous. Men have been lost at sea, in pit disasters. These are tragedies which bind closed communities but they can also lead to the development of a culture of masculinity that scoffs at people who complain as 'soft'. The attitude is 'stop moaning and get on with it'. Women's interests are submerged in priorities set by men. Possible worries about high child cancer rates are blunted by the unequal relationships between men and women, as well as everything else. (Bowman, 1987: 69)

Although we can recognize its relevance for understanding risks and attitudes to risks in the local community, we cannot, as interpreters of focus groups, transcripts and other texts, know exactly where this sense of solidarity and support comes from. What is clear is that the *kind* of talk, and the way in which debates develop, not just the content of people's conversations, have relevance if focus groups are being interpreted in a relational sense.

Negotiated identities and the researcher–researched relationship

Our last example illustrates that an important element to consider in analysing focus groups is the way that participants represent themselves in the context of the group. What sort of identities do they present? Why? And what can this tell us about the research? The focus group can be seen as a site of constant negotiation of identities and stances over a very intense one- or two-hour time period. The presence of researchers in the group and the way in which certain kinds of identification may reflect participants' relationship with the researcher needs to be part of that consideration. In a 'community' context, that researcher is usually an 'outsider' of one sort or another, even if 'the community' has been defined artificially for the needs of the research. It is even conceivable that the researcher, as 'outsider', may provide a coherent identity for an otherwise fairly disparate group of people through his/her 'otherness'. Again, we do not see the presence of the researcher as a negative 'noise' factor in any sense. Rather, negotiation of identity, in juxtaposition to others' ostensibly different (or similar) identities, is a part of that picture. Paying attention to this aspect of the focus group will add to, rather than detract from, the picture gradually being built up about community attitudes to risks.

For example, in a group consisting of 'middle-class' women who had children under eight years old and lived in the Whitehaven area (this was our a priori characterization of their identities), the point that one woman stressed about her own sense of identity in relation to Sellafield was that she *had chosen* to come and live there. She relates a story about being a relative newcomer to the area, and being unaware of any local radiation hazards. Ten years later, and having learnt a lot about the nearby presence of the industry, she is still in West Cumbria, through her own choice, as she sees it. The following excerpt from a focus group shows how, in making light of her initial naïvety, she is really asserting the fact that she is now much more knowledgeable, understands what the risks were and are supposed to be, yet has actively decided to stay. The second woman backs up her story, remembering the episode with her. She uses an 'outsider's expression' about 'glowing in the dark' in her part of the account. We interpret this as a way of scorning the idea that they might have received some contamination due to their naïvety ten years ago, and rejecting the identity that we as outsiders might impose upon them as risk 'victims'. But this is much easier to interpret having been present in the group (or by listening to the women's tone of voice on a tape-recording).

The second woman *could* be interpreted as being stoical about the probability of having received a dose, saying something more like: 'we weren't knowledgeable enough not to get a dose, but that's a part of living around here'.

First woman:	About ten year ago there'd been a big leak and there'd . . . we heard they'd even buried the bulldozers at sea, and we were sitting on this beach on a beautiful summer's afternoon . . . saying, 'Oh . . . this is a lovely beach! . . . Why isn't everybody else out?!' . . . I hadn't been long in Cumbria. . . .
Second woman	[*laughing*]: 'I'm surprised! A lovely beach like this and nobody's on it?!' It was closed! So we probably er, glow. Glow in the dark! (Group 4 Whitehaven)

Our interpretation is that the researchers' presence was keenly felt, and playing an important part in the way the discussion was taking place. In a very assertive way, the women were giving us quite a complete picture of themselves. The way that they presented a kind of double-act with a somewhat ironic little twist at the end (told in a rather mocking tone), suggests that they were delineating their complete difference from us as researchers. By using language that they don't normally subscribe to, indicated by the tone of voice (words such as 'glow'), they were both supporting each other in the belief that they were perfectly healthy (they didn't really believe that they had received any adverse health effects from the contaminated beach) and sharing an in-joke, perhaps (albeit benignly) at our expense (we, then, belonged to the outside community that *did* make jokes about Sellafield locals glowing in the dark).

The basic point that these two women had decided to stay and to live in this area despite such experiences, was underlain by a powerful defiance. They blatantly risked the possibility that we wouldn't understand their joking tone, that we would take them at face value and report that they had had a traumatic experience born of initial ignorance of conditions around Sellafield and that they were concerned that they might have received damaging doses of radiation! This defiance and resilience in the face of being 'researched' as risk 'victims' is again part of the picture we need to include about local perceptions of risk.

It is appropriate to mention that this exchange took place within the first ten or so minutes of the focus group discussion – that is at a point where participants were asserting their identities quite vigorously in the group. The timing of responses is often part of the implicit knowledge of the focus group researcher, and is rarely mentioned explicitly in reports or articles, although responses to recent calls to make more explicit the process of doing focus group research may begin to bring such tacit research knowledge to the fore. The desirability and practicality of so doing requires further debate.

Conclusion

Coming back to the question in the title of this chapter, 'can focus groups access community views?', we believe the answer is a qualified 'yes'. Our examples have highlighted aspects of people's attitudes to risks that would have been impossible to generate through quantitative polling or survey techniques. In the first example, we saw how the sharing of jokes, while seemingly downplaying a community's sense of risks, may actually demonstrate the extent to which risks are tied up with a sense of social worth and identity in a wider (non-professional) context. In this example, as in the second, there is an acute sense of awareness of the risk agenda as being much broader, and more fluid, than the question of whether individuals acknowledge health risks or feel 'safe'. A pervasive stigmatization associated with Sellafield (due in part to its image in the national media context) is an important factor here.

In the second example, where individuals were changing their stances in interaction with each other, the contribution of focus groups as opposed to interview or quantitative analyses lies in their capacity to permit wide-ranging interaction on a subject. The important point here is that this flexibility and fluidity of the focus group is seen not just as a means of expressing the wide-ranging nature of attitudes, but as a way of facilitating and recording the *active formation* of those values within the group setting. Therefore, the process of conducting focus groups deserves as much attention as their end-product (conventionally the transcript and resulting analysis).

Our third example looked at a piece of interactive discourse which conveyed hints of the complicated and subtle relationships between participants and group researchers. Although the force of this example would be much clearer from listening to the tape-recording of the discussion, by paying attention to the way in which the two women concerned were talking (in this example, they were acting, as if in a role play) and to the kind of words that they used, we can attempt to understand how they felt about talking about risks in relation to ourselves as researchers/outsiders. We can therefore try to understand how they initially saw our construction of them as risk 'victims' and how this features in the discussion – perhaps bringing about a certain element of defiance and rejection of that perceived construction of them. This would be completely undetectable in survey-based research. The example points to a key question for the kind of interpretative approach we adopt – how do we represent ourselves reflexively in the analysis as part-constructors of the focus group dialogue?

But what are our reservations about the ability of focus groups to access community views? Focus groups are not a panacea for the social sciences. As a research tool they can certainly help 'gain access' to some elements of the human condition and predicament that other methods cannot. On the other hand, as we have stated in this chapter, we think that the process of carrying out focus groups itself deserves analytical attention. Coming from the theoretical perspectives that we do, it would have been impossible to have made use of focus group data in a quantitative sense (although this is a surprisingly common research interest – see Agar and MacDonald, 1995), or to have fed data through a computer package for analytical purposes. Thus the suitability of focus group methodologies depends, in our view, very much upon prior commitments and on the way in which they are used and analysed (see Agar and MacDonald again on ethnographic research).

In the Sellafield area, the fluidity around the interactively negotiated construction of the meaning of 'risk' shows the extent to which different senses of collective identity (that is community) form around experiences of risk – including treatment by official bodies or by malign media. Therefore 'risk' and 'community' may mutually define each other, in varying ways, and in ways that are often only quasi-stable, and open to change. This emphasizes the problematic characters of both (assumed objective) 'risk' and 'community'. Hence, just as focus groups emphasize and allow explanation of the open-ended, multivalent, internally-tensioned and relational properties of attitudes to 'risk', they also show the open-ended, negotiable and constructed definition of 'community'. The fluid nature of these definitions means that they may be, in some ways, elusive of capture by social science techniques – even focus groups! Focus groups can offer us, however, a telling snapshot of attitudes-in-the-making, of the way that issues and identities interweave and of the sophisticated ways in which people manoeuvre and negotiate around the difficult issue of living with and talking about risks. A final consideration, relevant in terms of the policy use of research, is that perhaps the biggest challenge attached to the use of this methodology is how to convey such rich but untidy and unstable pictures to those (planners, policy makers and so on) democratically responsible for managing such risks.

Notes

1 Seascale is the nearest village (approximately 2 miles) to the Sellafield complex. Text and figures have been reproduced from the survey carried out by North East Market Surveys (1995: viii). The comments in brackets reflect on the percentage figures. Taking the first statement, for example, 79 percent of the sample on average

agree or agree strongly with the statement that it is safe living near Sellafield. However, the percentage is higher in sub-sample populations such as residents in Seascale and people working in the industry.

2 THORP stands for 'Thermal Oxide Reprocessing Plant'. THORP was built at Sellafield during the 1980s. Its opening was delayed because of a public controversy questioning the need for reprocessing. It finally began to operate in 1995.

10 Some issues arising in the systematic analysis of focus group materials

Jane Frankland and Michael Bloor

Until the 1980s, methods textbooks were largely silent on the technical task of analysing qualitative data. There were a few exceptions, notably Znaniecki's (1934) classic, *The Method of Sociology*, but many respected qualitative methods texts, for example, Cicourel's *Method and Measurement in Sociology* (1964), said almost nothing on the topic. The methodologist's gaze was elsewhere – on the researcher as an advocate for research subjects, on techniques of interviewing, on the negotiation of research access, and so on. This neglect of analytic techniques communicated a view of qualitative analysis as a craft skill, something learned piecemeal and progressively by apprenticeship and practice, rather than being a reproducible technology amenable to direct instruction. This earlier silence is now past and contemporary qualitative methods texts (for example, Silverman, 1993; Hammersley and Atkinson, 1995) all carry detailed instructions on research methods for analysing qualitative materials.

There remains perhaps one qualitative method that stands as an exception to this wealth of analytic instruction, namely the focus group method. Possibly the fact that focus groups have, historically, been developed within market research has inhibited explicit attention to analytic matters (see Sarah Cunningham Burley et al., Chapter 13; also Johnson, 1996). Certainly, current texts on focus groups (for example, Morgan, 1988) are more concerned with issues of composition and conduct than with analytic techniques. Typically, focus groups in market research are normally audio-recorded only for quality control purposes. The audiotapes are not transcribed: analysis is based on the debriefing of the group moderator by the report writer, so that group members' responses are filtered twice, first by the moderator and second by the report writer. This is clearly unsatisfactory: one of the potential advantages of focus group methods lies in the richness and complexity of the responses of group members so generated, and much of this richness is lost through a filtering process; further, there is a great danger of selective recall of, and attention to, some data and neglect of other contrasting or qualifying material. Focus groups can provide a rich, complex and extensive data set for social researchers. However, many of the potential advantages of these data are lost in the absence of appropriate methods of analysis. There is a need to retain something of the richness of transcript data, while ensuring that the great mass of data thus generated are analysed systematically and not selectively.

It is possible, of course, to analyse focus group transcripts from a conversation-analytic perspective, with the objective of throwing light on features of ordinary talk – turn-taking in conversations, for example – but our interest here will be in methods for analysing focus group materials in order to throw light on *substantive* issues, in this instance adolescents' group norms on smoking and quitting smoking. Myers and Macnaghten (Chapter 12) are concerned with a conversation analytic approach.

It will not be our suggestion that focus groups demand distinctive analytic techniques. However, we are concerned to show here that some special problems arise in the application to focus group data of analytic techniques developed to address other kinds of qualitative data (depth interviews and ethnographic fieldnotes). For simplicity's sake, we will concentrate in this chapter on one analytic technique, analytic induction, also sometimes known as deviant case analysis. We will discuss the advantages and difficulties in applying this method of analysis to focus group data and will illustrate the discussion with data from adolescents' focus groups concerned with smoking behaviour. We begin with a report of how these adolescents' focus group data were collected, indexed and analysed.

Data collection

Twelve focus groups were conducted with pupils in years 8 and 9 (aged 12 to 14 years) from four secondary schools in South Wales. The research aimed to establish the degree to which smoking and giving up smoking was a topic of discussion within the school setting. It was part of a wider, ongoing study of a schools-based, peer-led, smoking cessation intervention, with the intervention itself taking place some months after the focus groups. Focus groups are useful vehicles for collecting data on group norms, on the conformity, consensus, censorship and dispute surrounding such norms (Kitzinger, 1994b). These focus groups were set up to collect data, not on peer pressures to continue or quit smoking as such, but on public discourses about such peer pressures.

Groups ranged in size from four to eight, although the majority contained six pupils or fewer. Groups were differently composed by sex: five groups of girls, two groups of boys and five mixed groups. Earlier self-completion questionnaires had generated smoking histories and some groups were deliberately composed to include numbers of regular and/or experimental smokers. As group members were drawn from the same school and year-group, they were all known to each other, but they were not necessarily close friends.

Focusing materials were used in the form of photographs of pupils in school break-time settings. Groups were asked for their views of certain situations occurring within these settings: first of conversations to do with smoking between different groups of people; second, what they felt would happen if a member of a social group of smokers decided to quit smoking. Group sessions lasted for up to one hour and were tape-recorded and transcribed by the researcher who had moderated the groups.

Data Indexing

Many methods textbooks describe the processes used to index a qualitative data text (see, for example, Dey, 1993; Coffey and Atkinson, 1996). Since all analysis is essentially comparative, the purpose of indexing is simply to facilitate comparative analysis by gathering all data on a particular topic under one heading, in order to make the study of material manageable for analysis purposes. Indexing is, of course, an activity quite distinct from the exclusive coding of material: pieces of transcript are not assigned a single code in a final and arbitrary interpretative act; rather, each piece of transcript is assigned several, non-exclusive index-codes referring to the several analytic topics on which it may bear. There is no necessity, at the indexing stage, to settle on a final interpretation of an item of text, indeed the objective should be to simply pose a number of possible interpretations, deliberately postponing a final interpretion until the text item can be compared systematically with the entire universe of text items carrying the same index-code: the emphasis in the indexing act is on inclusiveness, on including initially all possibly relevant material, rather than on exclusiveness.

The indexing process generally follows a number of similar steps. The process employed here is described, while the example of data illustrates how the method was applied to the text:

1   The text was read through as a whole to refamiliarize the researcher/moderator with its content and to note patterns or themes of interest that were recurring in the data.

2   The data were then re-read and the process of attaching index-code words, or labels, that relate to the content of the text started. At the start of the indexing process, index-codes were quite broad and general. In the example below, quitting was considered to be the overall topic of the text, this index-code embracing the whole body of the data.

3   This process of indexing is cyclical. New index-codes may emerge in later transcripts and the researcher then returns to earlier texts to add this new index-code to them. In this case, on subsequent readings subcategories such as different types of peer pressure were noted and corresponding codes (such as bullying, exclusion, active encouragement by friends to continue smoking, and passive encouragement by friends to continue smoking) were added to the data set.

Indexing is therefore essentially inductive in nature, with categories emerging from the analyst's hermeneutic absorption in the text. Recalling the events of the focus group itself, the analyst has a participant's 'pre-understanding' of the transcript and understanding is deepened by submersion in the text. Analytic categories are generated through this understanding and these categories, applied to the text, deepen analytic understanding, which in turn stimulates greater elaboration of the analytic categories, which are in turn applied to the text, and so on. The process is not reductive: the data are retained in richness and context, but comparative analysis is facilitated. The progressive elaboration of index-codes is equivalent to that of chapter-headings and sub-headings. The later addition of new sub-headings to address emergent analytic interests is facilitated because the analyst has no need to re-read all the transcripts: only those text items indexed with the original 'chapter-heading' (for example 'peer pressure') need be re-inspected for possible re-indexing with the new sub-heading.

Data were entered into 'Ethnograph', a package for the analysis of qualitative data. This is one of a number of packages on the market that facilitates the organization and management of the data (see, for example, Tesch, 1990, for accounts of this and other available computer packages). Such packages do not, of course, *analyse* qualitative data, they simply facilitate such analysis. They ensure that analyses are based on a consideration of the entire universe of relevant textual material. In this respect packages like Ethnograph have only a limited advantage (instant electronic access to text) over a manual card index: it is true that computer packages can perform sophisticated tasks that a manual card index cannot (for example, one can access on the screen all the items of text indexed for 'X' where 'Y' is also co-present), but such sophistications are rarely an analytic requirement. So it may be the case that, for a small amount of transcript material, simple manual indexing may be an economical alternative to a qualitative data package. Manual indexing should carry the transcript number and page number as text locators.

In the example of indexed text below, abbreviated titles are given to the index codes for ease of study, but in practice index code numbers would be used. Thus, 'quitting' might be coded as 'A', with 'peer pressure' as 'A10'; 'exclusion' and 'bullying', as types of peer pressure, might carry codes such as 'A11', 'A12'. Sub-types of exclusion might be noted as 'A111', 'A112', and so on, if exclusion developed as a major analytical focus with a wide range of relevant transcript material available.

It should be recalled that the indexing process is simply an aid to analysis. It is therefore always provisional. For example, Lucy's statement in Figure 10.1 about the photo, that all the group in the photograph are 'looking at her [one member of the group] all weird', need not be viewed in the final analysis as 'bullying': the analyst may choose finally a more restrictive and physical definition of 'bullying'. The only requirement at the indexing stage is that items of text adopt provisionally a broad and

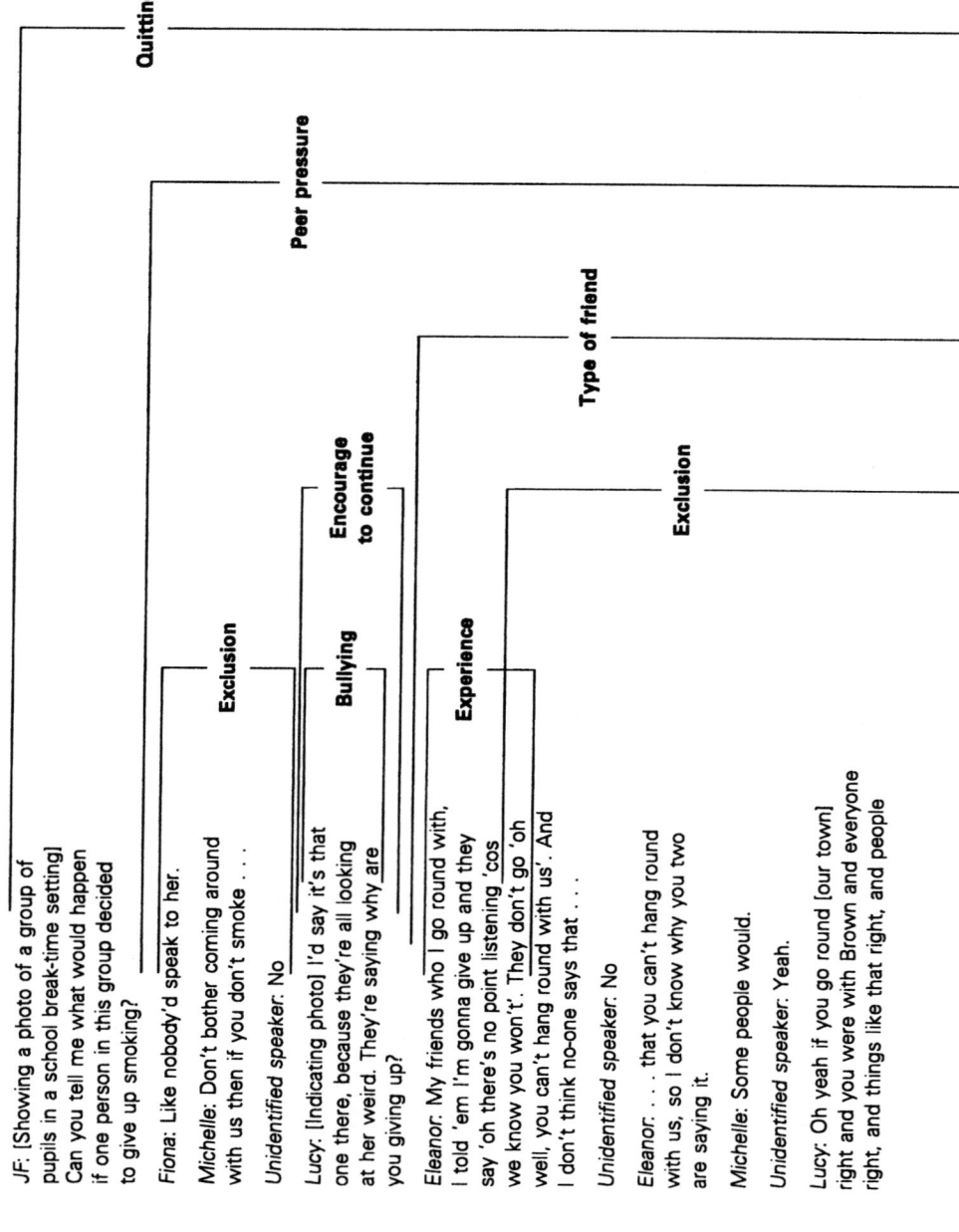

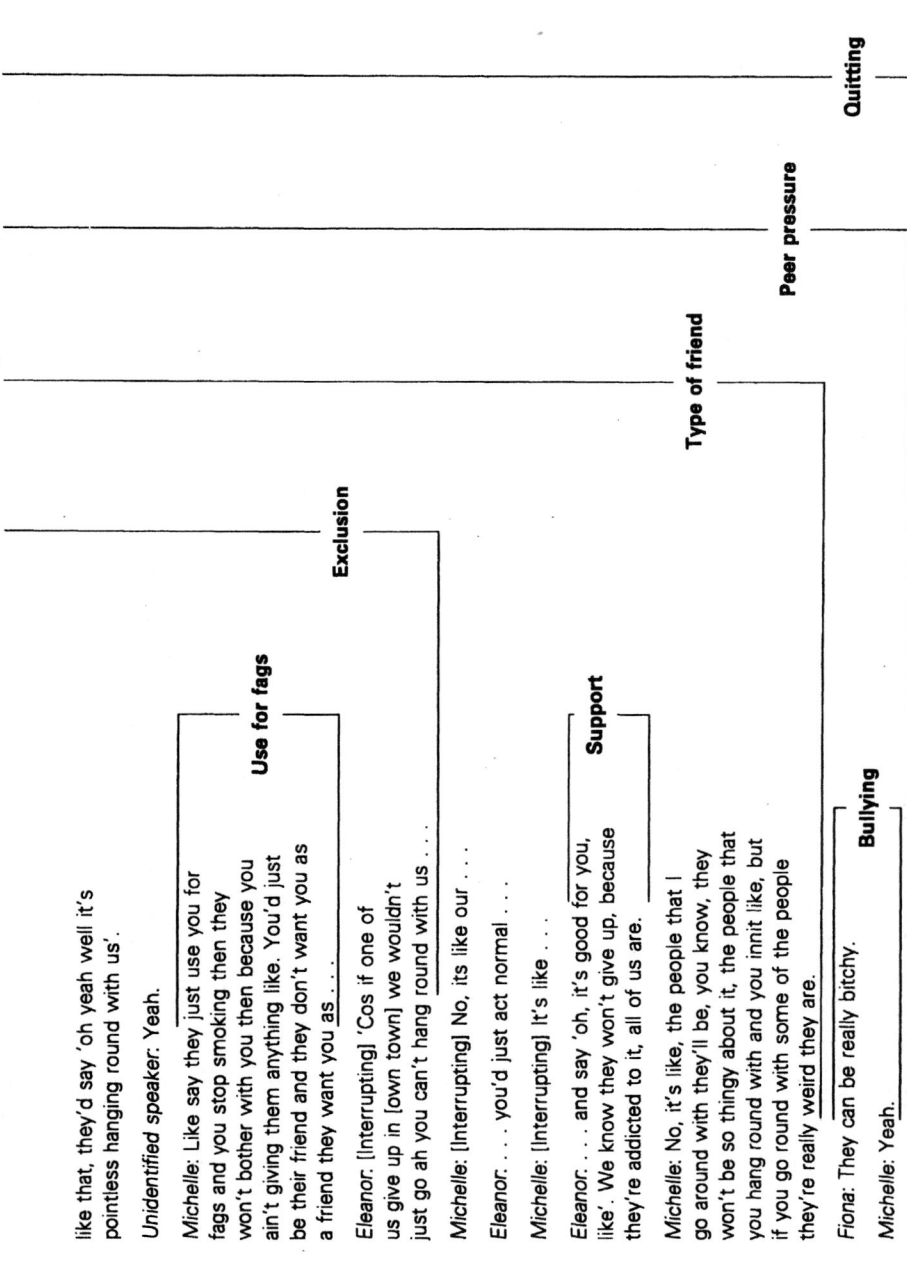

like that, they'd say 'oh yeah well it's pointless hanging round with us'.

Unidentified speaker: Yeah.

Michelle: Like say they just use you for fags and you stop smoking then they won't bother with you then because you ain't giving them anything like. You'd just be their friend and they don't want you as a friend they want you as ...

Eleanor: [Interrupting] 'Cos if one of us give up in [own town] we wouldn't just go ah you can't hang round with us ...

Michelle: [Interrupting] No, its like our ....

Eleanor: ... you'd just act normal ....

Michelle: [Interrupting] It's like ....

Eleanor: ... and say 'oh, it's good for you, like'. We know they won't give up, because they're addicted to it, all of us are.

Michelle: No, it's like, the people that I go around with they'll be, you know, they won't be so thingy about it, the people that you hang round with and you innit like, but if you go round with some of the people they're really weird they are.

Fiona: They can be really bitchy.

Michelle: Yeah.

Use for fags · **Exclusion** · **Support** · **Bullying** · **Type of friend** · **Peer pressure** · **Quitting**

FIGURE 10.1 *Indexed focus group extract*

inclusive definition of bullying to allow postponement of a final analytical decision until all the evidence is assembled. Similarly, there is no need for the indexer to agonize over whether to restrict the index-coding to the statement 'looking at her all weird' or to run the index-code on to include Lucy's next statement 'they're saying why are you giving up?' Since access to the index-coded items in their original text location remains an option for the analyst, no data is lost in the indexing process.

Interpreting the data

This section will describe in detail the method of analysis employed and illustrate the discussion with data from the study.

By the time the indexing is complete, the researcher has a good idea of the main focus of the analysis, but what is required now is a method of making systematic comparisons within the data, and of ensuring that all data from all cases contribute to the analysis, rather than selectively using some cases and ignoring others. The method of analysis used in this study followed the principles of analytic induction. Other methods of systematic analysis are available, for example, Williams's (1981, 1990) development of 'logical analysis'. The analytic induction approach was first adopted by Znaniecki (1934). Robinson (1951) provides a detailed description and assessment of the method. Its use has been described in a small number of studies, including Cressey's study of embezzlement (1953), Lindesmith's (1947) study of drug addiction and Bloor's study of ENT out-patient clinics (1978). The method is discussed extensively in modern textbooks on qualitative methods such as those of Silverman (1993) and Hammersley and Atkinson (1995). The purpose of the method is to derive propositions which apply generally across all the data to the entire universe of relevant cases or transcript items.

Generalizability of the analytical propositions is achieved by focusing on the 'deviant cases', those indexed items which appear to contradict the analytic proposition (hence the alternative term for analytic induction, 'deviant case analysis'). The analyst attempts to modify the analytic proposition to embrace the deviant cases – this can often be achieved by appending a qualifying clause to the original proposition (for example 'all non-smoking teenagers say they prefer the company of non-smoking friends, except where they have a boyfriend/girlfriend who smokes'). This may be a two- or a three-stage process: modification of the original analytic proposition may embrace most of the deviant cases; it may then be necessary to inspect the remaining deviant cases in order to introduce a further modification to eliminate further deviant cases; if there still remain a few deviant cases, then these must be inspected further to derive yet another modification of the analytic proposition, and so on. Alternatively, the deviant cases may be eliminated by modifying the definition of the population to which the analytic proposition applies. For example, it may be found that all the exceptions to the above proposition ('all non-smoking teenagers say they prefer the company of non-smoking friends, except where they have a boyfriend/girlfriend who smokes') are young people who currently do not smoke but who have tried a cigarette in the past, so the proposition may be restricted to teenagers who have never tried smoking. By both routes, modification of the defined population and modification of the analytic proposition, the deviant cases may be eliminated. The procedure both guards against selective attention to data and provides a systematic means of extending analytic thinking.

The present analysis centred on the stated importance of the concept of peer pressure for adolescents in attempts to give up smoking, and the aim of the analysis was to provide an elaboration of the meaning of this pressure. The analytical method that was adopted to achieve this was as follows:

1   The focus group was taken as the case for analysis purposes. Each case had already been index-coded according to types of peer pressure as described earlier.
2   For the first case, all data under each subcategory of peer pressure, for example bullying, was examined in turn in order to produce a provisional definition of the phenomena. (N.B. The Ethnograph can be used to search for data labelled under more than one index-code, so searches could be made, for example, for all data under the index-codes of peer pressure *and* bullying.)
3   By studying each of the subcategories of peer pressure, an initial proposition on peer pressure was formulated.
4   Subsequent cases were studied to see whether they confirmed or refuted in any way this initial proposition. Where a 'deviant' case, or one that contradicted the proposition, was found, then two options were considered: either the proposition could be altered or extended so that the deviant case was no longer excluded, or the earlier indexing decision was re-examined so that the deviant case was no longer defined as part of the population of peer pressure cases.
5   This process of considering the fit of data from a new case and reformulating the proposition/definition where applicable was then continued with the remainder of the cases.

An extended illustration will show how the definition of peer pressure was modified and developed. The first proposition formulated was that adolescents fear the threat of peer pressure on quitting smoking, in the form of bullying and exclusion from the group; that they expect active encouragement from peers to continue smoking; and that they perceive a passive pressure to smoke from seeing other people smoking.

This proposition needed to be modified once data from the next case were considered: this case showed perception of these pressures to be dependent on the ratio of quitters to smokers; pressures are greatest if only one person within a social group attempts to give up smoking, as this person would not have the resources to counteract the pressures; where more than one person quits, these people can support each other against the pressures.

The proposition had again to be modified because a number of cases stated that their friends wouldn't exclude an ex-smoker from their social group. This led the groups to differentiate between real friends and people who 'use you for fags', a distinction that was related to a difference between perception of pressures and actual experience of quitting (which is related to Michell and West's [1996] work on peer pressure and smoking initiation).

The proposition therefore needed to be modified to include this further distinction; however, at this point it became clear that there were insufficient data on this aspect of the process of peer pressure to take the proposition any further, that is to explore any further this notion of different types of friend. This touches on a limitation with the analytic induction method which is discussed further below.

Issues in the use of analytic induction for the analysis of focus group data

This section will draw on the above illustrative material to consider the advantages and limitations of analytic induction for analysis of focus group data.

Advantages

First, the analytical method used clearly ensures the systematic analysis of the data. The method lays out a prescribed process for analysis, following a number of clearly defined stages. Second, the requirement to either accommodate or eliminate all the deviant cases acts as a stimulus to extend the analysis, guarding against premature closure of the analytical task. And, third, another clear advantage of the method is its concentration on 'deviant' or contradictory cases. This forces the analyst to review both propositions and definitions used in the analysis and thus guards against a selective approach.

Disadvantages

First, analytic induction has traditionally been used for the analysis of case studies. The advantage of the case-study approach is that it allows for the collection of some data, removal from the field for preliminary analyses, then further data collection relevant to the hypothesis, and so on. Without the ability to return to subjects to collect additional data following initial analysis, the end point of data collection needs to be decided in advance of analysis. This creates the risk of either making the analysis more cumbersome than it need be by the collection of more data than necessary, or risking finding data lacking once the conduct of the analysis has begun. The data are situated in time and place. Analysts rarely have the opportunity to revisit their original focus groups in order to collect additional data to explore a new proposition or hypothesis, because it is seldom possible to exactly reconstitute an earlier group, although it may be possible to constitute a new group to act as proxy for the original members. In order to minimize the necessity for new data collection and in order to minimize the requirement to collect excessive amounts of data which may not be used in the final analysis, the focus of the analysis needs to be very clearly defined following piloting (Bloor, 1978).

Second, focus groups provide complex data sets, with distinct features stemming from the nature of group interaction, which set them apart from other qualitative data sets: focus groups typically contain instances of unfinished speech, such as when respondents are interrupted or where their views are silenced by disagreement from other members of the group (Kitzinger, 1994b). It is unclear to the analyst whether such instances are in fact statements that would form a 'deviant case' and which would therefore require reformation of the analyst's working propositions. Similarly, a member of a group may state an opinion, but other members, while not contradicting the first speaker, may underreact or go on to discuss other unrelated matters. It may be possible for the group moderator to clear up such ambiguities during the course of the group, but a researcher will be fortunate indeed if all such ambiguities are resolved prior to transcription. Once again, in such cases it may be unclear whether or not a group norm has been articulated and endorsed, and whether or not this group norm needs incorporation in an extended analysis. A degree of indeterminancy is introduced into an analytic system which is ill-designed to cope with it. It may therefore be necessary to consciously disregard a residual group of potentially 'deviant cases' because of irresolvable ambiguities in interpretation.

Conclusion

Focus group methods are an ideal source of data on the discursive practices surrounding group norms, particularly where they are drawn from pre-existing social groups. However, they do present particular difficulties in data analysis. Typical practice within market research organizations has not involved analysis of transcripts and, without transcription, the richness of the data is lost and the dangers of selectivity in analysis are self-evident. Transcription of data is much to be preferred but carries penalties in the form of increasing costs, an increasing time-frame for the analysis, and difficulties associated with the richness of the data. The richness of the data makes the application of some kind of systematic approach to analysis a practical necessity.

Analytic induction is one such systematic approach. The difficulties we have identified in the application of the analytic induction method to focus group data are not specific to this method. 'Logical analysis', as developed by Williams (1981, 1990) seeks to discover axiomatic statements or premisses in everyday speech and then explores and classifies the relationships between groups of premisses. It seems clear that the application of logical analysis to focus group data would run into related difficulties to those outlined earlier. The complexity and the situatedness of focus group data generate a degree of indeterminancy to analyses which sits ill with a systematic approach. An analytic approach which aims to elaborate the analysis by the progressive elimination of exceptional or anomalous findings cannot easily live with uncertainty about whether findings are indeed exceptional or anomalous. Clearly, it would be most unfortunate if an original analytic proposition or a series of original analytic propositions were elaborated purely to accomodate certain findings which could be interpreted in different ways, some of which were perfectly consistent with the original proposition(s).

Only partial resolutions of these difficulties are possible. Of course, no interpretative act is ever wholly determinate and every identification of similarity or dissimilarity is always provisional and defeasible, but these problems of interpretation are writ large in transcript data on group processes. Problems can be minimized, but not eliminated by the following strategies: by clear definition of the focus of the study after piloting, in order to concentrate data collection in depth on a narrow spectrum of projected analytical topics; by careful attention of the moderator to obvious ambiguities, latent disagreements and 'unfinished business' that arise in the course of the groups; and by acceptance by the analyst that some seeming 'deviant cases' must be dismissed as irresolvable ambiguities from which no analytic inferences should be drawn. If such strategies are adopted, then some sort of systematic approach to the analysis of focus group transcripts is both feasible and desirable. Unless a systematic approach of some kind (be it analytic induction or some other system) is undertaken, then it is difficult to see the advantages of audio-transcription of focus group interaction.

Acknowledgements

The peer-led smoking project was supported by the Medical Research Council, the Wales Office of Research and Development for Health and Social Care, Mid Glamorgan and Bro Taf Health Authorities and the European Commission (DGV). We are grateful to the pupils who trained as peer leaders and those who took part in the evaluation, the staff of the participating schools who undertook organizational tasks for us and the parents who gave their permission for their children to take part in the study.

11 The analytical potential of 'sensitive moments' in focus group discussions

Jenny Kitzinger and Clare Farquhar

A defining feature of focus group research is the use of interaction between research participants to generate data. It therefore follows that group dynamics should be given attention in the course of data analysis. It is useful to look closely at the different forms of interaction in the group such as arguments, mutual reinforcement, jokes and story-telling (see Kitzinger, 1994a). This chapter focuses on one specific aspect of group dynamics: the 'sensitive moment'. Where earlier chapters explored ways of identifying and managing sensitivity in focus groups (in particular Chapter 4), here we examine its analytical potential.

'Sensitive moments' may be indicated by explicit comments from research participants, hesitation and awkwardness, reactions of surprise or shock, individual defensiveness or tentative collective exploration. Paradoxically, the most sensitive discussion can occur when people are feeling comfortable in the group and choose to reveal experiences they have never mentioned before. Such moments indicate that discussion is going beyond the pre-rehearsed shared public knowledge described in Lynn Michell's chapter (Chapter 3). This may mean that the researcher needs to guide the discussion back on to safe ground or to pursue certain issues in interview or in a group composed in an different way (for example women only). Alternatively, it may be an opportunity for the researcher and research participants to explore issues usually evaded, isolated or censored.

Whether or not such sensitive moments are allowed to develop, they should neither be taken for granted nor be seen only as a problem. Such moments are sensitive in both senses of the word: they may be uncomfortable and exposing but they may also be sources of insight. If routine group talk displays the acceptable range of discourse, then sensitive moments map out the boundaries. They mark the limits of safe everyday conversation or the boundaries of conversation in this particular context (with both the opportunities and additional threats provided by the research context).

We demonstrate how focus groups can be used to unpack the social construction of sensitive issues, uncover different layers of discourse and illuminate group taboos and the routine silencing of certain views and experiences. Through attention to sensitive moments researchers can identify unspoken assumptions and question the nature of everyday talk. They can explore how people try to defend themselves and how new or deviant information is incorporated or sidelined, how boundaries are maintained, and how new knowledge or norms may be created. Attention to such issues is crucial for focus group researchers, whether they are concerned with the provision of services and the design of interventions or the articulation and policing of discourses, identities and knowledge itself.

The research projects which inform this discussion

The following discussion draws on half a dozen different research projects, five conducted by Jenny Kitzinger and one by Clare Farquhar. These are outlined in Figure 11.1. All six projects involved working with groups who had some pre-existing social connection – from being close friends to casual acquaintances, neighbours or co-residents. It was thus possible to note the contrast between what was revealed in focus groups, and what had previously been discussed in the existing social network.

Five of these projects involved discussion about sex, sexual identity and/ or sexual violence. Such topics are often assumed to be highly sensitive (although Chapter 4 questions this assumption). We focus on these five projects. However, we have included a sixth study, evaluating residential care for the elderly, to demonstrate that sensitive moments are not exclusive to the 'self-evidently sensitive' issues surrounding sexuality.

Sensitive topics and everyday conversation

Sensitivity in groups often occurs at several levels and group discussions may go through a process whereby the participants move from acknowledging the sensitivity of a topic, to analysing why specific details are so difficult to talk about. Sometimes a further shift will occur as the group tentatively explores breaking taboos. Sometimes in-depth discussion and 'shocking revelations' ensue. In this chapter we deal with each of these levels in turn, moving from analysis of when people shy away from a whole topic through to the more in-depth sensitive discussion that occurred in some groups.

The five projects that directly touched on sex, sexual identity and/or violence all generated a great many sensitive moments. Indeed, sometimes the whole topic was clearly seen as a rather awkward – or even dangerous – subject for discussion. For example, in project 3 (about sexual abuse), one group took time out in the middle of their session to comment on their difficulties. They noted the unusual in-depth concentration on a topic routinely passed over in everyday talk, the possibilities of heated argument and the emotional precariousness of the conversation.

Project 1 The lesbian sexual health project	15 focus groups conducted by Clare Farquhar with self-defined lesbian and bisexual women. Designed both to inform sexual health services and to explore lesbian community narratives (see Chapter 4).
Project 2 Public understandings of AIDS[2]	52 focus groups with a wide range of groups. Designed to explore the role of the media and health education in informing public understandings of AIDS (see Kitzinger, 1993).
Project 3 Child sexual abuse: the emergence of a public issue	49 focus groups. Designed to explore the role of the media, and other influences, on public understandings of sexual abuse (see discussion in Eldridge et al., 1997).
Project 4 Evaluation of the Zero Tolerance campaign	20 focus group discussions with a range of pre-existing groups. Designed to explore the impact of a public awareness campaign about violence against women (see Kitzinger, 1994c). These groups complemented a street survey (see Kitzinger and Hunt, 1993).
Project 5 Youth project: young people's ideas about violence, sex and relationships	10 focus groups with (apparently heterosexual) young people (aged 14–19). Designed to help develop a school anti-violence initiative (the groups complemented a questionnaire survey; for full discussion see Burton et al., 1997).
Project 6 Assessing hospital residential care for the elderly	6 focus group discussions in different residential institutions. Designed to inform a subsequent questionnaire survey to evaluate service provision.

FIGURE 11.1 *Outline of six projects which inform this chapter*[1]

> *F:* It's not a very nice subject though is it we're talking about, is it?
>
> *M:* It's an awkward subject to talk about too.
>
> *F:* Well yeah, I feel a bit awkward talking, I mean I'm laughing . . .
>
> *M:* It's not a subject you would talk about freely
>
> *M:* If you were sat here and you were serious about it, you'd end up bubbling.
>
> *F:* Yeah you would, you would, course you would [. . .]
>
> *M:* Touchy subject but . . .
>
> *M:* Awkward subject to talk about because it's not an everyday thing you . . .
>
> *M:* But it's an everyday thing that's happening. If you really got deep into a conversation you'd start arguing and . . .
>
> *M:* I mean you pass a remark while you're reading about it in the paper and that's as far as it goes.

However, topics may be experienced as sensitive even if they are not about traditionally taboo issues. For example, project 6 included group discussions with people in long-term hospital residential care for the elderly.

The sessions were designed to explore what they wanted from residential care and what they would like to see changed. For some research participants, the main research question was itself rather threatening. Participants sometimes commented that there was 'no point' thinking about what they disliked about their current situation. In the course of discussion it was evident that these boundaries were established in reaction to their limited choices. For example, one group agreed that there was no point 'looking forward' to having visitors, in case they were disappointed. Being asked to comment on staff was also seen by some as potentially dangerous. Some residents even tried to prevent others from criticizing staff. Complaints, when they were made, were often understated or qualified. For instance, it emerged that residents in one unit were unable to even have a glass of water until an hour after getting up because staff were too busy. However, they presented this information with comments such as: 'They are a wee bit short of nursing staff' and '[We are] lucky to get water at all'. The general attitude expressed in several of the groups was: 'You've just got to accept these things' and there seemed to be pressure not to be seen as 'a moaner', who would irritate both staff and co-residents. In one group, a particular woman felt under even more pressure than this. She became anxious during the session, repeatedly interrupted other participants with cries of 'the staff couldn't be nicer', and opted to leave the group. Later she expressed anxiety about being 'punished' for, in her words, 'being cheeky'.

Where a whole research topic is seen as sensitive, recruitment may be difficult and participation selective. Clearly this raises ethical and methodological problems, but it can also be a source of data. For example, there may appear to be patterns in who will or will not accept invitations to participate. In projects 3 and 5, both of which addressed the topic of sexual violence, it proved far easier to engage female than male participants in the research. Indeed, in the 'youth project' (project 5), it was exclusively male participants who refused invitations to participate or failed to show up after having agreed to come along. On several occasions the boys who failed to attend were identified (by those who did) as having particularly 'naff' attitudes toward women. In one group of school boys the absent individual was described by the others as 'a chauvinist pig', 'immature' with 'old-fashioned views.' Similar comments were made about three boys absent from another group.

> *M2*: There's no way David, Garry or Danny would have come along, they're so full of themselves.
> *M3*: He's got an attitude – 'I'm God's gift, I can get any girl I want, she'll do what I tell her.'

From the start, such comments indicate research participants' own assessments of the research frame and who might avoid engaging in discussion of a particular topic and why. Such comments also begin to locate the status of the research topic within everyday peer discussion. For example, the reluctance of some elderly hospital residents to articulate – or even think about – improvements, gave hints about the material and social conditions to which they are accommodating and, in some cases, an acute sense of powerlessness. The comments by some of the boys/young men invited to discuss sex, violence and relationships drew attention to the lack of opportunity they had for serious conversation about such issues. Indeed, several commented on the active resistance to, and obstruction of, such conversation from some of their peers.

> *M*: Boys haven't got the guts to ask – we try to look big [. . .]
>
> *M*: Girls talk about everything . . . how they feel, but boys . . .
>
> *F*: What do you talk about with David, Garry and Danny?
>
> *M*: Football.
>
> *M*: What we've done.
>
> *M*: Boys can't talk about relationships and sex.
>
> *F*: Do you talk to your older brother?
>
> *M*: No, he's always on the fucking computer.
>
> *M*: Guys just take the piss out of you.

Getting down to details: signalling sensitive moments within the broad topic

Regardless of the sensitivity of the basic topic outline there is always the potential for sensitive moments to arise in the course of discussion. For example, one of the unexpected sensitivities displayed in some of the focus groups about AIDS was embarrassment about 'knowing too much'. While in most circumstances ignorance is a socially undesirable state, the opposite was sometimes true when it came to discussing AIDS. In several groups people became embarrassed and were teased for 'excessive' knowledge about this topic and one (apparently heterosexual) woman commented that she would find it difficult to pursue information about AIDS, in case anyone thought she was lesbian. Seeking and giving information about AIDS thus clearly had implications for identity management.

Issues around identity and image management also proved important in the lesbian sexual health discussions (project 1). From the start it was obvious that talking about actual sexual practice was sensitive and many of the lesbian research participants would not have felt comfortable discussing this in a group with heterosexuals. This was not because of any 'inherent shyness' but because of the social status of lesbianism. As some explained, the clash between their own norms and values and those of the dominant heterosexual culture acted to silence them in the company of heterosexuals.

> *F*: If I get somebody who doesn't like that sexual practice, whether or not they share it actually, when they're heterosexual, I mind them knowing. But if she's lesbian and she doesn't like that actual practice, I don't mind. That's

> actually about image maintenance of lesbian sexuality in the face of heterosexuality, I guess.
>
> *F*: Mm hm.
>
> *F*: I think that there is a lot of lesbians who don't want straight people to know what they actually do in bed.

However, reticence did not only arise because of the dominance of heterosexuality and the prevalence of heterosexism. Concerns were also evident in the group discussions between lesbians themselves – but for a very different reason. The sensitivity around discussing actual sexual practice was in stark contrast to participants' confidence in other areas. Many confidently reclaimed words defined as negative in the mainstream culture (such as 'dyke') and some talked about wishing to be 'in your face' about their sexuality, refusing to be cowed by dominant cultural norms. Within the group, however, as discussion veered close to sexual practice, some women made nervous jokes, changed the subject or even leapt up declaring that the room was too hot or the window needed to be opened (see Chapter 4). It became clear that this awkwardness was partly due to the existence of widely differing definitions of acceptable sexual behaviour within the lesbian community. Examples of areas in which strong, competing views were held included bisexuality, sex with men, sado-masochism, and penetrative sex. Some women seemed frustrated by the silencing effect of such competing views. As one said: 'I'd just, I'd like to know things that I shouldn't be doing. Like, answer the question "Well, why not penetration?", and I don't, I *still* don't know, you know'.

Some women suggested that talking about sexual relationships may be particularly difficult for lesbians, as opposed to straight women. Heterosexual women may engage in raucous and detailed discussion about sex with their male partners during a 'girls' night out', while lesbian social worlds are organized differently.

> *F*: . . . women will often, heterosexual women will often meet up without husbands and husbands are, men are, a different, other group. Other. Whereas if we all sit and talk about our sexual relationships, you know, there's all links, you know, between us. And we know who it might be or, you know, there's something much . . .
>
> *F*: We're . . .
>
> *F*: There's a sameness about us, we're, we're . . .
>
> *F*: There's a sameness. Whereas I can, men are . . . very other.

Ironically, the fear of being judged (and found wanting) by other lesbians had led some participants to be reluctant to use services run by lesbians for lesbians, for example lesbian sexual health clinics.

> *F*: Well, I'd be worried, I'd be worried going along.
>
> *F*: You'd be worried about the politics that would be surrounding it.

> *F*: Yeah, it's like . . .
> *F*: About what counts as a lesbian, I suppose.
> *F*: Exactly.
> *F*: Would they pigeon-hole everyone outside . . .?

Transitory exploration of sensitive moments: doing the sensitive talking, rather than talking about the sensitivity

Sensitive areas may simply be noted, as has been illustrated, or individuals may begin tentative exploration, before retreating to (or being pushed on to) safer territory. Sensitivity is thus demonstrated rather than being explicitly acknowledged by the participants. One of the dynamics evident in several of the focus groups with elderly people in residential care was the way in which participants encouraged each other to be resigned and to adopt low expectations. For example, one woman began to talk about her sense of displacement, not only from her original home, but in being shifted between institutions (the unit in which she used to live had been closed down). However, she was repeatedly reassured and silenced by other group members.

> *JK*: If you have any problems or worries who do you talk to?
> *F?*: We would talk to the sister I would think, but I've never really had any problems, have you?
> *F1*: Well, just I wanted to go home.
> *F?*: Well, we all do, don't we, but we are here [. . .]
> *JK*: What are the sort of things you miss? [. . .]
> *F1*: I have lost all my friends. I've been shifted about so much [. . .]
> *F?*: We are friendly, it is up to yourself . . .
> *F1*: The neighbours [at the previous unit] were really great . . . before we came here, well you can't make the same neighbourliness in a place like this.
> *F?*: Well I think it is up to yourself how you mix with people.
> *F1*: It is, there is nothing wrong with it really, it's just eh . . . it's hard to get used to [. . .]
> *JK*: I have a few words [on cards] here I would like you to comment on [. . .] Let me choose one that you brought up earlier, Bessy . . . 'Independence'.
> *F1*: Yes.
> *JK*: That's important to you then?
> *F1*: Oh yes . . . oh yes, *very* much so.
> *JK*: And are there things that make you feel independent?
> *F1*: [There's] an unwritten law that you stay here, that, em, your independence, well, I couldn't say anything more . . . I like to be independent . . . but em . . . yes. . . .
> *JK*: Are there things that make you feel that you are *not* independent . . .?
> *F1*: Get out of here . . . no, no . . . it's not a bad place to be in . . . I'm as happy as the rest. It's just . . . where dignity is concerned, I don't know.
> *F?*: Well, you never use your dignity now, so much.

The discussion with young people about attitudes toward sex, violence and relationships involved a very different research population, under very different conditions, but here too similar dynamics were evident. Group members often made comments which silenced one another. Sometimes individuals who began to express 'deviant' perspectives appeared to lose courage and retreat from expressing their point of view. Indeed, the young men and women involved in this research often both commented on, but also displayed, conformity with standard gender roles. The following exchange occurred in a group of young men on a training scheme. Commenting on his feelings about trying to 'pick up' women, and his anger if he failed, one remarked:

> There's social pressure as well – like everybody's looking at you. Like going into the Rover's and getting a knock back and everybody else gets in [with a girl], you know what I mean? You're just so embarrassed you want to lash out at somebody.

His colleague asked 'Do you get knocked back?' At which he quickly became embarrassed and defensive, retorting: 'No [laughs] not me. In *general*, I was talking about *you*!'

Similar tentative explorations, closely followed by retractions, occurred in another male-only group discussion, this time with school students. In the example below, John (who is 17) and Eddie (who is 15) support each other in talking about not particularly having enjoyed their experience(s) of sexual intercourse. However, they are challenged by Andrew. (We use individual pseudonyms rather than F/M identifiers for some examples below to help readers to follow the process of interaction.)

John:	It [sexual intercourse] is highly overrated, anyway.
Eddie:	Yes, at our age it is anyway. I hope it gets better.
Andrew:	You can't be doing it right then! [to John]
Eddie:	Well, I'll tell you my tricks later. [to John]
John:	I do think it's highly overrated. Foreplay is better than the actual intercourse.
Eddie:	Aye [. . .] I mean sex is just like two minutes, that's it over.
Andrew:	Well, poor boy!
Eddie:	No, you know what I mean though, you can have like three and a half hours of foreplay, then sex lasts about five minutes or something.
Andrew:	I could show you a thing or two [. . .]
Eddie:	But girls that I've slept with say the sex is better than the foreplay, but the foreplay is also pretty good. It's like the sex blows them away into a different place. But what are you supposed to say? Right guys, are you supposed to say that you spent the whole night doing foreplay, and not finish it off with sex?

In this group both John and Eddie explicitly stated that they had 'had sex', Andrew implied experience, but never explicitly stated that he had. Over and above jockeying for the status associated with having 'done it', note how Eddie initially agrees with John, backtracks a little, briefly allies himself with Andrew against John and rephrases statements to protect his own image. He shifts from describing the length of intercourse as a 'couple of minutes' to 'five minutes' and he boasts about his effect on girls ('sex blows them away into a different place'). It is also he who references the issue of self-presentation ('are you supposed to say that you spent the whole night doing foreplay, and not finish it off with sex?').

This example illustrates a typical advance–retreat pattern to sensitive discussion. However, sometimes sensitive issues may be the subject of more sustained discussion, and revelations made which push the boundaries even further. In the young people's study this was most likely to occur in the groups including girls and young women because they, more than their male counterparts, often persisted in asking probing questions (of their male peers, themselves and each other). Conversation in female-only or mixed groups were thus often sustained long after a male-only group might have shifted to another topic.

In-depth exploration of sensitive moments: new data, new knowledge

When groups held or developed difficult moments this could lead to in-depth exploration of key issues. This, in turn, could lead to individuals, or the group as a whole, coming to articulate previously suppressed views, shift opinions or begin to present their own experiences in a new light. The example below occurred toward the end of a mixed-sex focus group discussion in a youth club. Only three research participants remained in the room at this point, the others having drifted away for the competing attractions of a pool game. The three who remained, Gordon, Doreen and Pearl, described themselves as close friends, but the following incident interrupted the relaxed and friendly nature of the discussion. Gordon started from the assumption that the two girls would share his agreement with the statement: 'Women call things sexual harassment which are only a bit of fun.'

> That happens at office parties. It's happened at my dad's works plenty of times. [. . .] Like pinched their bum, pinched the boob. [. . .] If women call things sexual harassment that have just been a bit of fun, like heat of the moment, bit drunk and everything [. . .] well, she's just in there to just get some attention really.

Pinching a girl's breast was just seen as something one does ('like scratching the wall paper'). As this boy went on to say:

> Like I mess . . ., I've done that [miming grabbing breasts] with Doreen and she hasn't messed about, she hasn't gone, 'Right that's it. I'm not speaking to you again, and I'll do you one'. Because some people take it as a pinch of salt, some people play on it.

In this case, however, the boy's views did not go unchallenged. Doreen, the subject of his 'attention' (who, it emerged, is regularly grabbed and sometimes left with bruises on her breasts) simply folded her arms in front of her chest, grinned and gazed at the floor. However, her friend, Pearl, launched an initially hesitant but increasingly confident attack on Gordon's attitudes and behaviour. During this exchange relations between the three friends became visibly strained.

Pearl initially challenged Gordon by declaring 'But there's no real need to do it is there, really? What's the point in pinching someone's breast?' She quickly defended herself from any suggestion that she might be taking on an unacceptable persona by adding 'I'm not really a prude, but I don't think that's funny really'. The conversation developed with Doreen initially defending Gordon but later agreeing with Pearl that, in fact, grabbing her breasts had 'gone beyond a joke' and could be distressing.

Doreen: It's just a bit of fun, it depends how the person takes it.
Pearl: Yeah, but Doreen, people do it to you all the time, I mean, every day.
Gordon: Not *every* day.
Doreen: Well, I do get a bit.
Pearl: Listen, nearly every day and you do get mad but you don't say so.
Gordon: Doreen knows it's just a bit of fun, isn't it. If it bothers her she should say something.
Pearl: It's because people do it to her all the time. Half the time she can't even be bothered by arguing back because Doreen don't like arguing, she doesn't like fighting. So Doreen don't say nothing. . . . You've got all your anger worked up, but, 'Oh no, the lad says, it's just a joke', so you're meant to forget it.

Clearly, focus group work can go further than merely eavesdropping. The researcher is creating a setting where, at the very least, a subject is addressed in greater depth than usual. Often research participants are discussing issues (such as sexual harassment, money, death) which are seldom mentioned in an everyday context beyond the routine exchange of jokes or platitudes. Sometimes this will be the first time that they have articulated certain views or experiences (to themselves, to each other, or to a particular friend in the group).

Indeed, focus group participants themselves sometimes identify the focus group as a special occasion and take the opportunity to discuss issues that are unconsciously censored or simply awkward to raise in more routine settings. In this sense the research session serves as liminal time and space where the new and unexpected may occur and where novel communication can be achieved. In the AIDS research, one young man used the group session to inform his brother that he had gone to be tested for HIV. In the lesbian sexual health project, one woman 'admitted' to having sought a sex-change operation, something she had never really talked openly about before but decided: 'I could maybe just say it here'.

The exchange of new and sensitive information about personal experience was particularly common in the two projects which focused on sexual violence (projects 3 and 4). In both projects research participants sometimes talked about unpleasant sexual encounters, their own childhood abuse, or the abuse of their children. There were particular patterns to, and effects of, these revelations which provided invaluable insights for both projects.

For example, one of the Zero Tolerance posters that was being evaluated in project 4 aimed to highlight the frequency with which children endured a range of sexual abuses (see Figure 11.2). This poster was quite controversial. Much criticism focused on the statement 'from flashing to rape'. Individually, people often criticized this caption for either 'hyping up' or 'diluting' abuse statistics ('you think, oh well they're only talking about flashing'). However, in the focus groups this statement frequently generated discussion between research participants about their own experiences of being flashed at – a process which often led them to state that it should not simply be dismissed as a joke. The caption also led to the gradual exchange of information previously excluded from common knowledge. For example, one group of friends initially dismissed the poster's suggestion that 50 percent of girls would encounter some form of abuse. They saw this as an exaggeration; until, that is, they tentatively began to reflect on their own experiences. This culminated in the following exchange:

> *F2:* . . . all these years I'd just thought: 'Oh that was the night I lost my virginity'. I hadn't even took the time to think about what actually happened. [. . .] He forced me. Now I'm thinking, for fuck's sake, when I lost my virginity I was raped. I remember actually thumping him to get him off me and he wouldn't get off. [. . .] He said: 'If you don't do it now, you'll never do it.' [. . .] I was too young, I didn't want to do it [. . .] I couldn't physically get him off me. I was beating him and I couldn't get him off. It was all over.
>
> *F1:* The first time I got drunk, I lost my virginity. I didn't want to do it either. I was pretty young as well.
>
> *F3:* You see, I'm the exact same. I was steaming [drunk] and in retrospect I wish it had never happened. [. . .] So that's every single person in this room.

In fact, at that stage it was not 'every single person' in the room. The only man present had not commented. However, later in the session he remarked:

> One thing, which I have never ever told anyone about [. . .] I was at a party when I was 16 [. . .] I was staying overnight [. . .] and I woke up and there was somebody in bed beside me, groping me. [. . .] It frightened the absolute life out of me.

The women's descriptions of 'losing their virginity' and the man's account of being 'groped' had not previously been discussed among this group of friends. The research participants' willingness to share these experiences at

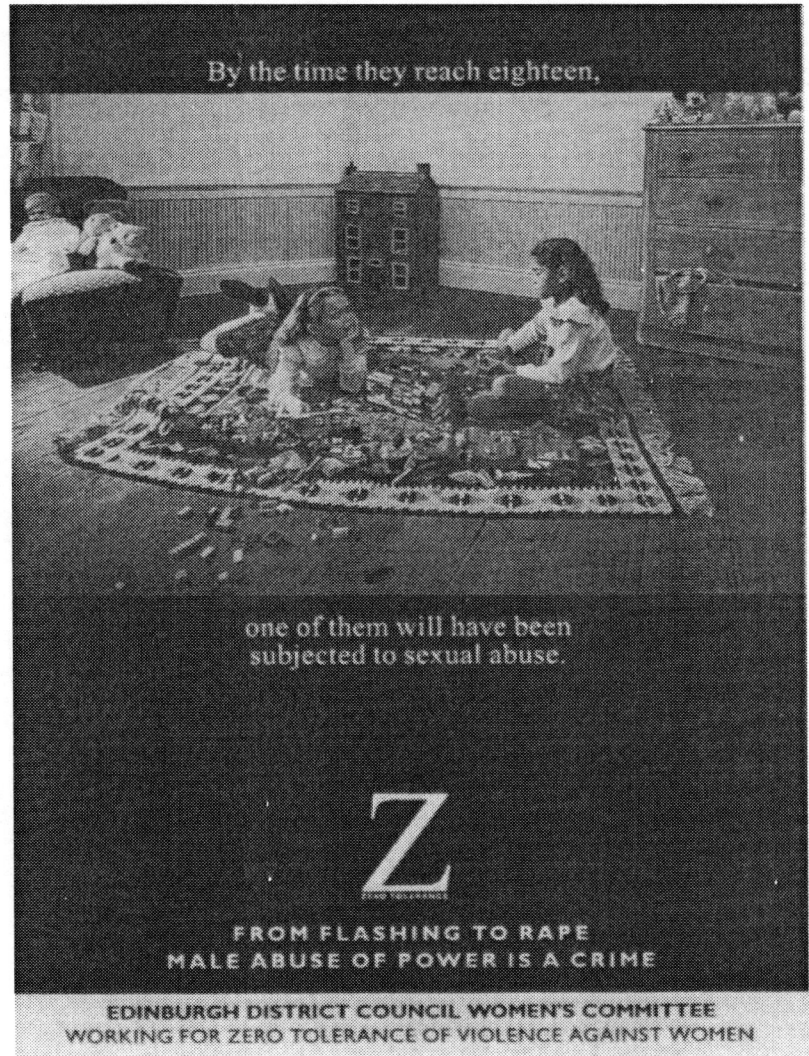

FIGURE 11.2 *One of the Zero Tolerance advertisements used in the focus groups. Reproduced by kind permission of the Zero Tolerance Charitable Trust*

this point was partly facilitated by the focus group discussion. However, it was actually triggered by the controversial caption – 'from flashing to rape . . .' – which seemed to give permission for a continuum of experiences to be explored. Had evaluation of the poster relied on individual interviews, the research participants might have maintained their initial negative assessment. However, the caption proved to have an interesting effect on dynamics within several groups, and often came to be positively evaluated by participants during the course of the discussion, precisely because they began to reflect on, and exchange, their own experiences.

Similar revelations and reframing of what people knew, thought or experienced occurred in group discussions about the media coverage of sexual abuse (project 3). For example, when group members talked about their own direct experiences of child sexual abuse, this often had the effect of impressing others with an emotional as well as intellectual acceptance of widespread abuse. Several members of groups in which these disclosures occurred wrote comments on their final post-group questionnaire such as: 'I now realize that it could be someone I know'.

Statements from those with personal (direct or indirect) experience of abuse also served to challenge conventional wisdom about causes, effects and blame. In the extract below, research participants were making a series of judgements about mothers of sexually abused children which included statements such as: 'How could the mother not know?', 'She *must* know'. (Such opinions were almost ritually exchanged in many of the sessions, certain phrases recurring across groups.) In this session, the group facilitator (JK) was aware of the growing discomfort of one member of the group and had been about to intervene to introduce some other perspectives (and, if necessary to change the subject). However, before she did so the woman herself ('Alison') cut across the conversation.

Jan: A lot of women stay with the guy and I can't understand that.

Mike: That's crazy, I don't understand that.

Christine: I mean if I had kids and a guy done anything to my wean [child] . . . you'd kill him.

Alison: That's easier said than done, that's crap, Christine, that's crap, that's crap.

Paula: Everybody's different, maybe Christine feels she could do that.

Alison: She must be a big person because I'll tell you something. . . .

Christine: I'm not big.

Alison: You must be, Christine, for the simple reason that my lassie was sexually abused by my father. I'd love to blow his brains off. I'd have loved to have stabbed him [. . .] Hey listen, there's not a night goes by but that I wish my Da would drop down dead for the things that he's done. [. . .]

Christine: Maybe I say that right, but maybe I might feel different if I was in the situation, right. But I've never been in the situation so I don't really know.

Alison: Ah well, I've been in the position, I'm in the position. I'm in the position and I've been in the position for years. I've been in the position for 8 years now.

Alison's revelation successfully challenged other participants, and led to one of the men present talking in-depth about his own feelings around the fact that his daughter too had been raped (by a neighbour).

Similar disruption and realignment occurred in another group when routine discussion of 'perverts' was disrupted by the revelation that a man some of them knew was a convicted child abuser. This challenged many of the assumptions other group members had been making up until this point, and opened up new ways of thinking about the problem and potential solutions.

One of the routine ways in which people discuss sexual abuse is the highly effective communication network, particularly among parents, for communicating unusual incidents in the streets or around the schools. These incidents were widely known about and often recalled and repeated long after the event ('Do you remember a man [. . .] [in] a white car that was going about [. . .] and it was down at the school, and he tried to drag in Alex McIntosh?'). Associated discussion of how sexual abuse might be prevented was framed exclusively in terms of monitoring the streets and keeping an eye on 'outsiders' (for example, by filming the number plates on strange cars coming on to the estate where they all lived). The routine nature of such discussion was in marked contrast to the same people's awkwardness in mentioning, or incredulous response to, examples where the abuser was a known member of their own community. Indeed, asked if they knew anyone who was an abuser, research participants were sometimes adamant that this could not possibly be the case:

F: They wouldn't be living up here if that's the case.
F: . . . No, I don't know of any
F: Because you all know one another, we all know their businesses and everything. Everybody knows – see, like if [anyone did anything] . . . everybody would know.

In the group quoted here, one woman did then reveal the information that a man they all knew had been convicted of abusing his daughters. This revelation was greeted with the shocked comment: 'Not Jimmy! You're joking?'

Such interactions proved invaluable to understanding public responses to sexual abuse and the role of media influence. The persistent focus of public discussion on stranger-danger and residual disbelief in incest is clearly encouraged by the disproportionate balance of media coverage (assaults by strangers receive far more attention, incest is often only newsworthy when the case is disputed; see Kitzinger and Skidmore, 1995). However, interaction such as that cited above highlighted another contributory factor: the social currency of different information. Public attitudes are informed by what information is routinely shared, and what is censured/censored within social exchange. Parents routinely warn each other about any stranger behaving 'suspiciously', but even close friends often do not talk about the 'dangerous' father, brother or grandfather in their own communities. Such dynamics have a direct impact on the ways in which communities identify threats, respond to them, and demand policy reactions. The findings from the focus group discussion about sexual abuse (conducted in the early 1990s) provided insights into community dynamics which predicted the recent furore about known abusers being relocated in 'the community' and the subsequent push for legislative change (Kitzinger, in press, b).

The contribution of sensitive moments: politics, theory and practice

Some people might interpret sensitive moments as an indication that focus groups are a dangerous method which is inappropriate for topics likely to stimulate strong emotions. Certainly, depending on the nature of your research question, group work will not always be appropriate (see Chapter 3). It is also true that focus groups should be handled with great care. There is a thin line between creating the opportunity for a group to discuss a difficult issue and foisting a discussion on people that they would really rather not have.

Many of the associated ethical problems and practical solutions have been discussed in previous chapters. Here we simply wish to add two points. First, researchers taking on obviously sensitive areas should have prior experience of in-depth qualitative work and should not come to the topic from a position of complete ignorance. For example, for the project on the media coverage of sexual abuse, Jenny Kitzinger's previous experience with focus groups alongside her prior interview-based research into sexual abuse was a necessary background for the confident conduct of the sessions. Second, we would argue that the style of facilitation is crucial. Obviously, there are ethical issues about asking people about sensitive areas. What is less often recognized is that there are also ethical issues about colluding to *evade* such areas. While it is usually inappropriate to ask highly personal questions in focus groups – for example about people's experiences of sexual abuse – it is also problematic to marginalize them by continually disregarding this possibility or assuming that no one could possibly want to reveal such experiences in public. Group facilitators should avoid using their power within the research setting either to close off sensitive possibilities or to push them too far. Where sensitive discussion areas are pursued in depth, the momentum should usually be maintained by the participants rather than the facilitator. Indeed, people will often clam up in the face of aggressive questioning. It is no coincidence that among the 13 interactive extracts used in this chapter only one cites an intervention from the facilitator (where JK sought to create space in the conversation for a particular individual in the face of silencing tactics from other group members).

With such caveats, we would argue that sensitive moments can be an invaluable part of the research process. Indeed, perhaps we should be aiming for *more* sensitive moments in focus groups, rather than *fewer*.

In our work, sensitive moments helped us to develop an understanding of the varied, conflicting and overlapping constructions of sensitivity and to map out the boundaries and transitions between public/private, acceptable/ unacceptable and routine/non-routine discourses among diverse groups in different situations. Often, they allowed us to go further than simply recognizing that an area might be awkward and achieve a greater understanding of when and why this may be so. Analysis of interactions between participants also allowed us to examine the construction and maintenance of boundaries in action. It highlighted the ways in which deviant experiences are silenced or incorporated and how discourses are policed (for example by association with stigmatized identities such as the 'prude' in project 5, the 'moaner' in project 6 or the person of 'dubious sexuality' in project 2).

Such analysis also directly informed the findings from each of the six projects in very practical ways. In the lesbian health project, it helped to identify obstacles to the use of sexual health services. In the group discussions with elderly hospital residents, it highlighted sensitivities around particular questions and the material conditions and concerns framing their expressed experiences. It thus helped to inform the design and interpretation of the subsequent questionnaire survey. Analysis of disruptive disclosures in the discussions of sexual abuse (project 3), documented the operation of particular social rules and dynamics within community groups which might influence how communities do (or do not) mobilize around different issues. Similar analysis in the other three projects provided crucial information about how people could relate to different campaign messages in specific social contexts, and this had clear implications for health promotion and public awareness strategies (see Kitzinger and Hunt, 1993; Miller et al., 1998).

Above all, when groups delved into and began to address sensitive issues in depth, this provided invaluable information about the place of personal experience within public discourse. The focus groups afforded access to the social processes through which the meaning of experience is constructed and reconstructed (whether this is the experience of being in long-term residential care or the experience of 'losing your virginity'). Unrehearsed talk about 'deviant' feelings or perspectives also provided invaluable insights into opportunities for change. Thus, in the study of young people's views of sex, violence and relationships, the research participants themselves at times began to experiment with different ways of challenging each other and understanding, communicating and accounting for themselves. Where group discussions go beyond conventional forms of routine public discourse they demonstrate possibilities for negotiating new forms of public knowledge.

On a general theoretical level, such work helps to clarify the distinction between common (but private) and shared (public) knowledge (Hughes and Dumont, 1993). It also throws up a series of questions about the relationship between individual experience, discourses, groups and society. Our focus group work suggests the need to relinquish assumptions about divisions such as private and public and to reconnect concepts such as personal and political. Instead of taking such categories for granted, we need to analyse what these categories mean in any given situation, how they are maintained and how they may be challenged and reframed.

In conclusion, sensitive moments may arise in any focus group research. Such moments should not be instantly shut down by the group facilitator, nor should they be ignored in the subsequent analysis. Whatever the topic of enquiry researchers can usefully ask: 'Why and when is an area sensitive or not?' 'Which aspects of the group process make people uneasy?' 'What allows them to discuss issues previously side-stepped?' 'Which opinions or experiences are seen as "skating on thin ice" and what happens when such opinions/experiences *are* discussed?' Such interrogation of focus group dynamics can be an invaluable part of any research project. Indeed, we believe that attending to sensitive moments in focus group discussion is an essential part of realizing the full potential of this method.

Notes

1 Some of these focus group studies were parts of larger projects. For example the AIDS and sexual abuse focus groups were conducted alongside analysis of the media coverage and interviews with journalists (see Eldridge et al., 1997; Miller et al., 1998). The 'youth project' focus groups complemented a large questionnaire survey (see Burton et al., 1997).

2 The bulk of the 127 groups included in projects number 2 to 6 were facilitated by Jenny Kitzinger herself. However, eight of the AIDS project groups, two of the youth project groups and sixteen of the sexual abuse groups were conducted by colleagues. Special thanks are due to Peter Beharrell, Hannah Bradby, Eddie Donaghy, Lesley Henderson and David Miller.

12 Can focus groups be analysed as talk?

Greg Myers and Phil Macnaghten

At some point, many focus group researchers find themselves sitting at a desk piled high with transcripts, wondering what to do with all this stuff. Most of the guides on focus group methodology (Morgan, 1988; Krueger, 1994) give a great deal of advice on setting up and conducting groups but say little about what to do after them. Recently some analysts have begun to focus on the complexity of interaction in focus groups (Beach, 1990; Kitzinger, 1994a, 1995; Agar and MacDonald, 1995; Myers, 1998). And there have been challenges to the idea that opinions and attitudes can be isolated from the conversational context in which they are generated (Waterton and Wynne, Chapter 9, this volume; Myers and Macnaghten, 1998).

There have been suggestions for content analysis (such as Bertrand et al., 1992; Knodel, 1993; Frankland and Bloor, Chapter 10, this volume) that address the complexity of focus group data, while still leading to quantitative results in categories that can support a case to a client. A coding system may, for instance, allow for the overlapping frames of reference for one utterance. But such analyses, however fine-grained, lose much of the context (and content) of the interaction: why just this was said just then. We propose that, along with other kinds of analysis, more attention be given to the transcripts as talk. There are a number of academic approaches to conversation in linguistics, sociology, and social psychology; we take our approach from the traditions of conversation analysis (for introductions, see Boden and Zimmerman, 1991; Drew and Heritage, 1993; Antaki, 1994; Psathas, 1995), and of discourse analysis (see Gilbert and Mulkay, 1984; Potter and Wetherell, 1987; Wetherell and Potter, 1992; Burningham, 1995). While these approaches differ in many respects, they share the assumptions that:

- Identities are negotiated in discourse (so in focus groups, we look at how they set up and work out roles).
- Talk is organized moment to moment by participants (so we look for ways they define sections, rather than defining sections as analysts).
- Talk is sequenced, one thing after another (so we must consider each utterance in terms of what came before and after).

How does such close attention to detail assist in developing a social analysis? Focus group studies that, like ours, are intended to inform social policy, aim to find out what people believe and how they act on the basis of what they say. But people say what they say, not in some abstract sphere of opinion, but in a variety of particular settings and situations; only through these specific settings do we have access to them.

In an influential critique of conventional conceptions of attitudes, Potter and Wetherell (1987; see also Wetherell and Potter, 1992; Potter, 1996) have argued that expressions of attitude are always situated in a particular discourse context, and that they should be interpreted within that context. Billig (1987, 1991, 1992) has characterized all thought as argumentative in character; people shape arguments in response to opposition, and take sides in discussion as part of the playing out of arguments. Burningham (1995) spells out the implications of this emphasis on discourse for attempts to gauge environmental attitudes. A survey aimed at finding out whether they approved or disapproved of new roads, or how much they valued the natural environment, would miss the complexity and ambivalence of people's relations to these issues by abstracting away from their situation (see Macnaghten, 1995). In Burningham's interview-based research, people talking about plans for a new road draw on various views of nature, risk and damage to justify one or another route, depending on whom they are talking to and what they are talking about. Focus groups offer a practical way of eliciting such complex talk, and in analysing the conversation we acknowledge the situatedness of opinion, and recover some of the richness and complexity with which people express, explore and use opinions.

The detailed analysis of focus group transcripts can follow from a developing critique within social psychology and sociology, of approaches that reify social attitudes, and assume that they remain fairly stable, that they determine opinions on specific cases, that they are linked to other traits, and that they can be elicited reliably. Focus groups are typically designed to elicit something less fixed, definite and coherent that lies beneath attitudes, something that the researcher may call feelings, or responses, or experiences, or world-views. Other researchers highlight focus group techniques for their ability to provide richer accounts of how people understand particular issues in the context of wider social concerns. So, for instance, a survey might ask respondents to rank air pollution among social problems, while a focus group might include discussion of various contexts in which participants might refer to air pollution (including, for instance, free-flowing talk on quality of life, locality, driving and leisure). But if we simply abstract attitudes from this discussion, we are treating them as we would in a survey.

A more practical reason for such detailed analyses of talk is to account for interpretations of focus group transcripts, and to allow for more comparison of different groups. There is always a danger, as with any method of social science research, of reproducing the expectations of policy-makers and researchers in the situation one sets up and the categories with which one analyses it. Analysts of focus groups need to be able to explain why they quoted just this passage, and how it relates to another passage from another group. In focus groups the processes of interaction can be made open and accountable. To trace the interactions, we must know more about how moderators set up a session and how participants interact with the moderator.

The great strength of focus groups as a technique is in the liveliness, complexity and unpredictability of the talk, where participants can make sudden connections that confuse the researchers' coding but open up their thinking. Agar and MacDonald (1995) give a good example, where their ethnographic work on youth drug taking seemed to give them an overview of the field, but where participants in a focus group discussion brought up something that had not yet been mentioned – the use of robitussin as a drug. Kitzinger (1994a) has similar examples where the interaction between participants led to topics that the moderator could not have raised. Holbrook and Jackson (1996) note how leaders emerged in their groups (they used groups of people who usually knew each other already), and how participants checked comments that might have remained unchallenged, or developed comments that might have seemed specific to one participant. Burgess et al. (1988a, b) give a detailed analysis of the group's response to the moderator's intervention. Such analyses enable us to explore how participants offer opinions, link topics and respond to the moderator, and through these processes we can reflect on how they engage with the topics brought by the researchers.

Much of the analysis of talk in such constrained situations starts by comparing talk in institutions (broadcasting, classrooms, medical interviews) with everyday talk (Boden and Zimmerman, 1991; Drew and Heritage, 1993). There are clearly ways focus groups are not like a casual conversation between friends. For our purposes, the key differences are that:

- The moderator can intervene to elicit responses and control turn-taking.
- The group displays opinions for the moderator.

On the other hand, participants in focus group discussions raise and shift topics, agree and disagree, select speakers and interrupt them, laugh and fall silent, in ways that they would in ordinary conversation. When the moderator intervenes, he or she follows not only the topic guide and specialist experience, but also his or her own instincts about how conversation usually works. We have argued that it is worth making some of this instinctive knowledge explicit, not only to moderate better and control for the moderator's effects, but also to understand in more detail what sort of talk and what sort of event any particular focus group is. In this chapter, we will consider three short examples showing how participants offer opinions in context, how they redefine topics, and how the moderator indicates whether a turn is on or off topic.[1] In the conclusion we will return to the practical problems and theoretical issues raised by detailed analysis of transcripts as talk.

Offering opinions

Here are two turns in different groups in which people say what seems to be the same thing in response to scientific assertions of the seriousness of environmental risks, the first from a group of unemployed middle-aged men in a city (Preston), and the second from retired people in a small town (Thornton).

> *B:*   So you've got to take a choice then of what you think.

> *M:*   So it's really you've got to take your choice who you believe.

If one interpreted statements as revealing attributes of subjects, one could code this as showing that very different groups of people (urban unemployed men and small-town retired people) hold the same attitude, sharing in the mounting scepticism of many people towards scientific authority. However, in the larger context of these discussions, these utterances can be seen to be different from each other, in a way that matters to interpreters and clients. How are these statements being used? In the first (Preston) example, the immediately preceding turns show how the participant was responding to the moderator's probing:

Transcription conventions:

<u>you</u>	stressed syllable
.	pause
/	onset of overlap
= =	turns following without any gap
( )	inaudible section
[ ]	comments added to transcription

Example 1

Mod:	so do you do you think when when one professor will say one thing another professor will say the other thing=
B:	=well who do you believe?
Mod:	well – who would <u>you</u> believe
B:	well you got two totally opposed different things
Mod:	yeah
→*B*:	so you've got to take a choice then of what <u>you</u> think
Mod:	yeah yeah

In the first turn here the moderator is reformulating B's previous comment and then asking him to make a choice. In the turns that follow, the way B and the moderator use 'well' suggests they are giving what are called *dispreferred* responses; that is, B is showing this isn't the direct or expected answer to the question, and the moderator is not answering B's question back to him. The participant's 'who do you believe?' is an interruption anticipating the moderator's question. But the moderator doesn't take it as a question to him. Instead, he responds by repeating these words, but now as a question to the participant 'who do *you* believe?' This is exactly how the handbooks tell moderators to respond to questions from participants to the moderator. The meaning of 'you' here shifts from general reference (anyone) to specific (B). The participant first returns to the problem he had earlier raised: 'you got two totally opposed different things'. The moderator responds with a continuer, 'yeah'. Only then does B state his opinion, the line we first quoted. 'So' is often used, as here, to mark a final statement or summary, a gist. What we find by this analysis is not just that he holds this opinion, but that he has to be pressed to state it; it is not something one normally needs to say. The idea that everyone has to choose for themselves among experts emerges only when he is challenged, and the challenge is seen in the form of the preceding turns.

In the second (Thornton) example, the utterance that interests us emerges as part of a lively interchange after one man has said that church officials should give the unbiased truth on environmental risks: 'you get somebody in a powerful position makes an opinion':

Example 2

Mod:	ok so so / people in ( )
F1:	/yeah but they don't do they [several at once]
M2:	cuz you get scientists who will have different views
M3:	/yeah
M2:	/on the same subject/
M3:	/exactly
→*M2*:	so it's really you've got to take
M3:	/yeah
M2:	/your choice who you believe
Mod:	well yeah but I mean I'm I mean given that these things might be a very real problem – who should be telling us . . .

The moderator has interrupted M1 with an indication that he has noted his point 'ok so so', usually the prelude to a reformulation of the participant's statement. Then there is evidently a confused attempt to get the floor, and M2, who gains the floor, frames his contribution as following from what has been said ('cuz'). He is supported at every possible completion point by continuers from other group members: 'yeah . . . exactly . . . yeah'. M2 starts the statement that interests us with another 'so', an indication that it is a summary or consequence of what he has been saying (Schiffrin, 1987). The moderator treats it this way, acknowledging 'these things' but returning to his earlier question. This time the statement 'you've got to take your choice who you believe' emerges as part of a shared general argument (what we have called a *commonplace* [Myers and Macnaghten, 1998]) in a collaborative production between two participants, responding to another participant's suggestion of an authority. It is framed not as a response to a challenge, but as a suitable summation. Attending to such details, we see not the general scepticism of authority shown in the surveys, but uses of scepticism in response to specific conversational situations, as bottom line or summation. Scepticism is not an attribute they already have, to be measured by suitable instruments, but a position they occupy in relation to other people and various attributions of authority (see also Waterton and Wynne, Chapter 9).

Topics

Analysts of focus group transcripts must pay attention to ways opinions are offered; they must also pay attention to what they are opinions of. It may seem that topics are set in the moderator's topic guide. But a closer look at transcripts from a conversation analysis perspective shows how participants shift the topic in step-wise transitions, sometimes in unpredictable ways, so there are often several potential topics in play. Consider the following passage from a group of retired professionals living in a village near the Lake District. They have just been shown a card containing words from a supermarket leaflet urging a variety of environmental actions, among them: 'Support tree-planting schemes, the development of wind-power and renewable sources of energy'. This is one section of their response (F1 and M1, and so on, are female and male participants; Mod 1 and Mod 2 are two moderators):

Example 3

> *F1:*   I don't know I don't know what um . I don't know enough about wind power now . xxx
> *M1:*   have you seen it?
> *F1:*   I've seen it yes . the main thing I would say about the bottom one is that . most conserva every time there's a wind power uh planning application . nearly every conservation body [Mod1: yeah] who is in the area [Mod1: mm] objects violently [?: mm] on the grounds that it's going to spoil . the visual impacts
> *?:*   the noise

F1: yes

Mod2: is that true or not?

M2: /these conservationists are putting things into this area/

F1: /I haven't been I don't know because I haven't /

M2: which are equally bad for

Mod2: Sorry what was it?

F1: I haven't I haven't actually seen a wind power station <u>working</u> so I can't speak from experience [Mod1: right] but I mean . if you want re<u>new</u>able power [Mod1: yeah] you've got to give a <u>price</u> . it's got it's got to be something in in . I mean it's not going to destroy the . ozone layer if you put wind . turbines . <u>so</u> . you've / got to balance it /

M1: /it it looks awful / [?:yeah] to people who <u>live</u> there =they say it's noisy . now /I don't know about that I <u>don't</u> know /

F2: /I don't know if it looks too bad / there's one on the other side of the other side of Skipton isn't there=

M1: =into <u>Lancaster</u> you can see it / xxx

M2: /I would rather see windpower [F2: yes I would] ((louder)) on Arnside Knot . which is doing some useful purpose [F2: yes I would] [Mod1: yeah] than what they put up there <u>now</u> . to protect the <u>cows</u> . from the draughts

?: ((laughter))

M1: but would you like Arnside Knot and Warton Crag and and Castle Bank to all have five windmills stuck on top=

M2: =oh no but I'm saying look I'm simply saying what they've <u>done</u> . up there . these conservationists is far worse . in my opinion [<u>xxx</u>]

M3: /nature will recover that it won't fall down over there /

F1: /but by the same token ((all talking together here)) / if you think about the view from Arnside Knot or anywhere around [Mod1: yeah] this area . looking across the bay . what spoils it most . is Heysham power station [Mod1: ahh that's] I mean you have this beautiful view [Mod1: yeah] and then you've got Heysham power station [Mod1: yeah] which will be here forever

At the beginning of each turn, participants acknowledge the given topic and the previous turn; by the end of their turn, they have often introduced a new topic that is to be taken as related. For instance, in her second turn, F1 both responds to the question, and goes on to talk about objections of conservation bodies; by stressing visual impacts she presents the new topic as relevant. In the last quoted turn, F1 moves from wind power to nuclear power by linking the view *of* Arnside Knot to the view *from* Arnside Knot; the continued reference to the place marks the new contribution as relevant. Thus the topic can shift as the discussion develops, while at each stage it remains relevant.

Such a set of transitions is typical of many long passages in the transcript in which the moderator does not intervene (see Waterton and Wynne,

Chapter 9, for a similar example). Each participant marks his or her new contribution at the beginning as relevant to the current topic. But within each turn, the participants can shift the context and interpretation for that topic. If we try to segment this flow into coded sections, we lose the connections, the way participants mark their contributions as appropriate at that particular point. For instance, in this case, we would lose the way in which the wind power stations are seen, simultaneously and ambivalently, in terms of renewable power, saving resources, preserving the climate *and* visual intrusion threatening the landscape. The ambivalence is like that in other focus groups on risk (see Waterton and Wynne, Chapter 9), illustrating the difficulty in drawing a priori the boundaries defining issues of social concern (as surveys do, by necessity). The ambivalence also shows the importance of sensitive listening, and of analysing people's own categories of experience (as focus groups aim to do).

Though these transitions may seem loose and wandering to observers and transcribers, the participants' own sense of the orderliness of topic shifts can be seen when the order is violated. That is how we interpret the laughter after M2's comment: 'what they put up there now . to protect the cows . from the draughts'. Here the remark can be seen as funny in itself (cows live outdoors and don't need protection from draughts). But it can also be seen as a response to an inappropriate attempt to shift the topic. So at first his contribution seems relevant to the current topic, 'I would rather see wind power', but by the end of the turn the other participants see he has linked it back to his own hobby horse, 'what they put up there now . to protect the cows . from the draughts'. Laughter, as in this case, is a complex interactional feature that occurs frequently in these transcripts; it often seems to function in mitigating disagreement, though it can also be interpreted in terms of ambivalence (see Waterton and Wynne, Chapter 9), tension, or solidarity.

Each of the turns after M2's comment begins with 'but', as participants try to reorient the previous contribution. Finally F1 ties the remarks of M2 and M1 back to the topic of visual impact: 'but by the same token – if you think about the view'. What this kind of example shows is that participants' ideas of topic, while very elastic, do not stretch indefinitely; there are mechanisms for marking some contributions as not on topic. One of the surprises of focus groups is the way that a group of strangers, after only an hour or so together, can show this kind of reflexive awareness of themselves as a group.

The moderator

Social science research methodologists give a great deal of attention to the possible effects of the researchers' intervention on the research data. Of course such intervention is unavoidable, if only through selection and idealization of the data. But it is particularly apparent in focus groups, where the moderator must get groups going and keep the discussion to a topic guide. (There are examples of leaderless groups, and groups moderated in different ways, see Morgan [1988: 48–53], but handbooks tend to describe groups with a strong moderator.) The work of the moderator, while recognized by researchers, is rendered invisible when the published reports on the research quote only the utterance of the participant, and not those leading up to it. If close analysis showed that the moderator controlled responses of focus group participants, focus groups would be seriously compromised as a social science research method. But what we see instead is a subtle process of interaction in which participants guide the moderator as well as the other way around.

The moderator remains a participant, though a quiet one, throughout the lively discussion in example 3 (one can compare it to the more interventionist moderating style in example 1). Nine times in this short passage Mod1 says things like 'right', 'mm', or his favourite, 'yeah'. These are what linguists call 'back channel utterances': the front channel is the stream of speech from whoever has the floor, while flowing the other way are the contentless sounds of other participants signalling to the speaker that they pass their turn to speak. (Back channel utterances are what you overhear when someone is on the phone and the person at the other end is doing most of the talking.) A 'yeah' spoken in this way is taken, not as agreement, but in the same way a nod might be taken, as a signal to continue talking. These utterances are spoken quietly, when the speaker with the floor pauses, and they never lead to a change of speaker. In transcription here, we have treated them as part of the main utterance, as if they were pauses.

Nearly all of the back channel utterances here are supplied by the moderator, suggesting he presents himself as the primary audience for participants' talk. Indeed, focus group moderators are trained to supply a stream of such utterances (at a training session we attended, the trainer put up an overhead projector slide saying 'yeah', 'right', 'okay'). These utterances are used with eye contact, body orientation and gesture to draw out responses beyond monosyllables, to suggest what our trainer called 'accurate empathy', without committing the moderator to view. If the moderator provided no back channel utterances at all, he would seem odd and detached. (Greatbatch [1988] points out how the absence of such utterances characterizes the display of objectivity in interviews with politicians on the radio news.)

These utterances, though expected and apparently ignored, still have an effect. The most striking feature of their distribution is not their content but their rhythm. In nearly every case, the moderator waits until the completion of the speaker's first main clause, and then almost every back channel utterance is at a point at which the speaker could stop and a new speaker take over. In one complex turn, for example, the moderator's 'right' and 'yeah' help mark F1 as the speaker with the floor, after she has competed with M2. The interventions also punctuate the parts of a two-part series.

> . . . if you think about the view from Arnside Knot or anywhere around [Mod1: yeah] this area . looking across the bay . what spoils it most . is Heysham power station [Mod1: ahh that's] I mean you have this beautiful view [Mod1: yeah] and then you've got Heysham power station [Mod1: yeah] which will be here forever.

F1 begins to construct a complex hypothetical statement with 'if'. The moderator says 'yeah' at the first possible place she could have completed her turn, indicating his receipt of this opening, acknowledging the reference to a particular local place. Then F1 continues with the rest of the construction. When that is possibly complete, the moderator says 'ahh that's', both acknowledging receipt and starting some comment on it. But F1 continues, without any overlap, by saying 'I mean', a form used for restatements and summaries (Schiffrin, 1987). Then she reformulates her view, now in three parts, again with the moderator acknowledging each part before she continues, but this time heightening the contrast with 'which will be here forever'. The form of the statement, including the hypothetical opening, contrast and heightening, are the result of complex interaction with the moderator. One way of looking at these back channel utterances is to note that the moderator uses them most in the participants' longer turns. But another way of looking at them is to ask whether the participants' turns become long because of this rhythmic background. The moderator signals, to the speaker and the other participants, not that he necessarily agrees, but that he is listening. Back channels from other participants have a somewhat different function; there the active involvement may signal (at least temporary) agreement.

The relevance of this observation to focus group methodology is that it enables us to trace the work of the moderator both as leader and as audience. The fact that the moderator is an audience for participants' talk may seem obvious enough – it was after all the researchers who invited the participants to attend. But it is not at all obvious that participants' talk is always to be interpreted as directed at the moderator. In fact we see complex shifting roles, not only of speakers, but also of chosen listeners. Back channel utterances, which are often not even transcribed, help us to trace these shifts in roles. The back channels are (with various non-verbal and lexical signals) one observable and accountable form of what focus group moderators may call 'empathy' or 'involvement'. They are also a mechanism for the focus of focus groups; participants respond, moment to moment, to such signals of whether they are on topic. These interventions can exclude as well as include; as we see in example 2, when responses bring one participant out, they also deny the floor to another. Thus, in any longer term, it can be important to the analyst to see just where the moderator intervenes, and where other participants break in or offer support, to see what parts the participants are assembling, and to see what potential statements there are at each point.

Implications: using and representing talk

A detailed analysis of focus group transcripts has implications both for other focus group researchers and for a wider range of social researchers who read focus group research. In our studies, we were interested in how people talked about environmental sustainability and about their own actions, and how this talk related to the language of policy documents and leaflets. We knew from earlier studies that people are aware of environmental issues (more aware than surveys might suggest) but that they present any action as depending on their sense of agency and their trust in other people and in organizations addressing them. Agency and trust are not general attributes that one does or does not have; they are contingent assessments that may differ from situation to situation and relation to relation. It is important for government bodies, businesses and campaign organizations to understand how people assess their power to act and their trust in others. We would argue that close attention to transcripts can illuminate the issues we were studying. For instance:

- *Offering opinions* – the way scepticism occurs in the transcripts shows that it is not news for the participants (though it may be news for the analyst): it occurs in commonplaces, and when participants are challenged to make a choice. In most conversational situations, when there is no direct challenge or need to find common ground, it can remain implicit.
- *Topics* – the way participants go from experience to aesthetic issues is an example of how they develop frames and links for topics not foreseen in the topic guide. The way they reject the offer of fences as a link is an example of how they bound the current topic – not everything for them can be lumped together as aesthetic.
- *Moderator* – the moderator's back channels show how he selected out a comment on the aesthetics of wind power stations from various comments competing for the floor, and how the elaborate contrast of this comment was constructed in interaction with him as the audience, marking each part.

It might be argued that all this could be seen by a sensitive moderator and interpreter, since they draw on the implicit awareness of conversational structure that this sort of analysis makes explicit. But there are always a number of possible interpretations, and it is important to be able to point to and discuss such patterns in explaining how one arrived at the interpretation one is presenting. To gloss all this automatically, to jump from the details to the interpretation, leaves out the focusing and responding work of the moderator, and the interactions of the participants that make one group different from another.

This raises the practical problem of just what should be in the transcript. We would argue that it can be useful, at least for some passages, to have much more detailed analysis and much larger chunks of quoted context. Most researchers are unlikely to take the transcription time needed for a full conversation analysis transcription, which could include indications of loudness, speed, voice quality, breathing and intonation, as well as timed pauses (for an example, see Atkinson and Heritage, 1984: ix–xvi); such a transcription takes about four times as long as a simple transcription in readable prose. But we did ask the transcriber (Elaine Hobson) to avoid the kinds of cleaning up she might usually do: we asked her to keep the repetitions, filled pauses and false starts, and to put down as much as possible of overlapping utterances. For sections used in publications, we enriched the transcription further and indicated pauses, interruptions, overlaps and back channel utterances. As in any transcription, researchers have to make decisions based on the costs of transcription against the benefits within their research framework (Cook, 1995).

Besides these questions of information and accuracy, transcription raises questions of readability and effects. Transcripts with standard spelling, capitalization and punctuation idealize the flow of talk by leaving out much of the data, but they are also more readable, for the researchers and the clients, than the more detailed transcripts suggested here. It has also been argued that the halting, broken appearance of speech transcribed in detail makes participants seem inarticulate. This warning also applies to our transcription of back channel utterances, which may overemphasize the effect these interjections have on the participants. Listeners (rather like *Hansard*, the official record of Parliamentary debates) edit speech as they hear it into flowing, coherent and uninterrupted messages. It takes some familiarity with the conventions of transcription before one can read detailed transcripts as conveying more of the sound and pace of speech. But such conventions do allow a practised reader to reconstruct much more of the flavour and detail of the talk, and arrive at better-grounded interpretations of utterances.

Our other suggestion is that longer quotations from the transcripts are often needed to support the analysts' interpretation. This too has a cost, in publication space and readers' patience. One might think this would lead, in the extreme case, to a quotation of the entire transcript to support one utterance. But one of the best-supported findings of conversation analysis is that speakers orient to the immediately preceding turn, answers following questions, assessments following assessments, response following accusation. In many cases it is that immediately preceding turn that is important to the analyst – the moderator's question, or a participant's example. For instance, F1's qualification in Example 3 that, 'I can't speak from experience', makes sense only in terms of the moderator's question, 'is that true or not?'. It is this question that focuses the response on evidence rather than opinion. We have argued further that it is often useful to look over the whole segment between major interventions by the moderator. Content analysis can tell us what they talked about, but conversation analysis can tell us how they talked about it, what it was linked to, how it would be presented to other people, what was necessary to support it.

Researching attitudes is big business in the social sciences, marketing and media. They are the raw material of surveys and talk shows, newspaper columns and phone-ins. But we as social science researchers should not necessarily take attitudes as objects that are out there in the subjects. Our attention to the talk in focus groups is part of a developing programme in the social sciences that treats opinions and attitudes rhetorically, as utterances produced in specific situations rather than as attributes of subjects. In social research, as in local radio, opinions are produced in context, for specific interactional purposes. On the radio, one may affirm one's identity, or provide entertainment, or promote a cause, often in response to some opposite point of view. In a focus group, one might be expressing solidarity, or playing devil's advocate, or changing the subject, or displaying one's special expertise or experience. These contexts do not make the discussions any less valuable to researchers or their clients, but it means that we must pay attention to the interaction if we want to understand what participants are doing when they display opinions.

Note

1 The passages of transcripts come from two studies conducted by the Centre for the Study of Environmental Change at Lancaster University. The first, on 'Public Perceptions and Sustainability in Lancashire', explored people's sense of quality of life and change in their environment to inform the development of sustainability indicators; it was funded by the Lancashire County Council, and involved eight groups in Lancashire in 1994, each of which met twice (see Macnaghten et al., 1995). The second, on 'Public Rhetorics of Sustainability', dealt with people's responses to organizations' appeals for environmental action, and the ways they themselves used these appeals; it was funded by the Economic and Social Research Council and involved eight groups in the North and South of England in 1995 (see Myers and Macnaghten, 1997; Macnaghten and Urry, 1998).

13 Theorizing subjects and subject matter in focus group research

Sarah Cunningham-Burley, Anne Kerr and Stephen Pavis

The ubiquity of focus groups as a research method clearly requires critical reflection about the complex sets of social relations in which they are embedded. At the same time as focus groups have grown in popularity in the social sciences, accessing the views of clients or consumers has become an important part of the planning process and public relations of both the private and public sectors. This chapter offers a critical analysis of the processes implicated in this trend, and a reflection on the position of sociology therein. Why, in the 1990s, does focus group research hold this prominent place across such a wide range of sectors? Is the increasing use of this qualitative research tool to be welcomed? Is the new focus on consumers' views a force for democracy? We begin with a critique of the current emphasis on the consumer in both policy and research. We then consider the positivist paradigm underpinning the use of focus group methods in both market and much of social research. This leads us to question the current emphasis on the consumer as opposed to the citizen and the positivist paradigm. In addition, we examine the role of the social researcher in this nexus of power relations between funders, consumers and citizens. We then go on to discuss how our own use of focus groups has been constrained by the prevailing market ideology, an appreciation of which has led us to argue for a sociology committed to reflecting multiple voices and to promoting participatory democracy, based on a redistribution of power and a promotion of citizenship as opposed to consumerism. To illustrate our argument, we reflect on the use of focus groups in one project in particular which was concerned with the social and cultural impact of the new genetics.[1] Our experience suggests that focus group research can be harnessed to challenge the power of experts and contribute towards greater public engagement with policy decisions. We conclude that social researchers involved in focus group research need to be open, reflexive and critical if their research is not to be used to support structures and processes which perpetuate inequality.

Consumerism and late modernity: the public and private sectors converge

The social transformations occurring from the 1970s have been characterized as a shift from modernism to post- or late modernism. Changes in production, accumulation and consumption, from Fordism to post-Fordism, have created pluralistic markets, flexible production processes and a reification of the consumer, choice and lifestyles. The breakdown of traditional structures has altered the relationships which individuals have with one another and with institutions, leading to a growth in individualization and the erosion of collective identities based on the traditional class structure. Gidden's thesis of reflexive modernity, for example, emphasizes agency and choice, where people themselves are central in reflexively constructing their identities and biographies from a diverse range of experiences and opportunities (Giddens, 1990, 1991).

The rise in consumerism and the breakdown of traditional production patterns have been reflected in the reconstitution of the health and welfare sectors: the 1990s are truly 'the decade of the consumer' (Popay and Williams, 1994: 3). The monolithic bureaucracies of the welfare state are being replaced by pluralism, internal markets and a new managerialism. The enterprise culture of the new welfare state replaces the client with the consumer, just as the wider social context emphasizes individuals as consumers, aggregated not in any traditional collective way, but as an amorphous mix of individual preferences and choices. The private and public sectors are converging, and their rhetoric reifies the public as consumers, whose needs must be identified and met through new products or services. In the UK this is embodied in the market/charter culture of the 1990s (Johnson, 1996), where citizens' rights become translated into consumer rights (Plamping and Delamothe, 1991), thus losing any critical edge in terms of entitlement or social benefit.

The unique combination of the requirement to 'listen to users' and the qualitative thrust of focus group research, gives social scientists using the technique an important niche in both the private and public sector. This is particularly evident in the health service, where structural changes have increased the funding of small-scale, local health service research, particularly studies of users and potential users of health care. Krueger, for example, states that 'Focus groups can provide them [professionals] with information about perceptions, feelings and attitudes of program clients. The procedure allows professionals to see clearly from a client's point of view' (1988: 21).

Epistemological issues: positivism prevails

The history of focus group research often typifies the technique as one which flourished in market research, yet was curtailed within the social sciences (Johnson, 1996). Traditionally, focus groups used by market researchers operate within a clear positivist paradigm. Participants in focus groups are constructed as passive subjects, who hold opinions and preferences on a range of matters important within the market-place. These opinions are considered to be objective facts, best expressed in group situations under the clever control of the moderator. The resultant knowledge is disembedded from the context within which it was generated. Participants are not active in the research process, and have no control over its use. They remain 'untouched' by participation – no further action is expected on their part. The emphasis is on the individual and his or her views, even though these may be expressed in groups; and the focus is on consumption rather than production.

Although focus groups are thought to have been less fashionable in social research until recently, there has been a rich but relatively undocumented use of the method throughout the post-war period (Morgan, 1988). They have been variously used in pilot work for many different types of studies (surveys and in-depth interview studies), and as a way of furthering the interpretation of research findings. Indeed, the positivist tradition, which underlies the use of focus groups within market research, has always been prevalent within social science, and is even experiencing a mini-renaissance in today's 'enterprise culture'. From our own experiences at a number of seminars on focus groups, we know that some social scientists are clearly operating within a market research paradigm – market researchers are sometimes even present at these meetings. This means that there is invariably an emphasis on recruitment (how to get people to attend) and technique (how to get people to talk). The participants tend to be treated as an aggregate of individuals, who are representatives of specific social groups (stratified according to class, age and gender). Some social scientists are even supplying alcohol to participants, or offering payments on a sliding scale (so that better-off people are paid more in recognition of their time being more expensive), both techniques from market research. In this model, the researcher's role in the research process is very much the enabler/moderator, or even the opportunist – the focus is on how to get the best data possible with this technique. There is little reflection on ontological or epistemological issues.

However, focus groups are not always used within a positivist framework. Indeed, their use in social research has been characterized as distinct from market research, precisely because of an allegiance to an interpretivist rather than positivist paradigm (Secker et al., 1995). Broadly, this involves a commitment to viewing reality as socially constructed, and to treating data as dependent on the social context of the research interview (in this case, focus groups). Particularly relevant is the primacy given to lay accounts as appropriate topics of research, and the diverse and multiple social realities that they generate. Emphasis here is upon active involvement and dialogue among participants, especially the free flowing nature of much of the discussion. The method is often viewed as empowering, because of this involvement of participants, particularly marginalized groups, for example, people with limited literacy (Kitzinger, 1994a, 1995). Freire (1972) among others (Padilla, 1993, quoted in Johnson, 1996) also highlights the usefulness of group techniques in the dialogic methods of community participation.

The rise in focus group research and the tensions between epistemological paradigms leads us to reflect on three key issues. First, we explore whether the current emphasis on consumer views really acts to 'empower' lay people. Second, we critique the positivism which underlies market and some social researchers' use of focus groups; questioning, in particular, the unproblematic acceptance of focus groups as a route to accessing 'user views' or 'lay knowledge'. Third, we discuss the role of the social researcher in this process: how are social scientists implicated in constructing the subjects and subject matter of their research?

The consumer and the citizen: empowerment or tokenism?

The discourse of empowerment is entangled within the consumer and marketing discourse (Grace, 1991); focus group research can also slide easily into these discourses. However, any equation between consumer choice and the redistribution of power is highly questionable. As Kelly notes, 'Consumerism is part of the rhetoric of the enterprise culture, one that deflects attention away from effective consumer participation through institutionalized means of representation' (1991: 137).

The enterprise culture of both the public and private sectors can give the appearance of empowerment by 'listening to the people' (Krueger, 1995). Instead, power is removed from, as opposed to granted to, many individuals when they become dependent on either the market or the goodwill of specific institutions and their representatives. Although these consumers might think of themselves as powerful, they are manipulated by experts, authorities and producers who present them with choices but strip them of the means by which to engender real change. As Beck argues, 'At the same moment as [the consumer] sinks into insignificance, he or she is elevated to the apparent throne of a world-shaper' (Beck, 1992: 137). Yet, the consumer and citizenship discourses are incompatible (Davison et al., 1997), and their conflation merely masks the erosion of citizens' rights.

This is particularly apparent in the health services. As we have already argued, there has been a growing emphasis on consumer views, as health services attempt to be more responsive to users' needs. However, even when empowerment is the aim, this has not been associated with increased democratization of health service planning, merely increased consultation. Put bluntly, it is still managers who choose (Klein, 1990), and the consumer has little influence (Winkler, 1987). Despite a significant number of rights-based consumer and pressure groups, very few user groups have been able to challenge seriously the centres of power, and research commissioned from the centre (the inside) is unlikely to provide the route to political activism. In this context consultation is unlikely to be empowering and, at worst, becomes little more than tokenism. Empowerment can only be engendered by institutional arrangements which embrace partnership between lay people and professionals and allow for democratic accountability (Bracht, 1991; Plamping and Delamothe, 1991).

The positivist approach: epistemological naïvety

As we have noted earlier, focus groups are most frequently used within a positivist paradigm, with its attendant positioning of the research subject as passive, with opinions which are tapped and documented through the use of good moderator skills. The positivist emphasis on documenting the consumers' point of view is not commensurate with interpretive under-standing or with public involvement in research and policy. It produces what Cain and Finch (1981) refer to as 'sociologically inert entities' still requiring theoretically informed, analytical attention from the researcher. This requirement cannot easily be met when more and more people are engaged in small-scale commissioned projects with little time for analytical reflection. Nor is it met when ontological and epistemological differences between interpretivism and positivism are blurred in the naïve assumption that focus groups must be interpretive because they access people's views in an informal group setting. In writing about the enthusiastic adoption of qualitative methods in health sciences, Thorne (1997) has expressed con-siderable concern about what she terms 'phenomenological positivism'. In other words, a 'phenomenological attitude' (wanting to find out about the subjective world of others) is being embedded in a positivist paradigm. Instead, she favours 'methodological integrity', whereby researchers acknowledge the complexity of the subjective world, including critically reflecting upon their own subjectivity.

An emphasis on qualitative methods, rather than upon epistemology, has led to a conflation of qualitative methods (here, focus groups) with interpretivism in social research. This unreflective position blurs important epistemological differences. Focus groups appear to cross the epistemo-logical divide with such ease that there can be a careless disregard of fundamental issues of power and control, the constitution of data and the positioning of all those participating in research. This means that the changing political, economic and social processes which may lead to the convergence of market and social research styles, as with the public and private sectors themselves, are effectively ignored.

Johnson (1996) argues that if social scientists are to use focus group techniques, then certain key issues must be addressed. For example, who is consulted; when are they consulted; who consults them; and how are their views assessed and represented? In particular, the social context within which research is commissioned, funded and conducted is crucial, as is the differential power relation between funders, researchers and research participants. These relations will all affect the research process, the questions asked and how the discussion is analysed. Importantly, they will also affect what happens after the research has been conducted. These issues need to be made explicit to those participating in focus group research, so that they are clear about the basis of their participation, and where it will lead.

If the rhetoric of listening to lay voices or consumers is adopted unreflectively, rather than critically challenged, the resulting knowledge will reinforce the dominant positions of those with power. Lay knowledge will be marginalized, often characterized as based on ignorance of the 'real issues', or important scientific or technical facts. It is undoubtedly the case that focus groups provide the room for participants to express their knowledge and views more fully than the traditional survey or questionnaire. However, any presumption of a lack of knowledge undermines a more interpretivist position where it is recognized that lay people have valid knowledge about a range of matters which affect their own lives.

Focus groups should not be seen as a way to access some static but as yet untapped set of opinions or preferences. The participants need to be considered as active subjects, who are involved in constructing social reality through interaction, both in their daily lives and in the focus group. They possess a dynamic 'stock of knowledge' (Schutz, 1970; Schutz and Luckmann, 1974), which can be mobilized in sensitive and comfortable environments where their views are not implicitly denigrated. When participants are truly active in the research process they are able to influence its direction and impact, for example the research itself may lead, or be allied, to some form of community action. In other words, participants in focus groups should be treated as citizens, rather than passive consumers.

The social researcher: clarifying positions

The convergence of market and social research within the market oriented health and welfare sectors provides ripe ground for 'naïve empiricism',[2] where little attention is paid to epistemological assumptions or the role of the researcher in the research process. As we have already argued, it is often considered enough to document consumer views and the research is characterized merely as the vector of these views. This can reinforce a set of social and research relationships which deny the expertise and active participation of research subjects. Social researchers, although arguing that theirs is a position of disinterested concern, are actually perpetuating the consumer culture when they treat participants as passive, thus deflecting critical debate.

Consumerism appears to privilege but, in fact, ignores the subject. Since social scientists are a part of the social relations which demand particular forms of knowledge, then we must reflect on that process. As Scambler points out: 'While the importance of reflexivity, as defined by Giddens, is now widely acknowledged by sociologists, it is less apparent that this acknowledgment translates into "appropriate" practices' (1996: 573). Scambler criticizes medical sociology in particular for its integration into the economy and the state, and for its 'systems-driven' projects, and calls for greater reflexivity and engagement in a 'reconstituted public sphere'. However, the argument is not just relevant to health-related research. Sociology, as a whole, is well placed to precipitate such reflexivity because of its critical stance and its understanding of social structure (Williams and Popay, 1994). This could occur within the discipline as a whole, and at the level of individual researchers who are operating in local environments and conducting specific research projects.

To summarize, while it would be inappropriate to overstate the role of focus groups in the market culture of the 1990s, their uncritical and enthusiastic use as a means to access 'user views' or 'lay knowledge' should be challenged. The alliance of the 'consumer culture' with focus groups is both disturbing and enabling. Social scientists are commissioned by purchasers, providers and users of health care; they operate in a climate which seems to privilege consumers and their views, but disempowers them in practice. On the positive side, research in this area can contribute to the planning process and to the nature of service provision in ways which are beneficial to users. On the other hand, such research may just play into the hands of planners and managers who, while commissioning such research, do not necessarily act on its results. This can give the appearance of public participation in decision-making, without generating any real change.

We now go on to reflect on our own experiences of these conflicting aspects of focus group research, describing how our views and approaches have unfolded over time as we sought to practise a more reflexive and progressive sociology in which participants are treated as active agents in the research process.

Using focus groups: some examples

In our work we have used focus groups on a number of occasions. This has always been based upon a commitment to the interpretivist position, which prioritizes subjective experience and views reality as socially constructed. However, this has inevitably been compromised by the realities of research funding. We have met some of the demands, by commissioning agencies, for research into lay or consumer views, and have used focus groups to obtain data on users' health needs and preferences for care. At the same time we have become increasingly aware that short research contracts, provided on a consultancy basis, often reinforce the user model and stand in tension with our commitment to treating research participants as socially located actors.

In research commissioned to investigate 'lay views of positive mental health', for example, Sarah and Steve[3] used focus groups alongside other qualitative techniques. The research highlighted the lack of salience of the concept of positive mental health among the participants, and the importance they accorded to both structural and individual factors as affecting mental well-being. The research process showed how lay people engage with complex research questions in a meaningful way: participants enthusiastically puzzled over the issues of 'positive mental health', giving freely of their analytical reflection, personal information and time (Pavis et al., 1996). At a more local level, Sarah and colleagues[4] have been involved in research commissioned by a local community health project, where focus groups were used to help assess the health needs of a deprived community (Curtice et al., 1994). In this research, engagement with the local population was immediate and interesting. Their lack of a voice was apparent, with a group of young men saying that no one had ever asked them their opinions on anything before.

While we welcome research commissioners' recognition of the need for this sort of research, we also realize that the way this is then fed back into any policy or planning is outside either the researchers' or the participants' control. The broad definition of health needs associated with this work is a positive step away from the narrowness of some epidemiological surveys. However, our experiences have taught us that such research efforts seldom have anything other than a marginal impact on those able to define policy and the allocation of resources.

These, along with other experiences, reinforce our arguments about the popularity of focus group research and its usefulness in assessing lay views. However, they also demonstrate that while social science research may now be integrated into the sets of relations which make up health care organizations, the subjects of the research, and often the social scientists themselves, remain outside of any meaningful engagement with decision-making. While we remain confident that our work remains sociologically informed, it is not automatically associated with effecting positive social change. Our next example provides a much more detailed exploration of these issues.

The social and cultural impact of the new genetics

Our experience, concerns and discontents reinforced our prior commitment to reflexive research practice, and to a critical sociology which does not take for granted the structure of authority and power within which it operates. We now go on to discuss Sarah and Anne's experiences of using focus groups in a project investigating the 'Social Impact of the New Genetics'.[5] This led us to reconsider the power of the method both in terms of accessing lay knowledge and in promoting lay participation in the public sphere.

The new genetics, especially as applied to medicine and health, raise many social and ethical issues for individuals and society. The research which we conducted involved interviews with scientists, clinicians and journalists; an analysis of selected written media coverage, including the specialist professional press; and focus group research with a range of population groups, or publics. This took place over two years and nine months and gave us access to a broad range of perspectives on the social and cultural impact of the new genetics. After the first stage of interviews with senior new genetics professionals it became apparent that this group held a very privileged position in negotiating the social impact of their knowledge and practice within the lab, the clinic and beyond. They utilized a series of flexible discursive boundaries around science, choice, control and responsibility to maintain this position. This means that these new genetics professionals, although clearly influencing clients' decisions, often disclaimed responsibility for this. These participants projected responsibility for the social impact of the new genetics on to an amorphous society, while at the same time arguing that they should have a privileged advisory and educational role in public debates and the policy realm (Kerr et al., 1997).

The current discussions about the public understanding of genetics must also be understood in the context of this professional boundary-work (Gieryn, 1983). Thus, professional appeals to the deficit in the public understanding of genetics reinforces their own expertise. The emphasis on educating the public is, of course, far removed from the citizen participation required to influence policy and practice. This is part of the process whereby professionals reinforce their cognitive authority in a world where trust in professional experts in diminishing (Wynne, 1991, 1995).

When setting up the interviews with lay people in this study, we felt that it was important to reflect critically upon this 'deficit model' of the public understanding of genetics. We deliberately sought to access a range of publics and chose to explore their knowledge and experiences of genetics and health in its broadest sense. This meant that we did not just want to speak to people with direct experience of genetic conditions, but to access the views of people with indirect links to genetic science and services and people with no obvious reasons to be interested in the topic. We chose focus groups because we felt that they would enable discussion and debate; they would encourage the participants to talk about something that they might not have previously considered in depth; they could access a range of population groups; and the discussion topics could be adapted to take account of the ongoing analysis as the project developed. Our perspective was that knowledge is not static, but contingent and relational: we considered lay knowledge to be valid in its own right, and a product of individuals' social experiences and environments.

However, we were also aware of some tensions within our research design. We were concerned that, by interviewing scientists individually and the lay public in focus groups, we were open to criticism for treating lay people's views as less important than those of professionals, and implicitly reinforcing the expert/lay divide. At the same time, we believed that certain attributes of focus groups (when used carefully and within an interpretivist framework) could actually empower lay people to express their views and contribute to policy debates. Group interviews in a supportive and relaxed atmosphere might make it easier for respondents to express their opinions and knowledge. Focus groups might also be less daunting than one-to-one interviews, as respondents may feel that they do not have to have an opinion on every issue or to answer all of the questions. Moreover, when respondents are new to a subject matter (in the sense that they do not consider it every day) the processes involved in group discussion can facilitate orientation and reflection. On a purely practical level, it is also difficult to convene focus groups with professional scientists and clinicians. Indeed, in the original research design we hoped to include some medical/ scientific professional groups in our 'publics', but in reality this proved very troublesome. As we shall discuss later, we were only able to convene one group of public health specialists and this proved to be an extremely difficult interview. This suggests that scientists' and clinicians' professional status often means that they prefer to be interviewed individually as opposed to in groups.

Our intention to reflect the diversity of publics, rather than to be representative in a more traditional sense, meant that we usually engaged with existing groups (for example, support groups or community groups). Groups were therefore small, and usually known to each other. We did not want simply to search for differences in participants' accounts in terms of class, gender or race, but sought to understand the way in which people's social location more broadly influenced their accounts (Kerr et al., 1998a). We therefore interviewed 20 groups – 6 who were directly affected by a genetic condition (such as people with disabilities, parents of children with Cystic Fibrosis); 4 with a professional interest in genetics (for example nurses and public health medicine specialists); 5 with an indirect link to genetics as their lifestyle or condition has been associated with genetics (for example, gay men and a support group for people with experience of heart disease); and 5 other community groups/friendship networks (for example, elderly people attending a day centre, and a group of Chinese students). No payment was made to group members to attend, although a financial contribution was made to one of the groups for the hire of a room in their building (the organization was a charity which promoted independent living for people with disabilities). The participants were engaged as actively as possible in the research process. The project was explained in detail and feedback was offered via reports. The work was conducted recursively, and the analysis was fed back to later groups to enable deeper and more pertinent theorizing. In the later focus groups we therefore developed techniques to enable detailed exploration of issues raised in the earlier sessions (Kerr et al., 1998b).

Philosophical and existential questions were asked, and group members reflected on services, practices and policy. This did not involve asking participants to give accounts of, or 'imagine', their courses of action as consumers of genetic services. Instead, they were asked to comment on the social and ethical issues raised by genetic tests and services. This allowed for a wide ranging discussion and did not put participants in an uncomfortable position by expecting them to disclose their personal views on sensitive subjects such as abortion.

As a result of these focus groups we began to see lay people's knowledge and views, drawn from a variety of experiences (both direct and indirect), as a form of expertise (which is, after all, the product of experience). This meant that people not only had expert knowledge about cultural attitudes and social relations related to the new genetics, but could also deal competently with technical and methodological issues without a strictly accurate and detailed knowledge of the subject. The level of sophistication of people's accounts was also related to the research technique, which allowed them to discuss and debate issues in-depth and not just to answer a narrow range of questions posed by researchers (or funders). The interaction between participants also meant that ambivalence and ambiguities were expressed and discussed in detail. Views were challenged and moderated; and shared and unique knowledge was revealed. Their accounts in focus groups, sometimes in the form of direct reflections, showed how people's varied social location influenced both their uptake of knowledge and its expression. The importance of people's perception of the *relevancy* of the new genetics was revealed. This suggests that, in sufficiently supportive and non-intimidating environments, the new genetics can become relevant to a broad range of lay people. These are necessary conditions for lay people to articulate or mobilize their relevant 'stock of knowledge', knowledge which constitutes lay expertise about genetics (Kerr et al., 1998a).

These focus groups also highlighted, as opposed to obscured, the powerful pressures to delineate professional expertise and lay ignorance. The group interview with public health professionals conducted by Anne was one of the most difficult research interactions she has ever encountered. The group was both hostile and defensive, refusing to be tape-recorded, criticizing the way questions were asked, and denigrating the entire interview process. It was clearly experienced as an infringement of the usual professional hierarchies by the participants, and they identified strongly with clinical genetics services whose practices they were being asked to comment upon.

In addition, there was a strong resistance among lay people and professionals alike to recognize that the accounts in these focus groups constitute a form of expertise which places a positive value on their opinions and experiences. Invariably, when the groups were being set up people expressed anxieties about their lack of relevant knowledge. A lot of reassurance was required to convince people that they would be able to talk about the new genetics whether or not they felt they had a high level of technical proficiency in the subject. People were also highly sceptical about their involvement in policy-making, arguing that their views were not considered to be important. This lack of confidence and history of exclusion means that, within the present structures, truly inclusive and meaningful debate about the new genetics would be very difficult. The processes of decision-making about funding and clinical application need to be revised if they are to become publicly accountable. This would require significant shifts in power and the creation of many more democratic fora. Research participants were already acutely aware of this.

Our experience of conducting these focus groups has led us to relate the research method to wider issues of participatory democracy in a more concrete fashion – we have begun to ask how do we create these fora and do focus groups help? As a direct result of our commitment actively to involve lay people in public debates and policy discussion about the new genetics, we organized a public discussion about some of the issues raised by our research at the Edinburgh International Science Festival 1997. This event, 'The Public Image of the New Genetics', involved a short panel discussion about the trustworthiness of geneticists, the role of the media and the level of public understanding of genetics, as well as the public's role in decision- and policy-making, followed by contributions from the audience. The event was open to the public, and research participants were invited to attend. Although this gave people who might otherwise have been silent an opportunity to express their views in public, it also highlighted the ease with which professionals can dominate public discussions. In addition it showed clearly (as did the focus groups) that there is no resolute public opinion about the new genetics (or any other issue for that matter). This suggests that fora which can deal with the inevitable ambivalence which a wider range of lay people will express, and the diversity present in different publics, need to be developed (Kerr et al., 1998b). Moreover, open contestation of expert knowledge should be a feature of all democratic processes (Wynne, 1995).

We have also had to reflect upon the other difficulties which arise from such a position. We must be mindful of raising the issue of public participation and walking away without actively campaigning for the setting up of such fora. And it would be all too easy to behave like 'unelected representatives'[6] of the lay populace if we did not try directly to involve them in the policy process. Furthermore, we must avoid totally relativizing lay and professional expertise, and recognize the enormous barriers to the provision of information to lay people, including problems as simple as physical access to the information, as well as the use of professional jargon and obscurantism.

We are also keenly aware that this research may not have been possible without the luxury of a two-year, nine-month grant, or a funding body that was sufficiently convinced by our arguments about the development of the research tools that we used. This is not the case for many researchers operating on a short-term consultancy basis and under greater constraints about the research design which they adopt. A radical shift in the use of focus groups, suggested by our research, and proposed by Johnson (1996), could also precipitate their dismissal as an appropriate way to access lay views by some of those commissioning or funding research. Any changes along the lines we are suggesting would be necessarily slow and piecemeal, and should preserve the position of sociology as a powerful force in both understanding relationships of power and knowledge and effecting social change. Otherwise both the discipline and those it should serve will become increasingly marginalized and manipulated by those with the power to define our involvement.

Conclusion

Focus groups are undoubtedly an important research tool for sociology when their use involves the consideration of the social context within which research is commissioned, funded and conducted; especially when the differential power relations between funders, researchers and research participants are acknowledged. These underpin the generation of data and therefore knowledge. If focus groups are embedded in the market-consumer discourse of the 1990s, there is a danger that their uncritical use will lead to the reproduction of, rather than challenges to, existing social relations. A reflexive stance is required where researchers must be positioned as active agents within the sets of social and cultural relations involved in the research process.

Focus groups can be an important tool in challenging the prevailing attitude to lay knowledge. Used carefully, they highlight lay expertise, not ignorance, and as such could be an important resource for policy-making. An interpretivist approach, where the social location of participants and the context of their accounts is recognized, is also a useful way of bridging the artificial divide between agency and structure in many social theories. In other words, focus groups position individuals' accounts of their consumption and identity formation in a group interaction and allow for the exploration of the way in which participants' social, cultural and economic location relates to the accounts which they provide. Perhaps most importantly, focus groups can be used to promote action of members instead of leaving participants untouched or underrepresented (Johnson, 1996).

Wynne (1992) has argued that it is only by engaging in research which reflexively problematizes 'science as well as publics' that 'potential forms of constructive public engagement with science' can be developed. This also applies to research on health care, and indeed it is required of social researchers themselves. 'Publics' stand in particular relationships to policy arenas, thus there can be no uncontaminated version of public opinion. Social science in general and sociology in particular, in this age of research-based public services, evaluation and charters, is not a disinterested vector of knowledge, but itself positional. If sociologists are to retrieve their critical stance, and contribute towards a better society (Seidman, 1994), we have to reflect upon our position within the political economy of consumer research (especially in relation to health and science/technology). Otherwise sociology is in danger of becoming an uncritical tool, manipulated by managers and policy-makers who solicit public opinion in order to manage public disquiet.

Notes

1 The new genetics refers to a body of knowledge and techniques arising out of the discovery of recombinant DNA in the 1970s. It principally involves research into the genetic components of a range of disease, illness and behaviour and its application in the clinic in the form of testing, screening and treatment.

2 This term is used by Thorne (1997), drawing on the work of Henwood and Pidgeon (1992).

3 This research, also conducted with Hugh Masters, was funded by the Health Education Board for Scotland 1995–6.

4 This research was funded by the Wester Hailes Health Project, 1992.

5 This research, also conducted with Amanda Amos, was funded under the ESRC Risk and Human Behaviour Research Programme, Grant No L211252003, 1994–7.

6 We would like to thank Brian Woods for this point.

Afterword

Putting this edited volume together has been a stimulating exercise. As editors we particularly enjoyed the opportunity to participate in intensive discussion with colleagues in diverse disciplines, with such a range of research interests and approaches. In classic focus group tradition, such discussion helped to clarify and develop our ideas; dialogue between participants was also integral to the evolution of the book as a whole.

We hope that this collection has helped readers to think positively and creatively about how they might use focus groups in the future. We have tried to include sufficient examples to convey a sense of the substantive process of focus group research as well as its theoretical potential. In the course of their chapters, the contributors have taken a fresh look at issues of access, recruitment, sampling, settings, running groups and collecting and analysing data. Rather than deal with these as mere technical issues, they have shown how such decisions are integral to shaping and interpreting research findings.

The analysis presented in this collection has identified pitfalls, but has also proposed solutions; it suggests a need for caution but also invites further experimentation. The contributors have questioned some emerging orthodoxies and at the same time demonstrated the versatility of focus groups and the benefits to be reaped from critical engagement with this data collection technique. While highlighting challenges, they also draw attention to opportunities. Often the challenges and opportunities of focus group research are, in fact, two sides of the same coin. Thus a central challenge such as the complex, fluid and elusive nature of focus group data is also the source of one of the most exciting opportunities of this type of work.

Focus groups have recently acquired the dubious distinction of being 'flavour of the month'. In the richness of data they can collect and the wide range of topics they can address, focus groups are certainly an invaluable addition to the traditional trinity of questionnaires, observation and interviews. However, having been the neglected 'Cinderella' of social science for so long, it is important they do not now become fashionable accessories that are adopted in an unquestioning style. Contributors to this volume warn of the dangers of misuse, and argue for the responsible and thoughtful employment of this method. The notion that focus groups are simply a quick and cheap alternative has been dispelled and contributors have unpacked some naïve assumptions about their inherently 'emancipatory' or 'participatory' nature. We need to continually examine the ramifications of diverse focus group methods and remain vigilant to the risks of co-option. While focus groups, in some form at least, are now becoming an established part of the methodological tool kit, how they are adopted and adapted remains of crucial concern. Ultimately, whether focus groups are simply added to a shopping list of potential methods or whether they are employed in a more challenging way depends on the extent to which researchers address the sort of debates presented in this book. Focus groups can be invaluable in the exploratory phase of quantitative projects or can be used principally for in-depth follow-up of findings from large-scale studies. However, the possibilities are much further reaching and there remains a great deal of work to be done in exploring and pushing forward the boundaries of focus group research.

Finally, we would note that in order to explore the full potential of focus groups it is necessary to ask questions about the research enterprise itself. Such enquiry should include questions about the relationship between research participants and group facilitators and between funding bodies and research teams, but it should also include questions about relationships within research teams themselves. All the chapters presented in this volume are written with hands-on experience of focus groups work (written by the main focus group facilitator on their own, or in collaboration between the researcher who facilitated the groups and grant-holders/senior researchers). This is, we believe, central to the value of the contributors' observations. A fragmented and hierarchical division of labour is destructive to understanding the organic whole of focus groups. There are clear disadvantages to research projects in which a (usually female) facilitator entirely relinquishes the 'data-package' to a (usually male) senior researcher who proceeds to analyse the data without discussion with colleagues. Such an approach fundamentally undermines the value of this method and limits its future. We hope to see on-going focus group research which challenges hierarchies within the 'knowledge production' process – both between research 'subjects' and researchers and between research 'assistants' and, the often misnamed, 'principal investigator'. Interesting new work could also evolve out of imaginative experimentation with facilitator styles and group exercises as well as innovation in overall research design. We would be interested to see focus group work building on interdisciplinary collaborations, exploring the possibilities of longitudinal research and repeat 'panel' groups as well as the development of action research plans and feminist initiatives. In rounding up this book we feel that some such initiatives are well-established (even though perhaps they have been unrecognized or under-theorized until recently). Other work in this field has, however, only just begun. We look forward to on-going debate about, and explorations in, focus group research design, discussion techniques, analysis and representation.

Rosaline S. Barbour
University of Hull

Jenny Kitzinger
University of Glasgow

References

Agar, M. and MacDonald, J. (1995) 'Focus groups and ethnography', *Human Organization*, 54 (1): 78–86.

Ahmed, B. (1996) 'Reflexivity, cultural membership and power in the research situation: tensions and contradictions when considering the researcher's role', *The British Psychological Society Psychology of Women Section Newsletter*, 7: 35–40.

Ahmed, W.I.U (1993) 'Making black people sick: "race", ideology and health research', in W.I.U. Ahmed (ed.), *'Race' and Health in Contemporary Britain*. Buckingham: Open University Press.

Alderson, P. (1995) *Listening to Children: Children, Ethics and Social Research*. London: Barnardos.

Anderson, N. (1992) 'Work group innovation: a state of the art review', in D.M. Hosking and N. Anderson (eds), *Organizational Change and Innovation: Psychological Perspectives and Practices in Europe*. London: Routledge. pp. 149–60.

Antaki, C. (1994) *Explaining and Arguing: The Social Organization of Accounts*. London: Sage.

ASA (1987) *Ethical Guidelines for Good Practice*. London: Association of Social Anthropologists.

Asbury, J.E. (1995) 'Overview of focus group research', *Qualitative Health Research*, 5 (4): 414–20.

Atkinson, J.M. and Heritage, J. (eds) (1984) *Structures of Social Action: Studies in Conversation Analysis*. Cambridge: Cambridge University Press.

Austin, J.L. (1962) *How to do Things with Words*. Reconstructed by J.G. Warnock. Cambridge, MA: Harvard University Press.

Bailey, M. and Brake, R. (eds) (1975) *Radical Social Work*. London: Edward Arnold.

Baker, R., Panter-Brick, C. et al. (1996) 'Methods used in research with children in Nepal', *Childhood*, 3 (2): 171–93. (Special issue 'Children out of Place', M. Connolly and J. Ennew [eds].)

Barbour, R.S. (1995) 'Using focus groups in general practice research', *Family Practice*, 12 (3): 328–34.

Barbour, R.S. (in press) 'The case for combining qualitative and quantitative approaches in health services research', *Journal of Health Services Research and Policy*.

Basch, C.E. (1987) 'Focus group interview: an under-utilised research technique for improving theory and practice in health education', *Health Education Quarterly*, 14: 411–48.

Beach, W.A. (1990) 'Language as and in technology: facilitating topic organization in a Videotex focus group meeting', in M.J. Medhurst, A. Gonzalez and T.R. Peterson (eds), *Communication and the Culture of Technology*. Pullman: Washington State University Press. pp. 197–219.

Beck, U. (1992) *Risk Society: Towards a New Modernity*. London: Sage.

Berger, P.L. and Luckmann, T. (1966) *The Social Construction of Reality: A Treatise in the Sociology of Knowledge*. New York: Doubleday.

Bers, T.H. (1987) 'Exploring institutional images through focus group interviews', in R.S. Lay and J.J. Endo (eds), *Designing and Using Market Research*. San Francisco, CA: Jossey-Bass. pp. 19–29.

Bertrand, J.T., Brown, J.E. and Ward, V.M. (1992) 'Techniques for analyzing focus group data', *Evaluation Review*, 16 (2): 198–209.

Bhopal, R., Phillmore, P. and Kohli, H. (1991) 'Inappropriate use of the term Asian: an obstacle to ethnicity and health research', *Journal of Public Health Medicine*, 13: 244–6.

Billig, M. (1987) *Arguing and Thinking: A Rhetorical Approach to Social Psychology*. Cambridge: Cambridge University Press.

Billig, M. (1991) *Ideology and Opinions*. London: Sage.

Billig, M. (1992) *Talking of the Royal Family*. London: Routledge.

Bloor, M. (1978) 'On the analysis of observational data: a discussion of the worth and uses of inductive techniques and respondent validation', *Sociology*, 12: 545–52.

Boden, D. and Zimmerman, D. (eds) (1991) *Talk and Social Structure*. Cambridge: Polity.

Bohan, J.S. (1992) 'Prologue: re-viewing psychology, re-placing women – an end searching for a means', in J.S. Bohan (ed.), *Seldom Seen, Rarely Heard: Women's Place in Psychology*. Boulder, CO: Westview Press. pp. 9–53.

Bowler, I.M.W. (1993) 'Stereotypes of women of Asian descent in midwifery: some evidence', *Midwifery*, 9 (1): 7–16.

Bowman, M. (1987) 'The Nuclear State of West Cumbria', in *A World's Waste: Cumbria, Sellafield and Reprocessing*. A Brewery Arts Centre Touring Exhibition.

Bracht, N. (1991) 'Citizen participation in community health: principles for effective partnership', in B. Badura and I. Kickbusch (eds), *Health Promotion Research: Towards a New Social Epidemiology*. Copenhagen: WHO. pp. 477–96.

Broom, G.M. and Dozier, D.M. (1990) *Using Research in Public Relations: Application to Program Management*. Englewood Cliffs, NJ: Prentice Hall.

Buckingham, D. (1993) 'What are words worth?', in D. Buckingham (ed.), *Children Talking Television: The Making of Television Literacy*. London: Falmer.

Burgess, J., Limb, M. and Harrison, C.M. (1988a) 'Exploring environmental values through the medium of small groups: 1: theory and practice', *Environment and Planning A*, 20: 309–26.

Burgess, J., Limb, M. and Harrison, C.M. (1988b) 'Exploring environmental values through the medium of small groups: 2. illustrations of a group at work', *Environment and Planning A*, 20: 457–76.

Burningham, K. (1995) 'Attitudes, accounts, and impact assessment', *The Sociological Review*, 43: 100–22.

Burton, S., Kitzinger, J., Kelly, L. and Regan, L. (1997) 'Questionnaire survey of 2000+ young people', report prepared for the Zero Tolerance Trust, Edinburgh.

Cain, M. and Finch, J. (1981) 'Towards a rehabilitation of data', in P. Abrams, R. Deen, J. Finch and P. Rock (eds), *Practice and Progress in British Sociology 1950–1980*. London: Allen and Unwin.

Campbell, R. and Schram, P.J. (1995) 'Feminist research methods: a content analysis of psychology and social science textbooks', *Psychology of Women Quarterly*, 19: 85–106.

Carey, M.A. (1994) 'The group effect in focus groups: planning, implementing and interpreting focus group research', in J.M. Morse (ed.), *Critical Issues in Qualitative Research Methods*. London: Sage. pp. 225–41.

Carey, M.A. (ed.) (1995) Special Issue of *Qualitative Health Research* on 'Issues and Applications of Focus Groups', 5 (4).

Carey, M.A. and Smith, M.W. (1994) 'Capturing the group effect in focus groups: a special concern in analysis', *Qualitative Health Research*, 4 (1): 123–7.

Cassell, C. and Symon, G. (1994) 'Qualitative research in work contexts', in C.

Cassell and G. Symon (eds), *Qualitative Methods in Organizational Research*. London: Sage. pp. 1–13.

Chambers, R. (1994) 'The origins and practice of participatory rural appraisal', *World Development*, 22 (7): 953–69.

Chapman, T. and Johnson, A. (1995) *Growing Old and Needing Care: A Health and Social Care Needs Audit*. London: Avebury.

Chiu, L.F. (ed.) (1993a) Communicating breast screening messages to minority women, Conference proceeding. Leeds Health Promotion Service.

Chiu, L.F., Knight, D. and Williams, S. (1993b) Breast screening training pack for minority women. Leeds Health Promotion Service.

Christensen, P. Haudrup (1993) 'The social construction of help among Danish school children', *Sociology of Health and Illness*, 15: 488–502.

Cicourel, A. (1964) *Method and Measurement in Sociology*. New York: Free Press.

Coffey, A. and Atkinson P. (1996) *Making Sense of Qualitative Data: Complementary Research Strategies*. London: Sage.

College of Health (1994) 'Focus groups', internal report. Hull: College of Health.

Cook, G. (1995) 'Theoretical issues: transcribing the untranscribable', in G. Leech, G. Myers and J. Thomas (eds), *Spoken English on Computer*. Harlow: Longman. pp. 35–53.

Cooper, P., Diamond, I. and High, S. (1993) 'Choosing and using contraceptives: integrating qualitative and quantitative methods in family planning', *Journal of the Market Research Society*, 35 (4): 325–39.

Coreil, J. (1995) 'Group interview methods in community health research', *Medical Anthropology*, 16: 193–210.

Cornwall, A. (1992) 'Tools for our trade? Rapid or participatory rural appraisal and anthropology', *Journal of the British Association for Social Anthropology in Policy and Practice*, 13: 12–14.

Cornwall, A. (1996) 'Towards participatory practice: participatory rural appraisal (PRA) and the participatory process', in K. De Koning and M. Mant (eds), *Participatory Research in Health: Issues and Experiences*. London: Zed Books.

Cotterill, P. (1992) 'Interviewing women: issues of friendship, vulnerability, and power', *Women's Studies International Forum*, 15 (5/6): 593–606.

Crabtree, B.F., Yanoshik, M.K., Miller, M.L. and O'Connor, P.J. (1993) 'Selecting individual or group interviews', in D.L. Morgan (ed.), *Successful Focus Groups: Advancing the State of the Art*. Newbury, CA: Sage. pp. 137–49.

Cressey, D.R. (1953) *Other Peoples' Money: A Study of the Social Psychology of Embezzlement*. New York: Free Press.

Curtice, L., Milburn, K. and Cunningham-Burley, S. (1994) 'Living a healthy life in Wester Hailes', final report. University of Edinburgh.

Dahlgren, P. (1988) 'What's the meaning of this? Viewers' plural sense-making of TV news', *Media, Culture & Society*, 10: 285–301.

Das, R. (1995) 'South Asian lesbians' perceptions of health and health care', paper presented at the British Sociological Association Medical Sociology Conference, September, York, UK.

Das, R. and Farquhar, C. (1996) 'Lesbians' conceptualisations of health and well-being', paper presented at Teaching to Promote Women's Health International Multidisciplinary Conference, June, Toronto, Canada.

Davison, A., Barns, I. and Schibeci, R. (1997) 'Problematic publics: a critical review of surveys of public attitudes to biotechnology', *Science, Technology and Human Values*, 22 (3): 317–48.

de Koning, K. and Martin, M. (1996) *Participatory Research in Health: Issues and Experiences*. London: Zed Books.

Devault, M.L. (1990) 'Talking and listening from women's standpoint: feminist strategies for interviewing and analysis', *Social Problems*, 37 (1): 96–116.

Dey, I. (1993) *Qualitative Data Analysis: A User-Friendly Guide for Social Scientists*. London: Routledge.

Dingwall, R. and Strong, P.M. (1997) 'The interactional study of organizations: a critique and reformulation', in G. Miller and R. Dingwall (eds), *Context and Method in Qualitative Research*. London: Sage. pp. 139–54.

Doyle, Y. (1991) 'A survey of the cervical screening service in a London district, including reasons for non-attendance, ethnic responses and views on the quality of service', *Social Science and Medicine*, 32: 953–7.

Drew, P. and Heritage, J. (eds) (1993) *Talk at Work*. Cambridge: Cambridge University Press.

Eade, P. and Williams, S. (1995) *The Oxfam Handbook of Development and Relief*. London: Oxfam Publications.

Edwards, M. (1996) 'Institutionalising children's participation in development', *PLA Notes*, 25: 47–51.

Edwards, R. (1990) 'Connecting method and epistemology: a white woman interviewing black women', *Women's Studies International Forum*, 13: 477–90.

Edwards, R. (1996) 'White woman researcher – Black women subjects', in S. Wilkinson and C. Kitzinger (eds), *Representing the Other: A Feminism & Psychology Reader*. London: Sage.

Eldridge, J., Kitzinger, J. and Williams, K. (1997) *Mass Media and Power in Modern Britain*. Oxford: Oxford University Press.

Ennew, J. (1994) *Street and Working Children*. London: Save the Children.

Ernecq, J.M. (1992) 'Planned and unplanned organizational change – consequences and implications', in D.M. Hosking and N. Anderson (eds), *Organizational Change and Innovation: Psychological Perspectives and Practices in Europe*. London: Routledge. pp. 276–87.

Espin, O.M. (1995) '"Race", racism and sexuality in the life narratives of immigrant women', *Feminism & Psychology*, 5 (2): 223–38.

Fals-Borda, O. and Rahman, M.A. (eds) (1991) *Action and Knowledge: Breaking the Monopoly with Participatory Action Research*. New York: Intermediate Technology/Apex.

Fardy, H.J. and Jeffs, D. (1994) 'Focus groups: a method for developing consensus guidelines in general practice', *Family Practice*, 11 (3): 325–9.

Farley, L. (1978) *Sexual Shakedown: The Sexual Harassment of Women on the Job*. New York: Warner Books.

Farquhar, C. (1996) 'Lesbian perspectives on HIV and sexual health', paper presented at Teaching to Promote Women's Health International Multidisciplinary Conference, June, Toronto, Canada.

Farquhar, C. and Das, R. (1995) 'Reflections on the use of focus groups in researching lesbian health care', paper presented at the British Sociological Association Medical Sociology Conference, September, York, UK.

Ferguson, E. (1996) 'Sceptics corner: focus groups distort reality', *Observer*, 8 September: 46.

Finch, J. (1984) 'It's great to have someone to talk to: the ethics and politics of interviewing women', in C. Bell and H. Roberts (eds), *Social Researching: Politics, Problems and Practice*. London: Routledge and Kegan Paul. pp. 70–87.

Fine, M. (1992) *Disruptive Voices: The Possibilities of Feminist Research*. Ann Arbor: The University of Michigan Press.

Fine, M. and Addelston, J. (1996) 'Containing questions of gender and power: the discursive limits of "sameness" and "difference"', in S. Wilkinson (ed.), *Feminist Social Psychologies: International Perspectives*. Buckingham and Bristol, PA: Open University Press. pp. 66–86.

Fine, M. and Gordon, S.M. (1989) 'Feminist transformations of/despite psychology', in M. Crawford and M. Gentry (eds), *Gender and Thought: Psychological Perspectives*. New York, NY: Springer-Verlag. pp. 146–74.

Fish, S. (1983) 'Short people got no reason to live: reading irony', *Daedalus*, 112 (1): 175–91.

Flexner, W.A., McLaughlin, C.P. and Littlefield, J.E. (1977) 'Discovering what the consumer really wants', *Health Care Management Review*, 1: 43–9.

Fonow, M.M. and Cook, J.A. (eds) (1991) *Beyond Methodology: Feminist Scholarship as Lived Research*. Bloomington: Indiana University Press.

Fontana, A. and Frey, J.H. (1994) 'Interviewing: the art of science', in N.K. Denzin and Y.S. Lincoln (eds), *Handbook of Qualitative Research*. Thousand Oaks, CA: Sage. pp. 361–76.

Foucault, M. (1990) *The History of Sexuality Volume 1: An Introduction*. New York: Vintage Books.

Francescato, D. and Tancredi, M. (1992) 'Methodologies of organizational change: the need for an integrated approach', in D.M. Hosking and N. Anderson (eds), *Organizational Change and Innovation: Psychological Perspectives and Practices in Europe*. London: Routledge. pp. 262–78.

Frazer, E. (1988) 'Teenage girls talking about class', *Sociology*, 22 (3): 343–58.

Freimuth, V.S. and Greenberg, R. (1986) 'Pretesting television advertisements for family planning products in developing countries: a case study', *Health Education Research*, 1 (1): 37–45.

Freire, P. (1970) *Pedagogy of the Oppressed*. New York: Continuum.

Freire, P. (1972) *Pedagogy of the Oppressed*. Harmondsworth: Penguin.

Freire, P. (1973) *Education for Critical Consciousness*. New York: Seabury Press.

Freire, P. (1985) *The Politics of Education, Culture Power and Liberation*. (Trans. Donaldo Macedo). Bergin & Garvey.

French, J. and Adams, L. (1986) 'From analysis to synthesis: theories of health education', *Health Education Journal*, 45: 71–4.

Frey, J.H. and Fontana, A. (1993) 'The group interview in social research', in D.L. Morgan (ed.), *Successful Focus Groups: Advancing the State of the Art*, Newbury Park, CA: Sage. pp. 20–34.

Fuller, T.D., Edwards, J.N., Vorakitphokatorn, S. and Sermsri, S. (1993) 'Using focus groups to adapt survey instruments to new populations: experience from a developing country', in D.L. Morgan (ed.), *Successful Focus Groups: Advancing the State of the Art*. Newbury Park, CA: Sage. pp. 89–104.

Geertz, C. (1983) *Local Knowledge*. New York: Basic Books.

Geist, P. (1994) 'Negotiating cultural understanding in health care communication', in L.A. Samovar and R.E. Porter (eds), *Intercultural Communication: A Reader*. 7th edn. California: Wadsworth. pp. 311–21.

Geraghty, G. (1980) 'Social research in Asia using focus group discussions: a case study', *Media Asia*, 7: 205–11.

Gergen, K. (1987) 'Toward self as relationship', in K. Yardley and T. Honess (eds), *Self and Identity: Psychosocial Perspectives*. Chichester: Wiley. pp. 52–67.

Giddens, A. (1990) *The Consequences of Modernity*. Cambridge: Polity Press.

Giddens, A. (1991) *Modernity and Self-Identity: Self and Society in the Late Modern Age*. Cambridge: Polity Press.

Gieryn, T. (1983) 'Boundary–work and the demarcation of science from non-science: strains and interests in professional ideologies of scientists', *American Sociological Review*, 48: 781–95.

Gilbert, N. and Mulkay, M. (1984) *Opening Pandora's Box: An Analysis of Scientists' Discourse*. Cambridge: Cambridge University Press.

Goffman, E. (1981) *Forms of Talk*. Oxford: Basil Blackwell.

Goffman, E. (1983) 'Felicity's condition', *American Journal of Sociology*, 83: 1–53.

Goldman, A.E. (1962) 'The group depth interview', *Journal of Marketing*, 26: 61–8.

Goldman, A.E. and McDonald, S.S. (1987) *The Group Depth Interview: Principles and Practice*. Englewood Cliffs, NJ: Prentice-Hall.

Gorna, R. (1996) *Vamps, Virgins and Victims: How can Women Fight AIDS?* Cassell: London.

Grace, V.M. (1991) 'The marketing of empowerment and the construction of the health consumer: a critique of health promotion', *International Journal of Health Services*, 21 (2): 329–42.

Graham, H. (1984) 'Surveying through stories', in C. Bell and H. Roberts (eds), *Social Researching, Politics, Problems, Practice*. London: Routledge and Kegan Paul. pp. 104–24.

Gray, B., Bougon, G. and Donellon, A. (1985) 'Organizations as constructions and destructions of meaning', *Journal of Management*, 11 (2): 83–98.

Greatbatch, D. (1988) 'A turn-taking system for British news interviews', *Language in Society*, 17: 401–30.

Green, G., Barbour, R.S., Barnard, M. and Kitzinger, J. (1993) 'Who wears the trousers? Sexual harassment in research settings', *Women's Studies International Forum*, 16 (6): 627–37.

Green, J. (1995) 'Accidents and the risk society', in R. Bunton, S. Nettleton and R. Burrows (eds), *The Sociology of Health Promotion*. London: Routledge. pp. 116–32.

Green, J. (1997) 'Risk and the construction of social identity: children's talk about accidents', *Sociology of Health and Illness*, 19: 14–21.

Green, J. and Hart, L. (1996) *Children's Views of Accident Risks: An Exploratory Study*. London: South Bank University.

Green, J. and Hart, L. (1998) 'Children's views of accient risk and prevention: a qualitative study', *Injury Prevention*, 4: 457–79.

Greenbaum, T. (1998) *The Handbook for Focus Group Research*, 2nd edn. London: Sage.

Griffin, C. (1985) 'Qualitative methods and cultural analysis: young women and the transition from school to un/employment', in R. Burgess (ed.), *Field Methods in the Study of Education*. London: Falmer Press.

Griffin, C. (1986) 'Qualitative methods and female experience: young women from school to the job market', in S. Wilkinson (ed.), *Feminist Social Psychology: Developing Theory and Practice*. Milton Keynes: Open University Press. pp. 173–91.

Guba, E.G. and Lincoln, Y.S. (1994) 'Competing paradigms in qualitative research', in N.K. Denzin and Y.S. Lincoln (eds), *Handbook of Qualitative Research*. Thousand Oaks, CA: Sage. pp. 105–17.

Hammersley, M. and Atkinson, P. (1995) *Ethnography: Principles in Practice*, 2nd edn. London: Routledge.

Hammersley, M. and Woods, P. (1984) *Life in School*. Milton Keynes: Open University Press.

Harding, S. (1986) *The Science Question in Feminism*. Milton Keynes: Open University Press.

Hare-Mustin, R.T. and Marecek, J. (eds) (1990) *Making a Difference: Psychology and the Construction of Gender*. New Haven, CT: Yale University Press.

Hargreaves, D. (1967) *Social Relations in a Secondary School*. London: Routledge and Kegan Paul.

Harrison, K. and Barlow, J. (1995) 'Focused group discussion: a "quality" method for health research?', *Health Psychology Update*, 20: 11–13.

Hart, E. and Bond, M. (1995) *Action Research for Health and Social Care: A Guide to Practice*. Buckingham: Open University Press.

Henning, J., Williams, J. and Haque, B.N. (1996) 'Exploring the health needs of Bangladeshi women: a case study in using qualitative research methods', *Health Education Journal*, 55: 11–23.

Henwood, K.L. and Pidgeon, N.F. (1992) 'Qualitative research and psychological theorizing', *British Journal of Psychiatry*, 83: 97–111.

Henwood, K. and Pidgeon, N. (1995) 'Remaking the link: qualitative research and feminist standpoint theory', *Feminism & Psychology*, 5 (1): 7–30.

Herbert, C.M.H. (1989) *Talking of Silence: The Sexual Harassment of Schoolgirls*. London: The Falmer Press.

Hinton, R (1995) 'Trades in different worlds: listening to refugee voices', *PLA Notes*, 24: 21–6.

Hinton, R. (1996) 'Using participatory methods for gender and health research', *Journal for Applied Anthropology in Policy and Practice. Anthropology and Refugees*, 3 (1): 24–34.

Hoare, T., Thomas, C., Biggs, A., Booth, M., Bradley, S. and Friedman, E. (1994) 'Can the uptake of breast screening be increased? A randomised controlled trial of a linkworker intervention', *Journal of Public Health Medicine*, 16: 179–85.

Holbrook, B. and Jackson, P. (1996) 'Shopping around: focus group research in North London', *Area*, 28 (2): 136–42.

Holland, J. and Ramazanoglu, C. (1994) 'Coming to conclusions: power and interpretation in researching young women's sexuality', in M. Maynard and J. Purvis (eds), *Researching Women's Lives from a Feminist Perspective*. London: Taylor and Francis. pp. 125–48.

Holland, J., Ramazanoglu, C., Sharpe, S. and Thomson, R. (1991) *Pressure, Resistance, Empowerment: Young Women and the Negotiation of Safer Sex*, WRAP Paper 6. London: Tufnell Press.

Holland, J., Ramazanoglu, C., Scott, S,. Sharpe, S. and Thomson, R. (1994) 'Methodological issues in researching young women's sexuality', in M. Boulton (ed.), *Challenge and Innovation: Methodological Advances in Social Research on HIV/AIDS*. London: Taylor and Francis.

Hoppe, M.J., Wells, E.A, Morrison, D.M., Gillmore, M.R. and Wilsdon, A. (1995) 'Using focus groups to discuss sensitive topics with children', *Evaluation Review*, 19 (1): 102–14.

Hughes D. and Dumont, K. (1993) 'Using focus groups to facilitate culturally anchored research', *American Journal of Community Psychology*, 21 (6): 775–806.

ICM (1991a) *Attitudes towards Nirex proposals: Sellafield, Cumbrian Residents*, prepared for Cumbria County Council, September, London: ICM Research.

ICM (1991b) *Environment Trends Monitor*. London: ICM Research.

ICM (1992) *Attitudes towards Nirex proposals: Sellafield, Cumbrian Residents*, prepared for Cumbria County Council, September. London: ICM Research.

ICM (1994a) *Nirex Opinion Poll Wave 3*, prepared for Cumbria County Council November. London: ICM Research.

ICM (1994b) *Report on Research to Monitor Public Attitudes to Proposed Nuclear Waste Facility at Sellafield*, prepared for Cumbria County Council. London: ICM Research.

Irwin, A. and Wynne, B. (eds) (1996) *Misunderstanding Science? The Public Reconstruction of Science and Technology*. Cambridge: Cambridge University Press.

James, A. (1995) 'Children and social competence', plenary paper presented at Children and Social Competence Conference, University of Surrey, July.

James, T. and Platzer, H. (1996) 'Ethical considerations in qualitative research with vulnerable groups: exploring lesbians' and gay men's experiences of health care', paper presented at the Third International Interdisciplinary Qualitative Health Research Conference, Bournemouth.

Jayaratne, T.E. and Stewart, A.J. (1991) 'Quantitative and qualitative methods in the social sciences: current feminist issues and practical strategies', in M.M. Fonow and J.A. Cook (eds), *Beyond Methodology: Feminist Scholarship as Lived Research*. Bloomington: Indiana University Press. pp. 85–106.

Jegede, D. (1996) 'Culture bound terminology in the interpretation of health and illness in the Yoruba community in Nigeria', *Journal of Contemporary Health*, 4, Summer: 74–5.

Jenkins, S. (1997) 'The curse of Chequers', *The Times*, 29 January. p. 46.

Johnson A. (1996) '"It's good to talk": the focus group and the sociological imagination', *The Sociological Review*, 44 (3): 517–38.

Jordan, J.V., Kaplan, A.G., Miller, J.B., Stiver, I.P. and Surrey, J.L. (1991) *Women's Growth in Connection: Writings from the Stone Center.* New York: Guilford Press.

Kalnins, I. et al. (1992) 'Children, empowerment and health promotion: some new directions in research and practice', *Health Promotion International*, 7 (1): 53—9.

Kefyalew, F. (1996) 'Child participation in research', *Childhood*, 3 (2): 203–13.

Kelly, A. (1991) 'The enterprise culture and the welfare state: restructuring the management of the health and personal social services', in R. Burrows (ed.), *Deciphering the Enterprise Culture: Entrepreneurship, Petty Capitalism and the Restructuring of Britain.* London: Routledge. pp. 126–48.

Kelly, L. (1988) *Surviving Sexual Violence.* Cambridge: Polity Press.

Kernohan, E.E.M. (1996) 'Evaluation of a pilot study for breast and cervical cancer screening with Bradford's minority ethnic women: a community development approach', *British Journal of Cancer*, 74: Supplement 24, S42–66.

Kerr, A., Cunningham-Burley, S., and Amos, A. (1997) 'The new genetics: professionals' discursive boundaries', *The Sociological Review*, 45 (2): 279–303.

Kerr, A., Cunningham-Burley, S. and Amos, A. (1998a) 'The new genetics and health: mobilising lay expertise', *Public Understanding of Science*, 7: 41–60.

Kerr, A., Cunningham-Burley, S. and Amos, A. (1998b) 'Drawing the line: an analysis of lay people's discussion about the new genetics', *Public Understanding of Science*, 7: 113–33.

Khan, M. and Manderson, L. (1992) 'Focus groups in tropical disease research', *Health Policy and Planning*, 7: 56–66.

Kitzinger, C. (1992) 'The individuated self concept: a critical analysis of social-constructionist writing on individualism', in G.M. Breakwell (ed.), *Social Psychology of Identity and the Self Concept.* London: Surrey University Press, in association with Academic Press. pp. 221–50.

Kitzinger, C. and Powell, D. (1995) 'Engendering infidelity: essentialist and social constructionist readings of a story completion task', *Feminism & Psychology*, 5 (3): 345–72.

Kitzinger, J. (1990) 'Audience understandings of AIDS media message: a discussion of methods', *Sociology of Health and Illness*, 12 (3): 319–35.

Kitzinger, J. (1993) 'Understanding AIDS: media messages and what people know about Acquired Immune Deficiency Syndrome', in J. Eldridge (ed.), *Getting the Message.* London: Routledge. pp. 271–304.

Kitzinger, J. (1994a) 'The methodology of focus groups: the importance of interaction between research participants', *Sociology of Health and Illness*, 16 (1): 103–21.

Kitzinger, J. (1994b) 'Focus groups: method or madness?', in M. Boulton (ed.), *Challenge and Innovation: Methodological Advances in Social Research on HIV/ AIDS.* London: Taylor & Francis. pp. 159–75.

Kitzinger, J. (1994c) 'Challenging sexual violence against girls: A public awareness approach to preventing sexual abuse', *Child Abuse Review*, 3: 246–8.

Kitzinger, J. (1995) 'Introducing focus groups', *British Medical Journal*, 311: 299–302.

Kitzinger, J. (in press, a) 'Media templates: patterns of association and the (re)construction of meaning over time', *Media, Culture and Society*.

Kitzinger, J. (in press, b) 'The media and the monitoring of paedophiles', in B. Franklin (ed.), *The Media and Social Policy.* London: Routledge.

Kitzinger, J. and Hunt, K. (1993) *Evaluation of Edinburgh Council's Zero Tolerance Campaign*.

Kitzinger, J. and Skidmore, P. (1995) 'Playing safe: media coverage of the prevention of child sexual abuse', *Child Abuse Review*, 4 (1): 47–56.

Klein, R. (1990) 'Looking after consumers in the new NHS', *British Medical Journal*, 300: 1351–2.

Knodel, J. (1993) 'The design and analysis of focus group studies: a practical approach', in D. Morgan (ed.), *Successful Focus Groups: Advancing the State of the Art*. Newbury Park: Sage. pp. 35–50.

Krimsky, S. and Golding, D. (eds) (1992) *Social Theories of Risk*. Westport, CT: Praeger.

Krueger, R.A. (1988) *Focus Groups: A Practical Guide for Applied Research*. Newbury Park, CA: Sage.

Krueger, R.A. (1993) 'Quality control in focus group research', in D.L. Morgan (ed.), *Successful Focus Groups: Advancing the State of the Art*. London: Sage. pp. 65–83.

Krueger, R.A. (1994) *Focus Groups: A Practical Guide for Applied Research*. Newbury Park, CA: Sage.

Krueger, R. (1995) 'The future of focus groups', *Qualitative Health Research*, 5 (4): 525–30.

Kuzel, A.J. (1992) 'Sampling in qualitative inquiry', in B.F. Crabtree and W.L. Miller (eds), *Doing Qualititative Research*. Newbury Park, CA: Sage. pp. 31–44.

Kvale, S. (1996) *Interviews: An Introduction to Qualitative Research Interviewing*. Thousand Oaks, CA: Sage.

Lago, C. and Thompson, J. (1996) *Race, Culture and Counselling*. Buckingham: Open University Press.

Lampon, D. (1995) 'Lesbians and safer sex practices', *Feminism & Psychology*, 5 (2): 170–6.

Lee, R.M. (1993) *Doing Research on Sensitive Topics*. London: Sage.

Lengua, L.J., Roosa, M.W., Schupakneuberg, E., Michaels, M.L., Berg, C.N. and Weschler, L.F. (1992) 'Using focus groups to guide the development of a parenting program for difficult-to-reach, high-risk families', *Family Relations*, 41: 163–8.

Lindesmith, A.L. (1947) *Opiate Addiction*. Bloomington, IN: Principia Press.

Lundberg, C.C. (1990) 'Surfacing organizational culture', *Journal of Managerial Psychology*, 5 (4): 19–36.

Lunt, P. and Livingstone, S. (1996) 'Focus groups in communication and media research', *Journal of Communication*, 42: 78–87.

Lykes, M.B. (1985) 'Gender and individualistic versus collectivist biases for notions about the self', *Journal of Personality*, 53: 356–83.

Lyon E.S. (1995) 'Dilemmas of power in post-graduate practice: a comment on research training', *Sociology*, 29 (3): 531–40.

McAvoy, B.R. and Raza, R. (1988) 'Asian women (1) Contraceptive knowledge, attitudes and usage, (2) Contraceptive services and cervical cytology', *Health Trends*, 20: 11–17.

McAvoy, B.R. and Raza, R. (1991) 'Can health education increase uptake of cervical smear testing among Asian women?', *British Medical Journal*, 302: 833–6.

McKeganey, N. and Bloor, M. (1991) 'Spotting the invisible male: the influence of male gender on fieldwork relations', *British Journal of Sociology*, 42: 195–210.

MacGill, S. (1987) *Sellafield's Cancer-Link Controversy: The Politics of Anxiety*. London: Pion.

Macnaghten, P. (1995) 'Public attitudes to countryside leisure: a case study of ambivalences', *Journal of Rural Studies*, 11: 135–47.

Macnaghten, P. and Urry, J. (1998) *Contested Natures*. Newbury Park, CA: Sage.

Macnaghten, P., Grove-White, R., Jacobs, M. and Wynne B. (1995) *Public*

Perceptions and Sustainability: Indicators, Institutions, Participation. Preston: Lancashire County Council.

Macpherson, P. and Fine, M. (1995) 'Hungry for an us: adolescent girls and adult women negotiating territories of race, gender, class and difference', *Feminism & Psychology*, 5 (2): 181–200.

Mariampolski, H. (1989) 'Focus groups on sensitive topics: how to get subjects to open up and feel good about telling the truth', *Applied Marketing Research*, 29 (1): 6–11.

Marshall, A. (1994) 'A study of the social construction of black female sexuality', in M. Maynard and J. Purvis (eds), *Researching Women's Lives from a Feminist Perspective*. London: Taylor and Francis.

Marshall, J. (1986) 'Exploring the experiences of women managers: towards rigour in qualitative research', in S. Wilkinson (ed.), *Feminist Social Psychology: Developing Theory and Practice*. Milton Keynes: Open University Press. pp. 193–209.

Martin, J.L. and Dean, L. (1993) 'Developing a community sample of gay men for an epidemiological study of AIDS', in C.M. Renzetti and R.M. Lee (eds), *Researching Sensitive Topics*. London: Sage.

Mason-John, V. (ed.) (1995) *Talking Black: Lesbians of African and Asian Descent Speak Out*. London: Cassell.

Mayall, B. (1993) 'Keeping healthy at home and school: "It's my body, so it's my job"', *Sociology of Health and Illness*, 15: 464–87.

Maynard, M. and Purvis, J. (eds) (1994) *Researching Women's Lives from a Feminist Perspective*. London: Taylor and Francis.

Mays, V.M., Cochran, S.D., Bellinger, G., Smith, R.G., Henley, N., Daniels, M., Tibbits, T., Victorianne, G.D., Osei, O.K. and Birt, D.K. (1992) 'The language of black gay men's sexual behavior: Implications for AIDS risk reduction', *The Journal of Sex Research*, 29 (3): 425–34.

Mechanic, D. (1962) 'Sources of power of lower participants in complex organizations', *Administrative Science Quarterly*, 7: 349–64.

Michell, L. (1997a) 'Pressure groups: young people's accounts of peer pressure to smoke', *Social Sciences in Health*, 3 (1): 3–17.

Michell, L. (1997b) 'Loud, sad or bad: young people's perceptions of their social worlds', *Health Education Research, Theory and Practice*, 12: 1–14.

Michell, L. and Amos, A. (1997) 'Girls, pecking order and smoking', *Social Science and Medicine*, 44 (12): 1861–9.

Michell, L. and West, P. (1996) 'Peer pressure to smoke: the meaning depends on the methods', *Health Education Research, Theory and Practice*, 11 (1): 39–49.

Mies, M. (1983) 'Towards a methodology for feminist research', in G. Bowles and R.D. Klein (eds), *Theories of Women's Studies*. London: Routledge & Kegan Paul. pp. 117–39.

Miller, C. with Treitel, C. (1991). *Feminist Research Methods: An Annotated Bibliography*. New York: Greenwood.

Miller, D., Kitzinger, J., Williams, K. and Beharrell, P. (1998) *The Circuit of Mass Communication*. London: Sage.

Morgan, D.L. (1988) *Focus Groups as Qualitative Research*. London: Sage.

Morgan, D.L. (ed.) (1993) *Successful Focus Groups: Advancing the State of the Art*. Newbury Park, CA: Sage.

Morgan, D.L. and Krueger, R.A. (1993) 'When to use focus groups and why', in D.L. Morgan (ed.), *Successful Focus Groups: Advancing the State of the Art*. London: Sage. pp. 1–19.

Morgan, D.L. and Krueger, R.A. (1997) *Focus Group Kit*, Vols 1–6. London: Sage.

Morgan, D.L. and Spanish, M. (1984) 'Focus groups: a new tool for qualitative research', *Qualitative Sociology*, 7 (3): 253–70.

Morrow, V. and Richards, M. (1996) 'The ethics of social research with children: an overview', *Children and Society*, 10: 90–105.

Mueke, D.C. (1970) *Irony*. London: Methuen.

Mulkay, M. and Gilbert, G.N. (1984) *Opening Pandora's Box*. Cambridge: Cambridge University Press.

Murphy, B., Cockburn, J. and Murphy, M. (1992) 'Focus groups in health research', *Health Promotion Journal of Australia*, 2 (2): 37–40.

Murray, S.A., Tapson, J., Turnbull, L., McCallum, J. and Little, A. (1994) 'Listening to local voices: adapting rapid appraisal to assess health and social needs in general practice', *British Medical Journal*, 308: 698–700.

Myers, G. (1998) 'Displaying opinions: disagreement and topic shifts in focus groups', *Language in Society*, 27 (1): 85–111.

Myers, G., and Macnaghten, P. (1998) 'Rhetorics of environmental sustainability: commonplace and places', *Environment and Planning A*, 30: 333–53.

Naish, J., Brown, J. and Denton, B. (1994) 'Intercultural consultations: investigation of factors that deter non-English speaking women from attending their general practitioners for cervical screening', *British Medical Journal*, 309: 1126–8.

National Association of Health Authorities (1988) *Action Not Words: A Strategy to Improve Health Services for Black and Minority Ethnic Groups*. Birmingham: NAHAT.

Nelson, N. and Wright, S. (1996) 'Participatory research and participant observation: two incompatible approaches', in N. Nelson and S. Wright (eds), *Power and Participatory Development: Theory and Practice*. London: Intermediate Technology Publications.

Nielsen, J.M. (1990) *Feminist Research Methods: Exemplary Readings in the Social Sciences*. Boulder, CO: Westview Press.

Norris, J., Nurius, P.S. and Dimeff, L.A. (1996) 'Through her eyes: factors affecting women's perception of and resistance to acquaintance sexual aggression threat', *Psychology of Women Quarterly*, 20 (1): 123–45.

North East Market Surveys (1995) *Socio-Economic Impact Study of the Nuclear Industry Among Residents* (on behalf of Copeland Borough Council, May). Cleveland: North East Market Surveys.

Oakley, A. (1981) 'Interviewing women: a contradiction in terms', in H. Roberts (ed.), *Doing Feminist Research*. London: Routledge and Kegan Paul. pp. 30–61.

O'Brien, K. (1993) 'Using focus groups to develop health surveys: an example from research on social relationships and AIDS-preventive behavior', *Health Education Quarterly*, 20 (3): 361–72.

Office for Public Management (1996) 'Responding to diversity, a study of commissioning issues and good practice in purchasing minority ethnic health'. London.

Olesen, V. (1994) 'Feminisms and models of qualitative research', in N.K. Denzin and Y.S. Lincoln (eds), *Handbook of Qualitative Research*. Thousand Oaks, CA: Sage. pp. 158–74.

Orr, J. (1992) 'Working with women's health', in P. Abbott and R. Sapsford (eds), *Research into Practice: A Reader for Nurses and the Caring Professions*. Buckingham: Open University Press. pp. 23–38.

Oxfam (1996) 'Refugee empowerment: a tool for participation'. (video). Oxford: Oxfam/Small World.

Padilla, R.V. (1993) 'Using dialogical research methods in group interviews', in D.L. Morgan (ed.), *Successful Focus Groups: Advancing the State of the Art*. Newbury Park, CA: Sage. pp. 153–66.

Parlee, M.B. (1979) 'Review essay: psychology and women', *SIGNS*, 5 (1): 121–9.

Patton, M.Q. (1990) *Qualitative Evaluation and Research Method*. Newbury Park, CA: Sage.

Paul, S. (1987) 'Community participation in development projects: the World Bank experience'. Discussion Paper No. 6. New York: World Bank.

Pavis, S., Masters, H. and Cunningham-Burley, S. (1996) *Lay Concepts of Positive Mental Health and How it can be Maintained. Final Report.* Edinburgh: Health Education Board for Scotland.

Pearson, M. (1983) 'The politics of ethnic minority health studies', in T. Rathwell and D. Phillips (eds), *Health, Race and Ethnicity.* London: Croom Helm.

Peplau, L.A. and Conrad, E. (1989) 'Beyond nonsexist research: the perils of feminist methods in psychology', *Psychology of Women Quarterly,* 13: 379–400.

Pettigrew, A. (1990) 'Longitudinal field research on change: theory and practice', *Organizational Science,* 1 (3): 267–92.

Pfeffer, N. and Moynihan, C. (1996) 'Ethnicity and health beliefs with respect to cancer: a criticl review of methodology', *British Journal of Cancer,* 74: Supplement 4, S66–72.

Phoenix, A. (1990) 'Social research in the context of feminist psychology', in E. Burman (ed.), *Feminists and Psychological Practice.* London: Sage. pp. 89–103.

Phoenix, A. (1994) 'Practising feminist research: the intersection of gender and "race" in the research process', in M. Maynard and J. Purvis (eds), *Researching Women's Lives from a Feminist Perspective.* London: Taylor and Francis. pp. 53–68.

Plamping, D. and Delamothe, T. (1991) 'The citizen's charter and the NHS', *British Medical Journal,* 303: 203–4.

Platzer, H. and James, T. (1997) 'Methodological issues conducting sensitive research on lesbian and gay men's experience of nursing care', *Journal of Advanced Nursing,* 25 (3): 626–33.

Plaut, T., Landis, S. and Trevor, J. (1993) 'Focus groups and community mobilization: a case study from rural North Carolina', in D.L. Morgan (ed.), *Successful Focus Groups: Advancing the State of the Art.* Newbury Park, CA: Sage. pp. 202–21.

Plummer, K. (1995) *Telling Sexual Stories: Power, Change and Social Worlds.* London: Routledge.

Pollner, M. (1975) '"The very coinage of your brain": the anatomy of reality disjunctures', *Philosophy of the Social Sciences,* 5: 411–30.

Popay, J. and Williams, G. (eds) (1994) *Researching the People's Health.* London: Routledge.

Potter, J. (1996) *Representing Reality.* London: Sage.

Potter, J. and Wetherell, M. (1987) *Discourse and Social Psychology: Beyond Attitudes and Behaviour.* London: Sage.

Psathas, G. (1995) *Conversation Analysis: The Study of Talk-in-Interaction.* Thousand Oaks and London: Sage.

Reason, P. (1994) 'Three approaches to participative inquiry', in N.K. Denzin and Y.S. Lincoln (eds), *Handbook of Qualitative Research.* London: Sage. pp. 261–91.

Reinharz, S. (1983) 'Experiential analysis: a contribution to feminist research', in G. Bowles and R.D. Klein (eds), *Theories of Women's Studies.* London: Routledge and Kegan Paul. pp. 162–91.

Reinharz, S. (1992) *Feminist Methods in Social Research.* New York, NY: Oxford University Press.

Renzetti, C.M. and Lee, R.M. (1993) *Researching Sensitive Topics.* London: Sage.

Ribbens, J. (1989) 'Interviewing – an "unnatural situation"?', *Women's Studies International Forum,* 12 (6): 579–92.

Ritchie, J. and Spencer, L. (1994) 'Qualitative data analysis for applied policy research', in A. Bryman and R.G. Burgess (eds), *Analyzing Qualitative Data.* London: Routledge. pp. 173–94.

Roberts, H. (ed.) (1981) *Doing Feminist Research.* London: Routledge.

Robinson, W.S. (1951) 'The logical structure of analytic induction', *American Sociological Review*, 16: 812–18.

Rosen, M. (1991) 'Coming to terms with the field: understanding and doing organizational ethnography', *Journal of Management Studies*, 28 (1): 1–24.

Royal Society (1992) *Risk: Analysis, Perception and Management*. London: The Royal Society.

Rubin, H.J. and Rubin, I.S. (1995) *Qualitative Interviewing: The Art of Hearing Data*. Thousand Oaks, CA: Sage.

Rudat, K./MORI Health Research Unit (1994) 'Report on the health and lifestyles survey on black and minority ethnic groups in England'. Health Education Authority.

Scambler, P. (1996) 'The "project of modernity" and the parameters for a critical sociology', *Sociology*, 30 (3): 567–81.

ScanLink Report (1996) ScanLink in Newham Report on a year of raising community health awareness.

Schiffrin, D. (1987) *Discourse Markers*. Cambridge: Cambridge University Press.

Schlesinger, P., Dobash, R.E., Dobash, R.P. and Weaver, C.K. (1992) *Women Viewing Violence*. London: British Film Institute.

Schon, D.A. (1991) *The Reflective Practitioner: How Professionals Think in Action*. Aldershot: Avebury.

Schutz, A. (1970) *Reflections on the Problem of Relevance*. New Haven, CT: Yale University Press.

Schutz, A. and Luckmann, T. (1974) *The Structures of the Life World*. London: Heinemann.

Seals, B.F., Sowell, R.L., Demi, A.S., Moneyham, L., Cohen, L. and Guillory, J. (1995) 'Falling through the cracks: social service concerns of women infected with HIV', *Qualitative Health Research*, 5 (4): 496–515.

Searle, J.R. (1969) *Speech Acts*. New York: Cambridge University Press.

Secker, J., Wimbush, E., Watson, J. and Milburn, K. (1995) 'Qualitative methods in health promotion research: some criteria for quality', *Health Education Journal*, 54: 74–87.

Seidman, S. (1994) *Contested Knowledge. Social Theory in the Post Modern Era*. Oxford: Blackwell.

Segal, L. (1994) *Straight Sex: The Politics of Pleasure*. London: Virago.

Sheldon, T.A. and Parker, H. (1992) 'Race and ethnicity in health research', *Journal of Public Health Medicine*, 14: 104–10.

Siebold, C., Richards, L. and Simon, D. (1994) 'Feminist method and qualitative research about midlife', *Journal of Advanced Nursing*, 19: 394–402.

Silverman, D. (1993) *Interpreting Qualitative Data: Methods for Analysing Talk, Text and Interaction*. London: Sage.

Singleton, V. (1993) 'Science, Women and Ambivalence – An Actor Network Theory Analysis of the Cervical Smear Test'. PhD dissertation, Lancaster University.

Song, M. and Parker, D. (1995) 'Cultural identity: disclosing commonality and difference in in-depth interviewing', *Sociology*, 29 (2): 241–56.

Spencer, L., Faulkner, A. and Keegan, J. (1988) *Talking about Sex*. London: Social and Community Planning Research.

Standfield, J.H. (1994) 'Ethnic modelling in qualitative research', in N.K. Denzin and Y.S. Lincoln (eds), *Handbook of Qualitative Research*. London: Sage.

Stanley, L. (1995) *Sex Surveyed 1949–1994: From Mass Observation's "Little Kinsey" to the National Survey and Hite Reports*. Basingstoke: Taylor and Francis.

Stevens, P.E. (1993) 'Lesbian health care research: a review of the literature from 1970–1990', in P.N. Stern (ed.), *Lesbian Health: What Are the Issues?* London: Taylor and Francis. pp. 1–30.

Stewart, D.W. and Shamdasani, P.N. (1990) *Focus Groups: Theory and Practice.* London: Sage.

Steyaert, C. and Bouwen, R. (1994) 'Group methods of organizational analysis', in C. Cassell and G. Symon (eds), *Qualitative Methods in Organizational Research.* London: Sage. pp. 123–46.

Strathern, M. (1987) 'An awkward relationship: the case of feminism and anthropology', *SIGNS: Journal of Women in Culture and Society,* 12 (2): 276–92.

Strauss, A. (1978) *Negotiations: Varieties, Contexts, Processes and Social Order.* San Francisco: Jossey-Bass.

Stubbs, P. (1993) '"Ethnically sensitive" or "anti-racist"? Models for health research and service delivery', in W.I.U. Ahmed (ed.), *'Race' and Health in Contemporary Britain.* Buckingham: Open University Press.

Sudarkasa, N. (1986) 'In a world of women: field work in a Toruba community', in P. Golde (ed.), *Women in the Field: Anthropological Experiences.* Berkeley: University of California Press.

Taylor, J.M., Gilligan, C. and Sullivan, Amy M. (1996) 'Missing voices, changing meanings: developing a voice-centred relational method and creating an interpretive community', in S. Wilkinson (ed.), *Feminist Social Psychologies: International Perspectives.* Buckingham and Bristol, PA: Open University Press. pp. 233–57.

Tesch, R. (1990) *Qualitative Research: Analysis Types and Software Tools.* London: Falmer Press.

Thorne, S. (1997) 'Phenomenological positivism and other problematic trends in health science research', *Qualitative Health Research,* 7 (2): 287–93.

Traweek, S. (1992) 'Border crossings: narrative strategies in science studies and among physicists in Tsukuba Science City, Japan', in A. Pickering (ed.) *Science as Practice and Culture.* Chicago, IL: University of Chicago Press. pp. 429–65.

Tritter, J. with Bell, S., Brada, M., Miles, B. and Richards, M. (1996) 'Patient-centred cancer services? What patients say', *Medical Sociology News,* 21 (3): 19–23.

Unger, R.K. (1983) 'Through the looking glass: No wonderland yet! (The reciprocal relationship between methodology and models of reality.)', *Psychology of Women Quarterly,* 8: 9–32.

Vaughn, S., Schumm, J.S. and Sinagub, J. (1996) *Focus Group Interviews in Education and Psychology.* Thousand Oaks, CA: Sage.

Vera, E.M., Reese, L.E., Paikoff, R.L. and Jarrett, R.L. (1996) 'Contextual factors of sexual risk-taking in urban African American preadolescent children', in B.J.R. Leadbetter and N. Way (eds), *Urban Girls: Resisting Stereotypes, Creating Identities.* New York, NY: New York University Press. pp. 291–304.

Watts, M. and Ebbutt, D. (1987) 'More than the sum of the parts: research methods in group interviewing', *British Educational Research Journal,* 13 (1): 25–34.

Weeks, J. (1985) *Sexuality and its Discontents: Meanings, Myths and Modern Sexualities.* London: Routledge.

Weeks, J. and Holland, J. (eds) (1996) *Sexual Cultures: Communities, Values and Intimacy.* Explorations in Sociology 48, British Sociological Association. London: Macmillan.

Weisstein, N. (1993) 'Psychology constructs the female; or, the fantasy life of the male psychologist (with some attention to the fantasies of his friends, the male biologist and the male anthropologist)', *Feminism & Psychology,* 3 (2): 195–210. (Orig. 1968.)

Wells, W.D. (1974) 'Group interviewing', in R. Ferber (ed.), *Handbook of Marketing Research.* New York: McGraw Hill. pp. 2–146.

West, C. and Zimmerman, D. (1991) 'Doing gender', *Gender and Society,* 1: 125–51.

Wetherell, M. and Potter, J. (1992) *Mapping the Language of Racism: Discourse and the Legitimation of Exploitation.* Hemel Hempstead: Harvester; New York: Columbia University Press.

Whitehead, T.L. (1986) 'Breakdown, resolution and coherence: the fieldwork experiences of a big, brown, pretty-talking man in a West Indian community', in T.L. Whitehead and M.E. Conaway (eds), *Self, Sex and Gender in Cross-cultural Fieldwork.* Urbana, IL: University of Illinois Press.

Whitehead, T. and Conaway, M. (eds) (1986) *Self, Sex and Gender in Cross-Cultural Fieldwork.* Urbana: University of Illinois Press.

Wilkinson, S. (ed.) (1986) *Feminist Social Psychology: Developing Theory and Practice.* Milton Keynes: Open University Press.

Wilkinson, S. (1998a) 'Focus groups in feminist research: power, interaction and the co-construction of meaning', *Women's Studies International Forum*, 21 (1): 111–25.

Wilkinson, S. (1998b) 'Focus groups in health research: exploring the meanings of health and illness', *Journal of Health Psychology*, 3 (3): 329–48.

Wilkinson, S. (1998c) 'Focus groups: a feminist method', *Psychology of Women Quarterly*, 23 (2).

Wilkinson, S. and Kitzinger, C. (eds) (1995) *Feminism and Discourse: Psychological Perspectives.* London: Sage.

Wilkinson, S. and Kitzinger, C. (1996) *Representing the Other: A Feminism & Psychology Reader.* London: Sage.

Williams, G. and Popay, J. (1994) 'Researching the people's health: dilemmas and opportunities for social scientists', in J. Popay and G. Williams (eds), *Researching the People's Health.* London: Routledge.

Williams, R. (1981) 'Logical analysis as a qualitative method', *Sociology of Health and Illness*, 3: 141–87.

Williams, R. (1990) *A Protestant Legacy: Attitudes to Death and Illness among Older Aberdonians.* Oxford: Clarendon Press.

Willis, P. (1977) *Learning to Labour.* London: Gower Press.

Winkler, F. (1987) 'Consumerism in health care: beyond the supermarket model', *Policy and Politics*, 25 (1): 9–16.

Wong, G.C., Li, V.C., Burris, M.A. and Xiang, Y. (1995) 'Seeking women's voices: setting the context for women's health interventions in two rural counties in Yunnan, China', *Social Science and Medicine*, 41 (8): 1147–57.

Woolgar, S.W. (1983) 'Irony in the social study of science', in K. Knorr-Cetina and M. Mulkay (eds), *Science Observed.* London: Sage.

Worrell, J. and Etaugh, C. (1994) 'Transforming theory and research with women: themes and variations', *Psychology of Women Quarterly*, 18 (4): 433–50.

Wynne, B. (1991) 'Knowledges in context', *Science, Technology and Human Values*, 19 (1): 1–17.

Wynne, B. (1992) 'Misunderstood misunderstanding: social identities and public uptake of science', *Public Understanding of Science*, 1: 281–304.

Wynne, B. (1995) 'Public understanding of science', in S. Jasanoff, G.E. Markle, J. Petersen and T. Pinch (eds), *Handbook of Science and Technology Studies.* London: Sage.

Wynne, B. (1996) 'Misunderstood misunderstandings: social identities and public uptake of science', in A. Irwin and B. Wynne (eds), *Misunderstanding Science? The Public Reconstruction of Science and Technology.* Cambridge: Cambridge University Press. pp. 19–46.

Wynne, B., Waterton, C. and Grove-White, R. (1993) *Public Perceptions and the Nuclear Industry in West Cumbria.* CSEC report. Lancaster: CSEC, Lancaster University.

Yelland, J. and Gifford, S. (1995) 'Problems of focus group methods in cross-

cultural research: a case study of beliefs about sudden infant death syndrome',
Australian Journal of Public Health, 19 (3): 257–63.

Zeller, R.A. (1993) 'Focus group research on sensitive topics: setting the agenda
without setting the agenda', in D.L. Morgan (ed.), *Successful Focus Groups:
Advancing the State of the Art*. London: Sage. pp. 167–83.

Znaniecki, F. (1934) *The Method of Sociology*. New York: Farrar and Rinehart.

Name index

Subject index

9 780761 955689